P9-CMN-221

NOVANETICS

HOW TO USE ADVANCED WEALTH TECHNIQUES & YOUR SUBCONSCIOUS MIND TO GET RICH

THE BEST BOOK IN THE WHOLE WORLD

DAVID BENDAH

INCLUDES A FREE SPECIAL "START-UP" SECTION ON TEN MORTGAGE ASSISTANCE PLANS TO PAY YOUR MORTGAGE PAYMENTS & A SECOND FREE SPECIAL "START UP" SECTION ON HIGH PROFIT RENTAL REAL ESTATE & "NO MONEY DOWN" OFFERS

David Bendah   San Diego   USA

Copyright © 2020 by David Bendah, San Diego, California, USA.   All rights reserved.   Printed in the United States of America.   Previous title "*How To Use Your Hidden Potential To Get Rich*." Copyright © 1985.   No part of this publication may be reproduced, or distributed in any form or stored in a data base or retrieval system, or transmitted in any form or by any means, like, electronic, mechanical, photocopying, recording or otherwise, without prior written permission from the publisher. Write: David Bendah, PO Box 152808, Dept. DD2, San Diego, CA   92195.

ISBN: 978-1-7354357-0-1

This publication is designed to provide accurate and authoritative information in regard to the subject matter covered. It is sold with the understanding that the publisher is not engaged in rendering legal, accounting, construction or other professional service.   The services of a competent professional should be sought, if legal advice or other expert assistance is required.   This book expresses the author's views and opinions.   The information contained in this book is provided without any express, statutory, or implied warranties.   Neither the authors David Bendah, nor its resellers, or distributors will be held liable for any damages caused or alleged to be caused directly or indirectly by this book.

The intention of the book is to help the reading with sound, practical and valuable advice, with the intention of helping the reader increase their net worth and improve their life.   The author does offer his book material to the reader so they can become successful.   The author requests if there is anything further he can do to assist he readers, they can write or call to obtain the assistance they need.   The author does extend his wishes that readers contact him regarding their experiences and success stories due to this book, "*NOVANETICS*".   He would especially like to know, how much readers benefited and what monetary gains readers obtained due to this book. The author further states that reader feedback and stories would have a good meaning to him and if readers write the author, he will add readers to his mailing list and send his latest opportunities to the readers.   Write the author at: David Bendah, PO Box 152808, Dept. DD2, San Diego, CA   92195.

ORDERING BOOKS

David Bendah books are available at very special quantity discounts to use for mail order or internet sales or as premiums, sales promotions, in corporate training programs or for educational uses.   If you would like to purchase books and become registered students send $34.95 USD plus $3.95 USD for shipping for any quantity of books. For international orders send $34.95 USD + $15 USD for shipping.   For more information or sales please write, David Bendah, PO Box 152808, Dept. DD2, San Diego, CA   92195.

BECOMING A REGISTERED STUDENT

"*NOVANETICS*" is an educational school course, whose purpose is to increase your income.   In order to take the final examination and earn the "*NOVANETICS*" certificate you must be a registered student.   Buying this book makes you a registered student.   To become a registered student and buy the book "*NOVANETICS*" send $34.95 USD plus $3.95 USD for shipping for any quantity of books.   For international registered students send $34.95 USD plus $15 USD for shipping.   If you have bought the book through a book store or other retail outlet send a copy of your sales receipt or proof of purchase.   Write, David Bendah, PO Box 152808, Dept. DD2, San Diego, CA 92195.

NOVANETICS:

HOW TO USE ADVANCED WEALTH TECHNIQUES & YOUR SUBCONSCIOUS MIND TO GET RICH

TABLE OF CONTENTS

Contributions

I would like to make special mention of the talented employees who helped me make the book a success.

Andrew Jowers
Susanna Vega
Michele Howard
David Brauner
Barbie Scheurenbrand
Pnina Bendah

I would also like to make special mention of the influential people in my life that inspired me to write the book.

James A. Belasco, Ph.D.
Howard R. Mueller, Ph.D.
Courtland Bovee, M.S.
Robert B. Settle, Ph.D.
William A. Nye, Ph.D.
Douglas A. Peterson, Ms T., M.A.
Michael Dean Ph.D.
Wayne McMahon
Gary Silver
Michael Kelly
Sherry L. Stillwater
Pamela J. Lawrence
Donna Gilbert
Bart Polin
Sam Glassman

What This Book Can Do For You

Success need not elude you. It is not hard to attain. People just like you have become successful. What do they have that you don't? They have the key to success. It is the key that unlocks prosperity's mysterious doors. You are holding that key. It is the same key that has made fortunes and empires for people all over the world. Use this key wisely and you will prosper.

You may be asking yourself why should you read this book. Let me ask you one question. Why shouldn't you read it? I am giving you the chance of a lifetime. A chance to become everything you want to be. I can tell you, thousands upon thousands of people have studied the concepts in this book and are now very successful. Would you risk being like them? Make the decision that will make you rich and successful and read this book.

What secrets does this book hold? There is no mystery. It shows you how you can use the magical powers of your mind to get what you want. You see, most people have the potential to become successful. The reason they are not successful is because their hidden powers are asleep. Waking up your hidden powers is the first step. The second step is to expose them and show you how to harness their energy so that you can become successful.

Let this book, *"Novanetics"* "The Best Book In The Whole World" unlock your hidden potential.

NOTE: *The slogan "The Best Book In The Whole World" is based on a contest with a "$3,000 reward" on books that increase income.*

Chapter One

Tapping Into The Power Of Novanetics

Your search is over. The advanced wealth techniques and other advanced methods that use your subconscious mind to get rich, are now yours. They are utterly amazing and I think you will find that this book is one of the best books that you own. I implore you to read this book from back to back until you have finished it. This way you will get the most from the educational money making programs this book has to offer you. There is a road to acquiring wealth, success and happiness and it is *Novanetics*. You have made the right choice.

Novanetics is a fabulous success system that uses advanced wealth techniques and your subconscious mind, and has created wealth and happiness for myself, as well as for many successful people. What's more, in this book, I will guide you every step of the way, just like I have guided myself and thousands of others just like you. *Novanetics* can make your life amazingly better. It really works and I absolutely assure you that it is the right book for you and I know it can really help you. Novanetics has worked for me, and it will work for you. Let me tell you more.

What Is Novanetics

Novanetics is a method of tapping into your subconscious mind to unleash your total potential. *Novanetics* will give you substantial success, prosperity and significant happiness. It is a compilation of the greatest secrets for success ever assembled in one book. It contains knowledge from the greatest minds on earth and knowledge from the mystical philosophy of the Far East to the wisdom of Christianity. *Novanetics* will show you the secrets of ultimate success. Much of *Novanetics* is being used by the Japanese in their quest to become the most successful nation on this earth; and it has worked. The Japanese have the highest income of any group in the United States, and as a society, the Japanese can boast at having the lowest crime rate and the greatest longevity of any people on earth. They understand *Novanetics* and use it. It is time for the whole world to use this advanced knowledge to better themselves. Let me tell you more about *Novanetics*.

Novanetics could be your key to success. After reading *Novanetics,* you will be able to tap into your powerful, hidden potential locked inside of your mind. You could be using it to enrich your life. *Novanetics* will show you how to release your infinite wisdom to become successful. That's right, you will learn how to use your subconscious mind to achieve prosperity and happiness. You will learn the same secrets that the rich and powerful use to achieve their success. As Sigmund Freud said, "There is a powerful force within us, an un-illuminated part of the mind - separate from the conscious mind that is constantly at work molding our thought, feelings, and actions."

Let me first tell you a little about success so that you can thoroughly understand it. There are three types of success.

1)   Success with yourself.
2)   Success with other people.
3)   Success with material things, such

as money.

All of these types of successes have to do with a relationship between yourself and something else. Once you are able to master the fundamentals of success, you will be able to master any and all of the three types of successful relationships. Many things that you wanted could be yours once you master the fundamentals of a successful relationship.

Here is a list:

1) Love yourself and be happy with yourself and with everything you do.
2) Have very caring and loving relationships with your friends and with everybody around you.
3) Increase your wealth and overall prosperity.

Do you want to achieve these three types of success? If the answer is yes, then you need *Novanetics*. *Novanetics* can change your life. I have all of these things and they arrived when I was able to master *Novanetics*. *Novanetics* is simple to master, yet it's results are astounding. Let me tell you more.

I am very happy, I have many friends and I have earned millions of dollars. Many years ago, I struggled to make ends meet and I was unhappy. I knew I needed to make changes in my life. It was then that I discovered *Novanetics*. When I discovered these principals for success, my life changed. You can make the same drastic changes in your life by using my revolutionary methods of *Novanetics*.

Many of you probably believe that wealthy people are better educated, or smarter, or simply have had more breaks in life than those who haven't achieved as much. You may be surprised to know that I haven't had those breaks. I grew up poor, in a downtown section of Toronto. The house I lived in has since been demolished due to its poor condition and became part of a small park by a railway on Dundas. My father worked hard to move our family to a northern part of Toronto, called Downsview when I was 8 years old. It was a richer neighborhood with better opportunities for the future. All through high school I could average no better than Bs and Cs in my class work. I wasn't proud of my English and Math grades. By no means was I ever considered an overly

intelligent person, but that changed when I applied myself. You can do the same with your life when you apply yourself.

My family moved to the United States, California in 1978. I attended university in San Diego as a business major. My life started to change in the 80's. While I was in the university called SDSU, I started a small mail order company. I wrote the book "*How To Use Your Hidden Potential To Get Rich*" during that time. I dreamed and set my goals on having a large company. I repeated my goals to myself everyday and I worked hard at building a book company. My company grew quickly over a period of a few years. By 1986 my company had over a hundred employees and published about a hundred different books and two national magazines.

David Bendah

Since then I, David Bendah have earned millions of dollars for himself and millions of dollars for many others. I have earned so much money that I was featured on "Life Styles Of The Rich And Famous" in 1990 and I was also featured in Rolling Stones Magazine as well as other magazines and television shows. I am an expert when it comes to making money quickly and effortlessly for other people. Very few know as much as me in setting other people up in their own business. I only became wealthy and successful by mastering the art of *Novanetics,* which are the same techniques that you will learn in this book.

The Quiz

You are now on the road to success. In this book, I am going to tell you how to get many of the luxurious things that you want. But before we start, I will give you a quiz so that you can begin to evaluate yourself. It will only take a few minutes and it will reveal just how well you understand the principles of success.

This quiz was made for you. This quiz will tell you about yourself and where you stand in relation to the people around you. Take the quiz it will be good for you.

Since you have decided to take this quiz willingly, I am going to make it very easy. Simply answer each question with either an "A", if you *agree* with the sentence, or with a "D" if you *disagree* with the sentence.

When you take the quiz, remember that the first thing that comes to your mind is probably the best answer. Use this technique of answering the questions and you can have the best possible answers. Be spontaneous. If you think seriously about a question, you may end up with the wrong answer. Good Luck!

The Quiz

1) The power of your mind can give you many things that you want.

2) Luck has a lot to do with getting rich.

3) Some people are poor by their own choice.

4) Recognizing and admitting to your weaknesses is wise?

5) It is not necessary to write down a goal to finish it effectively.

6) Specific goals are unnecessary.

7) Planning ahead takes the fun out of activities.

8) Visualizing or dreaming of your desires is natural?

9) Commonly made decisions should be solved at your first compulsion.

10) Hunches are valid only some of the time.

11) No specific time limit should be placed on goals.

12) Perusing a goal will make you happy?

13) For the most part, you should fully expose your feelings to supportive people.

14) You should give to others because they expect you to.

15) Speaking about anything on your mind is healthy.

16) High expectations are not good because they lead to disappointments.

17) Creating a funny and cheerful personality will make you less likable with friends, because this is not a serious personality.

18) It is better do a funny "ballet" dance when doing something peculiar in front of people like sneaking away?

19) A person begin to be funnier within one hour with the comedy techniques in Novanetics.

20) It is to your advantage to concentrate on more than one thing at a time.

21) Strong persistence will not help you get what you want because it irritates people.

22) You learn more when you feel that you know nothing or don't have a set opinion.

23) It is better to know something about everything then to specialize in one area.

24) Scientific studies show that the power of the mind may improve body healing by 30%.

25) You can drastically reduce your debt to creditors and still keep some of assets without declaring bankruptcy with a wage earners plan.

26) Can a person earn a rental income of $9,600 a year with a $975 investment that includes locks on two doors and installing one exterior door?

27) Of the five ways to earn money from income property which are cash flow, equity, depreciation, appreciation and interest payments, can depreciation and interest payments be deducted on your tax return.

28) Refinancing your mortgage at a higher interest rate is a great way to lower your monthly mortgage payments.

29) Will building a rental apartment on your property guarantee that the market price of your home will go up?

30) You can bring your mortgage payment down to zero, and earn a rental income, even after the cost of the construction, by building accessory apartments.

31) The government doesn't offer special home financing programs that can reduce the mortgage payment for home owners.

32) Some people just lock the doors in a section of their home that has a separate entry way, then rent out that part of the house to save 60% on their mortgage payments.

33) Can anyone with little money and the right instructions become a millionaire from real estate?

About the Answers

Fun, wasn't it? You see, I told you the quiz would be simple. Now for the part you have been waiting for.

Here are the answers: 1-A, 2-D, 3-A, 4-A, 5-D, 6-D, 7-D, 8-A, 9-A, 10-D, 11-D, 12-A, 13-A, 14-D, 15-A, 16-D, 17-D, 18-A, 19-A, 20.-D, 21-D, 22-A, 23-D, 24-A, 25-A, 26-A, 27-A, 28-D, 29-A, 30-A, 31-D, 32-A, 33-A.

Here is what these scores mean? Multiply your score by three to see your score as a percentage of 100. So if you got 30, that would be 90% and if you got 25, that would be 75%. A score of over 90% is an A+. A score of 80% to 89% is an A. A score of over 70% to 79% is a B. A score of 60% to 69% is a C.

If you scored less than 33, you need *Novanetics*. A score of less than 33 means you don't know something that you should know.

All the answers to these questions can be found in this course. As you read further, you will notice that the various topics I cover correspond to each question. This test was designed to show you how well you understand the principles of success.

I have provided quizzes and summaries all the way through this excellent course. This was done to teach you, what you will need to be successful in your life. Good luck with this exciting course. After you have finished this educational course you may want a "*NOVANETICS*" certificate to hang on your wall in the same decorative frame you would use for a college degree. With this certificate you can show others you have completed the "*NOVANETICS*" course. A "*NOVANETICS*" certificate is impressive with family and friends. This certificate may also get you jobs and business opportunities with people that will see the certificate. The final 200 question examination is in the back of this book, NOVANETICS. Write David Bendah, PO Box 152808, Dept. DD2, San Diego, CA 92195 and send your name and address in capital letters and the completed scantron test sheets for the NOVANETICS Real Estate and Business certificate. Submit a total of $9 for the grading of the exam and the NOVANETICS personalized educational certificate which includes shipping & handling.

The Beginning

What is the first thing that you need to be successful? Take a guess before you read the answer. It is the first thing you need. If you possess this one thing, you will be more successful and happier than might have ever imagined. What is it? It is a strong burning desire.

You Must Have A Strong, Burning Desire To Be Successful

An ordinary desire is not enough; you need a strong, burning desire for success. You need a desire that makes you want to become successful and wealthy so badly that you are willing to learn new ideas and accept new ways. Have you felt this burning desire? I hope the answer is yes, because without this burning desire you will not be able to succeed. First, you must really want success. If you want to succeed, you must accept the fact that your life will change; and realize too, that you must really want these changes in order to succeed.

The First Step

The first step to getting what you want is, "knowing what you want." Once you know what you want, then you should feel a strong desire to complete your goals. Do you know what you want? You do want the total success and the prosperity that we discussed earlier; don't you? Of course you do. Your personal success is what *Novanetics* offers you. Repeat to yourself that *"success and prosperity is what you want and that it is something for which you are willing to pay a price."* Go ahead, I will wait. Repeat those words.

What is the price you have to pay? That price is to follow the educational *Novanetics* method of success. In as much time as it takes to read *Novanetics,* your life can begin to change significantly for the better.

Believe In Yourself

The only thing that will stop you from succeeding are the limitations you put on yourself. I know this because time and time again I have seen people who could have done well, but didn't succeed. The only reason they didn't succeed is because they did not believe that they could do anything but fail. When you limit your expectations, you limit the amount of money and happiness you can achieve through *Novanetics.* Believe you can succeed. Believe in yourself.

Limiting Your Mind

The power of your mind can give you many things that you want and I mean, many things. You have within you the power to accumulate wealth. What is it that keeps some people from attaining wealth? If you think you can't get something, you record it in your mind as, *"I can't do it."* One of the reasons you may not have thousands upon thousands of dollars, is because the limits you put on yourself. One of the reasons you don't have loving relationships, is because your limits. You must try to get whatever you need.

I struggled through some low paying jobs. I went to work with the feeling that there was no way I could get better wages, so why would I try to change jobs? I stayed with the same job. I expected to do badly, and so I did badly. My employers had very little faith in me. Later, I made more money than any of them would have dreamed. *The mistake was mine for not believing in myself.* I urge you to follow this simple advice: *Believe In Yourself.* As my friend Mat would say, *"Don't go through life making peanuts when you could be making cashews."* If you think that all you will ever make is peanuts, then that is all you will ever make.

The Man Who Learned How to Believe

I am going to share with you the story of a man who you've probably heard of, but don't know much about. As a boy, this man wanted to be a Presbyterian minister. He was unable to go into that profession, so he turned to one of his other interests which was music. He was a music teacher most of his life. He limited his expectations. He believed that he would never be anything more than a music teacher, then one day he changed; that was the day he began having high expectations and believing in himself. He became successful only when he began to believe that he could be more than a teacher. In his late 30's, he stopped limiting his thoughts. He developed a burning desire to be successful. At 41, with no business experience, Dwight Hamilton Baldwin began selling pianos. His belief in himself and his determination to forge ahead, made his company what it is today.

Even when times were bad, he kept pushing. His dream began with a belief in himself. He fulfilled his first dream and made a lot of money. His second dream was to manufacture pianos. At age 68, Mr. Baldwin realized his dream. You may have heard of the Baldwin Company. They manufacture beautiful pianos It all began when Baldwin began believing in himself.

Key To Success

Your mind has the potential to get you many things that you desired. I am going to show you how to use the full potential of your mind. You will be amazed at how well your mind performs. There is only one thing that I will ask of you. It is one small thing I must insist so that you will get the most out of this program. It is to believe in yourself.

Believing

Believe in yourself and Novanetics. You may be skeptical. You may ask yourself, *"Why should I?"* I ask you this one question, "*Why shouldn't you*?" You have nothing to lose. I am guaranteeing your success or I will refund the purchase price of this book. Follow my success system and you will do well. If you decide not to follow my program, your life will not change. But tell me, is that what you want? I am sure you want to be successful.

Success can be yours, and I am giving you the chance of a lifetime, so take the opportunity. Some people feel that they will go nowhere in life. They have that negative attitude. Is that what you want? Is it to go nowhere in life? I don't think so. You are different. You are reading *"Novanetics"* because you want to get ahead in life. You have

an advantage over most people. Your desire to get ahead will get you ahead.

I suggest that you take notes as you read. I would also like you to use a marker to highlight any points that you think will benefit you. I also urge you to memorize anything that you feel should be incorporated into your life. Follow these simple steps and success will be yours. It will be yours because *"Novanetics"* will show you the business techniques necessary to become successful.

The Successful You

I am going to show you how to change your beliefs, and how to make your new beliefs help you to become successful. However, before we can change your beliefs, you must look at yourself. I want you to examine your beliefs. Do you have any beliefs that are negative that you should change? What are your beliefs regarding other people or relationships in your life? How do you feel about money and other material things? What are your beliefs about happiness and love?

Examine your beliefs, because we will keep the positive beliefs and cast off the negative beliefs. Sit down and look at yourself carefully, and ask, *"What am I like?"* Just being able to see yourself can help you recognize *positive* beliefs which you should keep, and those beliefs that should be discarded or changed because they are *negative*.

Ask yourself another question: *Why am I this way?* This will start you thinking about the reasons your beliefs are the way they are. You can begin working on your problems when you've answered this question. Do you genuinely want to succeed? If the answer is yes, then we can begin working on your problems and the solutions. Let me tell you what certain people that I know did after asking themselves these questions.

Pete Had No Belief

Pete, a friend of mine, wanted to buy magazine advertising for computer equipment he wanted to sell. Every time the magazine deadline neared, he made some excuse for not placing the advertising. He made all sorts of excuses. He called the magazine sales representative to discuss the terms of the advertising, but didn't submit the advertising. Three months went by and Pete still couldn't decide if he was going to submit the advertising.

One Wednesday morning, Pete discussed his ad with Joe, the representative from the magazine. Joe asked Pete, "Why aren't you placing the advertising; are you afraid of losing money? Don't you believe in your product? There are people who are selling similar products and they are making money." Pete got off the phone and was infuriated with Joe, but this conversation made him think. He took a look at himself and realized that he really didn't believe that his advertising would do well. He was stalling because he didn't believe in his product. When he realized that, he called Joe back and said he was going to place the advertising.

Pete did place the advertising; and it made him a lot of money. His advertising helped him double his sales for a product. It took belief in himself and in his product to place that advertising, and it was this belief that enabled Pete to make a lot of money.

Belief In The Razor

How strong is belief? At the age of 32, King C. Gillette, a traveling salesman, struggled with his old-fashioned straight razor. He believed he could create a disposable razor that would always stay sharp. One day in 1895, he thought of sharpening both edges of a piece of metal. He told his wife, "I've got it! Our fortune is made." He had a belief in his razor. He had so much belief in his razor that he persisted, even when people told him to forget his *crazy idea.* No one would invest in Gillette's idea because no one believed in him.

King Gillette, however, believed in himself. He had more than an ordinary belief in himself and in his idea, he also had a *burning desire* to be successful; and no one was going to stop him. It took him eleven years to make his first cent from his razor business. He was over 40 years old before he started making money at it, but I'm sure you will agree, the wait was well worth it.

What Can Your Mind Do?

I have told you about two very successful people. Gillette, who made it when he was 40,

SUMMARY

- Novanetics will show you how to be successful, happy and prosperous.
- To be rich, you must have a burning desire to obtain wealth.
- Negative thoughts limit the wealth-creating powers of your mind.
- Believe in yourself and in your efforts and you will surely succeed.
- Your mind has the power to give you many things that you want.
- If you make the effort to use *Novanetics, y*ou will see results.

and Baldwin, who made it when he was 41. Why weren't these men successful earlier? Why did they wait until they were in their 40's to be successful? The answer is simple. *They didn't realize their full potential.* If you don't realize your full potential now, *when will you?* You know you have what it takes to become successful. Commit yourself to *"Novanetics" and* give it your maximum effort. You will free the valuable potential that is locked up in your mind. If you make an effort, you will see results. These results are real. These results will bring you success.

Are you unhappy with what you have right now? If you are, then take this opportunity to change your life around. Get the prosperity and success that you want and to make your dreams come true. You can have these things. Your dreams can be realized and wealth and prosperity could be yours. How do you get what you want in your life? With *"Novanetics"*. *"Novanetics"* can give you what you have always wanted. That is what I am going to show you in this book. I will work with you to help ensure your success. Believe me, that you and I can do it. Trust me and together we will work for your success.

Chapter Two

Wealth Is Your Choice

Wealth is a choice. It is not fate that some are wealthy, it is a choice. If you choose to be wealthy, you will have more money. Let me show you what I mean. If you believe that you will earn only $24,000 a year, those instructions are sent to your subconscious mind, and it will try to ensure that you just earn $24,000 a year. Your subconscious mind interprets your beliefs as being your wishes. It complies with what you want. It doesn't know the difference between right and wrong. Your subconscious mind will obey your thinking program. At this point, there is no way that you will earn more than $24,000. Your subconscious mind not change the instructions, you gave it. It must follow them.

Let me explain why positive thinking is so important. Any positive statement you make will be sent to your subconscious mind, and it will try to ensure that positive statements are carried out. Your mind does whatever it is told. Positive people always get ahead because they give their minds positive suggestions.

Your mind will obey negative statements as well as positive statements; it doesn't know the difference between the two. It just does what you tell it to do. What happens when you give yourself negative statements? Your mind carries out those negative instructions. If you tell yourself that something is impossible or can't be done, your mind will be convinced that you won't be able to do it. It interprets "impossible" as, 'this task should not be done'; and it will never get done. You can be sure of that.

Anything Can Be Carried Out

Almost anything that you tell your mind will be carried out. If you want riches, you must tell your mind that you want riches. Your mind will try to follow your instructions; and it will immediately begin formulating a plan for obtaining riches. It does all the work for you. Convey your desire for riches to your mind, as outlined in this book and it will attempt to comply with your wishes. You will be amazed at what the miracle-producing power of your mind can do.

I am going to show you the best way to send instructions to your subconscious mind. It's called *"Novanetics"*. I will show you how to use the same techniques used by the world's greatest men and women. These methods are at your disposal, and in order for you to be successful, they must be used. You will be aware of the methods used by those who have obtained success; you will have the very same advantage.

You Must Be Positive To Succeed

Being rich is positive. Having a great family is positive. Having a beautiful house is positive. Having a fancy Mercedes sports car is positive. When the atmosphere is positive then the outcome will be positive. It is important to send positive instructions to your mind. You will always gain more when positive things happen to you. Smile and act positive and speak in positive terms, so that positive instructions are sent to your subconscious mind. When you create a win-win attitude, you will start to win. Develop a positive nature so your whole life will start to be positive and you will start to win.

What Can Go Wrong?

If you try the *"Novanetics"* techniques, you can succeed. I have talked to many people and some have told me of their marvelous results. I have helped many people better their lives by inspiring them to give *"Novanetics"* a try. *"Novanetics"* can help you. What happens if this system doesn't work for you? I guarantee your success or you can always get your money returned for the purchase price of this book.

There are some ways you will fail to succeed. Let's find out if you fall into that category. A man told me that he tried these techniques and nothing happened. At the time, he was the manager of a car rental company. He was renting a small house for himself and his family when he decided to try to improve his life through these wealth techniques. I asked him to tell me what he was doing. He told me he repeated his goals to himself three times a day. He said he told his mind that he wanted to have $200,000, but that money never came. *"Why"*, he wanted to know. I questioned him further and discovered something interesting.

This man told me that he wanted $200,000, but that he knew he couldn't have it. He didn't think he could earn it. His subconscious mind was instructed not to produce $200,000. The message he was sending his mind, didn't work. *You have to believe that you can get what you want.* This man didn't believe he was worth $200,000. He got what he felt he was worth; so he got little. You can't play with your mind. You can't ask your mind for something and expect to receive it, when deep down you don't believe that you will earn it.

You must have faith, you must believe in yourself. Acknowledge the fact that the wealth is there, all you have to do is ask your subconscious to give it to you. You must have confidence in yourself. Thinking that you will not be able to have something creates a *negative possession* in your mind. Having a *negative possession* will put you right back to where you started.

I want to finish telling you my story about the man who had negative thoughts. I explained to him that he had to believe in himself in order to get what he wanted. Later, he told me that he had raised his goals. He now wanted $500,000. He came back to me a few years later and told me how he had followed all my instructions to the tee.

Today, this man is worth about $600,000. He owns a large house with a swimming pool, and a car rental company. How's that for success? You could do the same with *"Novanetics"*.

The Destroyer Of Success

Believing in yourself will bring you riches and that's only if you believe in yourself. Guess what disbelief will give you? It will give you failure and poverty. *Is that what you want? No, I think not.*

If you don't think or believe that you will make it, then you won't. Your subconscious mind is so powerful, that it will obey commands that you give it. Giving your mind negative commands will only prompt it to perform negative acts. Having a negative attitude will get you nowhere. I'm sure you have heard this statement before. I heard it hundreds of times when I was negative. I heard it, but I should have acted on it and become positive and believed in myself. A positive attitude is much more productive.

I had no plans for myself when I left high school. I didn't think I was going to college. Why? Because I felt that I wasn't clever enough to make it through college. When people asked me why I wasn't going on to college, I told them that I had different career plans. I didn't really. I made excuses for not being college material. I believed that I would never amount to much, so why not just settle for what I had and make the best of it. When I believed that I would be a failure, I was a failure. When I believed I would be successful, I was successful. When I had a negative attitude, I sent those messages to my subconscious mind. Do you ever give yourself negative suggestions?

I got tired of low paying jobs. I made an effort to change. I wanted to go places and I wanted to be someone successful. I knew that I had it in me. I just needed to learn how to let it out. It was then that I learned one of the most important lessons of my life. When I believed in myself, I excelled in my life. When I didn't believe in myself, I failed.

I worked for different companies. Somehow, I felt I would get higher paying jobs. As the years went by, my jobs didn't get that much better. I was so unhappy with myself that I made an effort to change. I realized that the choice was mine. I made the choices and the changes were good.

If I wanted to fail, all I had to do was to think negative thoughts. If I wanted to succeed, all I had to do was think positive thoughts. Let me ask you something: What do you want? What type of expectations *do you* have for yourself? I am sure you want to succeed. I am sure you want more money or a higher paying job.

How To Deal With Fear

Why do we limit ourselves? We limit ourselves because of fear. The fear of rejection or loss is one of the greatest de-motivators. But remember what President Franklin Roosevelt said: *The only thing we have to fear, is fear itself.* How true he was.

In my life, I have lost many thousands of dollars and many relationships with people that I liked, but I learned something. You are probably asking yourself what. Every time I failed, I learned a great deal. Failure, isn't good but it is one of the best teachers I know. There was a time when I lost more than $10,000. That was a lot of money to owe a bunch of hungry creditors. What else could go wrong?

My health started to fail on me. While I was sick in bed, I realized that the only thing I had left was myself; and even that was failing. I realized that I'm all I have, and at that point I began to appreciate the small things that life has to offer. When I had lost family members, my health and my money, I realized that I had been taking for granted all that life has to offer.

I made a commitment to myself. I vowed that I would regain everything I had lost and that I would go one step further. I wanted to have stronger, closer more meaningful relationships with everyone I knew. Later, I had more meaningful, loving relationships with my family and friends. I wanted to be healthier. What is family or money without your health? You need your good health. Later, I was healthier than I ever have been. I could go to work without feeling run down and exhausted. I could run easily. I could go out without feeling irritable or flustered. I also wanted to make more money than I had ever made before. Making more money was easier and less aggravating. I was earning more money and feeling better about myself. Later bought a new house and a new car with my money, and I still had money to invest in other ventures.

So, you see, losing everything, which is a terrible thing to happen to anyone, made me a better person. Today, each time I suffer a setback, I pick myself up. First, I figure out why I fell. Then I push forward more strongly than before. The truth is that failure helped me to learn. If you learn the lessons of your failures, you will become a better person. The Hindus say that *you will make the same mistake over and over again until you learn your lesson.* Learn your lesson. Learn from failure. It is a great teacher.

I earned back all of the money I lost and earned quite a bit more. Since that time I have done so well in the business community that I have earned millions of dollars for other people and myself. I was featured on television and in magazines. I had become famous, but all of that business experience has made me an expert in the business world. Few know as much as me when it comes time to make a lot of money easily and effortlessly. I am an expert in setting someone up in their own business so they are prosperous and they stay successful. Many loopholes, secrets and techniques for becoming wealthy that is closely guarded by the very rich is in this book. You have the money secrets of the ages to use for yourself, so that you can become more successful that you ever dreamed you could be. Use them wisely and you can count on being one of the select few who have become exceeding wealthy, just by following the techniques and concepts in this book.

How This Man Beat Failure

I want to tell you a story about a man who failed more times than you or I could tolerate. He was born in Pennsylvania in 1857. When he was seven, his parent's farm was taken away because of a defaulted mortgage. When he was 14, he was fired from his printing job because of his poor aptitude. He spent four years working for a confectionery store. In 1876, at the age 19, he felt it was time to make it on his own.

With the help of his aunt, he set up his own candy kitchen. He sold penny candies from his shop and did so well, that a year later he moved to a larger space. He had problems getting labor and working capital and his business started to slide. He was very depressed and devastated by the poor performance of his business. He was losing his health and he nearly died. He almost didn't make it, but with his mother's nursing and because of his courage, he pulled through. Seven years later, he expanded into the wholesale candy market, but he couldn't collect the money that was owed to him. The sugar refineries wouldn't extend him credit and his aunt couldn't help him financially. His business failed and was sold.

Instead of being discouraged, he became even more determined than ever to succeed. He had a dream that he would be successful. He would not rest until his dream was real. He decided he wanted to sell caramels and started his new business in a basement in Chicago. He worked long hours, selling his candies through street vendors. While he was struggling, he got a letter from his father telling him of the wonderful opportunities in the West. He left everything and got on a west-bound train, only to be disappointed. The opportunities in the West were grim and so disappointing that he set out for New York.

This man now began his third venture. He wasn't going to let the first two failures get in his way. He opened a small factory in New York City where he made caramels. He was doing so well that he moved to a larger unit and hired more people. Unfortunately, he over-stayed his first lease by a few days. His former landlord sued him for a full year's rent and he couldn't afford the extra expense. In 1886, at age 29, he was forced into bankruptcy.

Even after this third failure, he was determined to be successful. Failure taught him how to be a good businessman. He had so much faith in himself that he was able to convince his uncles to back him on his fourth venture. This ambitious man believed in himself a great deal. His uncle felt anyone with that much determination and persistence would succeed.

He started with four employees and a small factory. Milton Hershey, the man who suffered so many failures, did so well that within a few years the Lancaster Caramel Co. took up one entire city block and employed 2,000 workers. Mr. Hershey later became the king of chocolate bars. What do you think would have happened if Hershey had given up? He would not have been as successful. If you give up when you experience a setback, think of Hershey's determination and courage. It may do the same for you as it did for him.

How You Can Beat Failure

One great cause of failure are the mistakes that we make. We all make mistakes. Your success will be determined by how you handle your mistakes. Successful people learn from their mistakes. If you don't make mistakes, you wouldn't learn. Mistakes teach you, so learn from them; they are the greatest teachers you have. Consider a guided missile on route its target. Every now and then, it gets off course. It makes mistakes. It has a self-adjusting system that puts it back on track. Your mind acts in the same way. It gets off track by making an error. It is your duty to correct that error and continue your course until you hit your target.

We all fail. The more successful you become, the more you will fail. That's right. Your ability to succeed depends on your ability to tolerate failure and to learn from it. You can beat failure. You can beat it with a simple method. Concentrate on your successes. This method will enable you to tolerate failure and will give you the courage to continue with your goals. Use it. Think about how good you felt when you succeeded. Let that image stay in your mind. Too many of us forget our successes and remember only our failures. Do you know what this does? It makes you fail even more. Do you dwell on your failure? Don't dwell on your failures.

The next time you make a mistake, learn from that mistake. Understand why you made the mistake and make provisions so that it doesn't happen again. Most importantly of all, think of your past successes. Let your mind visualize the feeling of positive success. Do this, and you will be more successful.

Poverty Is A Disease

You have the potential to have almost everything you ever wanted. Your mind has the ability to play ball. Your mind will pitch baseballs to you and all you have to do is catch them. You will hear them slap in your leather mitt as you do better in your life. If you have the ability to catch those balls then you can get wealth. The game of life is succeeding and doing well.

We all try to stay as healthy as possible, don't we? If you are sick, you must try to get better and do everything you can to stay healthy. Do you know why? It is because we must be healthy to live and when we are healthier we are happier. Another reason is our society tells us that being sick is not good for us. We want to do what is good, so we stay healthy. Let me ask you something. If you are sick, do you go to the doctor? Do you work on your health to make yourself better? I think your answer is "yes." We all do the things that make us healthier. We eat the right foods, we exercise and we brush our teeth.

Poverty is a disease. When we are poor we must prevent this disease. A good education and a good job are cures for poverty. A cure for poverty lies front of you. *Novanetics is your cure.* You can choose to use this medicine to get the prosperity that you wanted, or you can believe that you are what you are and that nothing can change you. The terminally ill believe that. Their health doesn't improve and it usually gets worse with time. You must do the best you can with what you have.

What do you think will happen to your financial position in time? Are you going to adopt a sickly attitude, or a healthy one? It has to be a healthy one. Your financial situation can get better or it can get worse. This book was designed to improve your wealth and your health. What do you have to lose if you are lacking things in your life? Use this book wisely and you could have plenty of both.

IMPORTANT

It is important that you keep this program confidential. I mean this sincerely. The only person you should speak to are supportive people that are going to participate in it with you. This way you have support. Some people close to you will, unknowingly de-motivate you. They will have negative feelings toward success. It is just the way some people are.

Success seems to scare some people.

SUMMARY

- Wealth is a choice, so make the right choice and choose wealth. Your future depends on it.
- When the atmosphere is positive then the outcome is positive. You must be positive to succeed.
- Fear can lead to disbelief. Disbelief leads to failure.
- Failure can be useful. It teaches us. Learn the lessons of failure and become more successful.
- We all make mistakes. A successful person learns from his mistakes and corrects them.
- Poverty is a disease. Having or not having, the best wealth and health is your choice.
- You should keep this program confidential. Many people unintentional will de-motivate you.

Internal changes that will make you successful will begin to occur. Change is not always easy for others to accept. The changes in you will benefit them after they have had time to accept the new you. Confide in people when you have completed this program and you have many of the things that you want. Your success will depend on your silence. There is one exception to talking. You may confide in the people who are supportive of you.

Chapter Three

The Power Of Novanetics Is Within You

You have a hidden power within you, a power that can assist you in doing anything you want. This power is your subconscious mind and *Novanetics* can release it. It is so mighty that it can help create wealth and power for you, if you dare to use it. There are two parts of your mind that do your thinking for you. One is the conscious mind. This is the part of your mind that you are consciously aware of and is used in everyday thinking. It is the part of your mind that reasons and takes your instructions.

The other is the part of your mind of which you are not aware of, is the subconscious mind. It is quicker and much more powerful than the conscious mind. It performs some of the same functions as the conscious mind, but you are not aware of its influence. Together, their magical powers work to give you anything you want.

Your Subconscious Mind

The conscious mind is the reasoning part of your mind, that you are aware of and the part that follows your instructions. No matter what the instructions are, they will be carried out by your mind. If you want to move your hand, you think then you act by moving your hand. If you want to run, you then think then you move your legs and start to run. Almost any instructions you give to your mind will be obeyed. If you keep saying, "I can't love. I can't love," your mind not let you love. If you keep saying, "I won't be rich. I won't be rich." Your mind will not let you be rich. It is better to keep saying you will be rich.

Let me show you what I mean. Think of your subconscious mind as the captain of your mind that we will call a ship. The subconscious mind sends instructions for the ship's course. This ship will do what you tell it to do. If you tell this ship to go south, it will. If you tell it to stop, it will do that too. What happens if you tell the captain to send his ship off course? It will try to do this. Any instruction you give this ship will be carried out.

Your subconscious mind doesn't know the difference between right and wrong or between good and bad; it is not a reasoning mind. If you keep telling your mind the wrong thing, you will brainwash yourself into continuously doing the wrong things. Your mind obeys your instructions and orders. The orders that you give to your mind will determine whether you succeed or fail. Tell your mind to sail full-speed ahead toward the land of prosperity, and you will be sailing into the waters of success to prosperity. Tell your mind that you are unsure about the existence of that Promised Land, and you may be lost.

Choose success and give your mind positive suggestions. If you feel negative about yourself in any way, remove those feelings. A negative outcome is not good for you. You don't want that. I am sure you will agree that removing these negative feelings will only lead you to your success.

How The Mind Works

I want to show you my interpretation of how the mind works so that you can understand exactly what your mind is capable of doing. First, I am going to draw you a diagram of the mind and its basic components.

Let me go through the diagram with you so that you know what I am talking about. Information is the first thing that enters your mind. It is sensed by the part of your mind that I call *paying attention:* Paying attention, that is, to the exact, present moment. Your mind can only focus on the present; what else could you pay attention to except the things that are happening right now. Things you think of in the past or in the future are brought up from your memory. If you are bringing things up from your memory, you are thinking or using your mental processes. If you are thinking, you will not be able to focus on the exact present moment.

The Mind

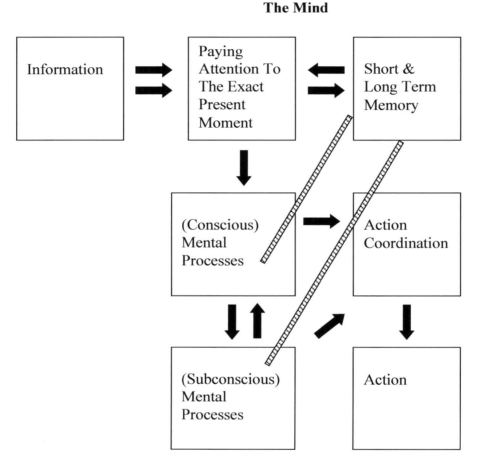

Next comes *conscious thinking.* This is the type of thinking that you do every day. This is the type of thinking that you can see in your mind. Next, there is *Subconscious thinking.* You do this every day, too, but you are not fully aware of it. In fact, it is called 'subconscious' because you are not aware of it. Your thinking is then converted into action by your action coordinator. Simple, isn't it?

Your Memory System

Your mind is a huge memory system, a memory so vast that it contains information and thousands of *thought programs.* A *thought program* is like a computer program. An electronic computer program allows a computer to carry out a function like playing a movie or processing information. The mind can carry out all types of functions and thoughts, and can combine to create some very intricate functions.

Let me show you what I mean. The other day I went to buy a movie at a video store. A *thought program* showed me what sequence of events I needed in order to get to the video store: walking, seeing, touching, etc. Another one showed me how to find the video, while one showed me how to take the video off the shelf, how to buy the video and how to get back home.

20

Do We Program Ourselves?

Our *thought programs* are programs that we create in our mind. We create them with our ability to think. The more you work with a *thought program*, the better it gets. That is why we say, *"practice makes perfect."* Doing something over and over again helps us remember the task. A task like driving is practiced again and again, so you become an excellent driver. If you do it enough times, you don't even have to think about the activity.

Have you ever driven a car and realized after getting to your destination that you hadn't really thought about the actual process of driving, but just drove? Your mind programs you to drive so well that you are able to occasionally talk to your friends and listen to all sorts of things like the radio, while performing a difficult task like driving. Your mind has created a *thought program* for driving. I am sure that you have done this. This is one of the functions of your mind. It will program an activity for you, so that you don't have to think about it.

Your mind does this so that you can pay attention to what is happening .at the exact, present moment. It puts your mind in the automatic-pilot mode so that you can do other things. Let's talk about using the full potential of your powerful mind. If you know exactly what it does and how to operate it, you will be able to utilize its full

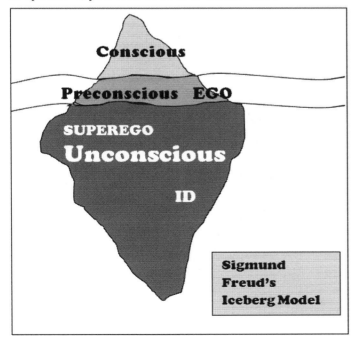

potential. Using your mind's full potential will bring you more success. If success is your goal, then read on carefully.

Sigmund Freud's Iceberg Model

Sigmund Freud postulated that that the unconscious mind and preconscious mind took up 6/7 or six-sevenths of the human mind. The mind is like an iceberg, it floats with one-seventh of its bulk above water. The preconscious contains part of the ego. The Unconscious mind contains the SUPEREGO, THE ID and a part of the ego.

Sigmund Freud's Subconscious Mind

The concept of the unconscious was central to Freud's account of the mind. Freud believed that while poets and thinkers had long known of the existence of the unconscious, he had ensured that it received scientific recognition in the field of psychology.

Sigmund Freud, that was born in Austria and spoke German, states explicitly that his concept of the unconscious as he first formulated was based on the theory of repression. He postulated a cycle in which ideas are repressed, but remain in the mind, removed from consciousness yet operative, then reappear in consciousness under certain circumstances.

In Freud's psychoanalytic theory of personality, the unconscious mind is a reservoir of feelings, thoughts, urges, and memories that are outside of our conscious awareness. Most of the contents of the unconscious are unacceptable or unpleasant, such as feelings of pain, anxiety, or conflict.

Can We Listen When We Are Not Paying Attention

There is evidence to substantiate that people can pay attention or hear information, even if they are not paying attention or listening. How is this possible? I don't know. Some say that your subconscious mind can actually pay attention and secretly listen for you when we are busy doing things. Some say your subconscious mind can even listen for you while you are asleep. They say they can subconsciously listen to tiny bits of conversations and/or events.

What does that mean? Let's say you are

having a conversation with Judy, and at the same time another person behind you named Simon, that you don't hear is trying to talk to you. Would you vaguely hear with your subconscious mind, what Simon said to you even if you didn't listen to him and even if you were busy talking to Judy. Some people say that, they have a vague summary of what other people that they don't hear said to them. Does your subconscious mind do this?

If you are at a party and two people not far from you (about fifteen feet), that you can't hear are talking about you. Can your subconscious mind get an idea of what they said, by evaluating bits of information? Many people say yes. Let's say you are at a party, and many people are talking to each other. Though, you can't hear these people the air seems to have a simple summary of their conversations as their private conversations fills the party room. It is the atmosphere of the party. Do you feel that certain restaurants or certain parts of the city are fun or have a great atmosphere? I think places like Disneyland, a beach or a park are fun places with a happy atmosphere.

Some say when expressing their emotions or intuition, which are influenced by the subconscious mind, they have a vague idea of what others said. What does this mean? It means that just talking can give you an understanding of any topic, from your point of view and from another person's point of view.

Try going to a party of about 50 people and then have a private conversation with one person, in a corner of the room. In this private conversation you would talk about yourself in strong positive statements. Do you think other people not listening to you in the room; can subconsciously hear tiny bits of that conversation? There is evidence to prove they can. This could make you popular. Well, what do you think of subliminal listening and how popular it can make you?

Two Types Of Thinkers

There are two types of thinkers. They are distinguished by their ability to change their *thought programs*. Structured thinkers prefer to stay with the same *thought programs*. They don't want to think. They always have the same point of view. Creative thinkers know that everything around them is constantly changing. That is why their *thought programs* are constantly changing. Let me discuss the structural thinker, which is more common.

The Structural Thinker

A structural thinker prefers to use the same *thought programs* over and over again, because they do the same type of work over and over again. Such a person prefers to think in a very structured way. This person is opinionated. They believe that they are right when they do things. This type of person lacks curiosity and doesn't ask many questions but are good at certain things. In their world, they are more correct than others and things are either right or wrong or black or white. This person could have a job like factory worker, electrician or plumber. They could be blue collar workers where a worker performs skilled or unskilled manual labor.

Many years ago, Sam, a good friend of mine, who was a very successful stockbroker in Toronto, told me, "Structured people think in black and white only. Seeing colors requires thinking. Creative people can see colors." In fact, he always tells his clients that not everything is black and white, that they have to see the colors, too. He sells more stocks then other brokers. A structural thinker tries to do the same things. This person closes their mind to certain facts. They sometimes will feel uncomfortable in unfamiliar situations or uncomfortable around people they don't know.

The Creative Thinker

A creative thinker doesn't always stay with the same *thought programs* and they could be in upper management of a company. They are constantly thinking and re-evaluating all of their opinions. They are not afraid to admit that they are wrong. They may admit to their mistakes and correct them. They acknowledge their weaknesses and strengthen them. They are critical and supportive.

A creative thinker always looks for new and better ways to do everything. They may be curious by nature. They do not form an opinion until they have evaluated many aspects of an issue, including arguments. Their opinions, when formed, are never set in stone sometimes their opinions are only a temporary view or belief. A creative thinker likes to think and they use their minds to accomplish tasks. They know that to be successful, they must be creative thinkers. Success and creative thinking go hand in hand. This person could perform professional managerial or administrative work. They could be business owner, executive or manager. They could be white collar workers.

The Perfect Structurer

Ron was a veteran printer with his own printing business. He had good prices and did great work. There was just one thing about Ron that customers disliked. He was a structured thinker. If you agreed with Ron, then the two of you would get along just fine. Ron, you see, had to be right. He structured his thoughts so that he had an answer for everything. As long as he had the answer, he didn't care if his answer was logical or correct. He was argumentative. Once, he had a big argument with a customer over the merits of his favorite football team. The Vikings are a poor reason to lose a customer.

Ron was moderately successful. He worked long hours and was not really moving up in his field. He had a very small shop with a few customers and as you might expect, he had a high turnover of pressmen. His business declined until finally one cold December day, his business folded. He didn't have enough cash flow to keep the doors of his shop open. Everything he had worked for, his whole life was gone. He said he cried the day he closed his shop, and how he swore that he would change his life around.

Ron's Decision

It was then that he decided that he had to make some changes in his life. He talked to many of the most successful people in his community. He also picked up many self-improvement books that he could find and read them long into the night. He really wanted to change. Within a matter of months, Ron did change. "Everyone makes

SUMMARY

- Your mind will obey positive suggestions or negative suggestions.
- Your mind is a ship and your subconscious mind is the captain.
- Your memory system contains *though programs* which are similar to computer programs.
- You can program your mind to perform different tasks.
- In Sigmund Freud's iceberg model he postulated that the unconscious mind or subconscious mind takes up 6/7 of the human mind.
- Some say the subconscious mind can hear tiny bits of conversations, even if you are not listening.
- There are two types of thinkers, they are the structural thinker and the creative thinker.
- The structural thinker keeps the same routine. They tend to keep a structured work regiment where they concentrate on tasks.
- The creative thinker likes to think. They analyze different problems and come to different solutions.

mistakes," he said. "I look at the mistakes I make now, and try to correct them. I try not to accept anything if I am not sure about it. There was a time when I just accepted what other people said. I'm not saying I don't listen to other people. I listen to them more than ever, but with a third ear. I evaluate what they say after they say it. I want to make sure that what they are telling me makes sense. I am more confident now in my beliefs. In my business, I used to accept the fact that I wasn't making much money. I used to tell myself that it was because of the economy. Do you think I could have admitted that it was because of me? No way. I now make it a point to look at my business inside out. If my competitors are making money, then, so will I."

"I set aside one day a week as a time when I

examine my business to try and discover ways that I can make it more profitable. I spend two hours looking for ways to serve my customers better and increase profits. Because of these two hours, I now have an increase in sales every month. I offer my customers typesetting, and that makes me more money. I even sell magnetic signs. These signs bring in an average of $72 a month. That's pretty good for a few hours a week. The time I now set aside for reflection has wound up making me a lot of money."

Today, Ron is doing very well. He was single and is now happily married. He owns several printing shops, and doesn't even work that much anymore. He just overlooks the shops to make sure that they are running well. I forgot to mention that he still conducts his two-hour-a-week thinking sessions. Ron's case is a good example of what a little creative thinking can do.

Let me ask you this. Are your thoughts structured or creative? Do you accept what people tell you without thinking about it, or do you evaluate a thought before accepting it? I want you to think seriously about the questions I have asked. If you feel you have any structured thoughts, make the effort to re-evaluate them. Examine your ways. Be successful.

Chapter Four

How To Get The Wealth You Want

This chapter of *Novanetics* contains the methods necessary for becoming successful and prosperous. The instructions are in simple workbook form. Follow these steps and you may see immense success. This section will show you how to imprint instructions to your subconscious mind. This is an imprint that will last a lifetime and that can bring you wealth and prosperity.

The Two Things You Must Know

There are two things that you must do to get what you want. FIRST, *you must know exactly what you want.* SECOND, *you need to work faithfully for what you want.* Let's talk about what happens when you lack one of these qualities. If you know exactly what you want and make no attempt to get it, you will not get what you want. If you don't know what you want, but you work hard, you will be wasting your time going in circles. So you see, you have to know what you want and then you have to work for it. In this chapter I will tell you how to do both.

Working Faithfully

After you know what you want you must devote yourself to your goals and work faithfully to complete your goals. Working faithfully means putting your heart into your work and caring about your work, so you can be quick at your job and you can produce good quality work. You could start at a young age and work towards your career and your work specialty so that you will be successful when you are older. If you are older then start devoting yourself to your work at a older age. You are never too old. Any age is fine to devote yourself to your work. Working hard and being faithful to your work always pays off in the end.

Carnegie Worked Faithfully

Andrew Carnegie was born in Dunfermline, Scotland, in a small weaver's cottage by a family of impoverished laborers. At age 12 Carnegie's family who wanted a better life, immigrated to America in 1848. Times were hard and at the age of 13, his father who was a handloom weaver was out of work. His mother helped her brother and sold potted meats at her sweetie-shop and was the main breadwinner. Carnegie got little school education, but his family was so poor, so in 1849 at the age 13, he got his first job as a bobbin boy changing spools of thread. He only earned $1.20 a week, that helped his family, but he had a burning desire to become successful. He wanted to do better in his life and opportunity struck when only 14, Carnegie got a better job. In Pittsburg in 1849, he worked for the Ohio Telegraph Company as a telegraph messenger boy for $2.50 per week. All of his faithful hard work had paid off. Four years later in 1853 at the age of 18, he landed on a great opportunity. He worked for Thomas Scott as secretary and telegraph operator for $4.00 a week.

The Scottish-American, Andrew Carnegie was determined to make wealth his choice and succeed. He worked hard at his job to excel at his work. At the age of 24, he was a superintendent for the Pennsylvania railroad. He cared about family and got many family members jobs. That year he hired his sixteen year old brother Tom as secretary and telegraph operator. With the help of Scott, Carnegie invested $500 in a railroad passenger company called Adams Express. He didn't have enough money so his mother put a $600 mortgage on the family's $700 home.

Carnegie's choice was to become very rich. He had a dream and knew that his many years of hard faithful work would guarantee his success. He made his dreams come to life and he became a very rich man. In the 1860's Carnegie had investments in railroads, bridges and oil derricks and during that time, he raised money for an American enterprise in Europe as a bond salesman. In 1901 Andrew Carnegie sold the Pittsburg Carnegie Steel company to J.P. Morgan for $303,450,000, which later became U. S. Steel Corporation. Due to that sale, he became the richest American for several years, even surpassing John D. Rockefeller. His hard work starting at a young age paid off. His dreams of prosperity had come true. In the United States and Great Britain, in the last 18 years of his life he became a top philanthropist, giving away $350,000,000 dollars to libraries, charities, foundations and universities.

A Man Who Knew What He Wanted

In 1806, 23-year-old William Colgate opened up his own little soap shop. His new company was called Colgate and Company. He hung a little sign outside his window to attract customers. Colgate's previous job was working for a soap maker; now he was determined to make money with his own business. He knew how to make soap and wanted to use his skills to create a successful little store. Colgate had some ideas that he thought he could sell to his customers. On his first day of business, Colgate waited for his customers. He waited, and he waited. Half way through his first day, there still had not been a single customer. Later in the day, an old man walked in to his store and purchased a two-pound bar of soap. Colgate asked his first customer where he wanted his soap delivered. The man was very surprised. At that time, free delivery was unheard of. Young Colgate then told the man that *service* was the motto of this business. This man, who lived a mile from Colgate's shop, gave his address to Colgate. Colgate had to close his shop one hour early that evening because the delivery

had to be made on foot. He said afterwards: "It may have cost me double my profit on that first sale to make the delivery, but I won a good customer and I have kept him ever since."

Colgate knew what he wanted. He had decided that good service was necessary for his business, and he wanted his shop to be a success. He wanted a profitable soap shop, and that is exactly what he got. Colgate gained other customers quickly with his good service. News of his shop got around and more people walked through his doors. Colgate worked hard to create his business. He sold so much soap in the years that followed that he opened a large soap making factory. This eager man created an empire. He knew what he wanted and went after it. Look what knowing "*what you want*" and "*working faithfully*" did for Colgate. Do you know what you want and will you work faithfully for it?

Know What You Want

Before you can reach any of your goals, you have to know what you want. That is why this step is one of the most important of all. You will probably do better at the functions in which you are interested in or that you are good at. They often tend to be the same functions anyways. Getting involved in these areas will bring out all of your good points. You should put 100% of your efforts towards your goals. If you are good at certain work or you like certain work, then you can "*work faithfully*" towards your goals.

I have included an exercise that will help you understand what you want. I have included this step for a good reason. I want you to know yourself better. I want you to know all of your positive qualities and all of your strengths. Discovering more about yourself will make you a more positive person and will increase your self-confidence. If you have trouble completing this exercise, then that is more reason enough to bear down and complete this step properly. I would not have included this exercise if I didn't feel it would benefit you greatly. After you have become successful you will look back and realize how important a step it was on your road to success. The process is easy. Write down your strengths or the functions you do well in one column and your likes or the functions you enjoy in another. Follow my example.

My Strengths	Your Strengths
Functions I Do Well	**Functions You Do Well**
Write Poetry	
Speak In Public	
Write Music	
Help Other People	
Plan A Family Function	
Sculpt	
Type	
Manage My Time	
Organize My Items	
Get Along With Other People	
Design	
Communicate With Other People	
Work With A Computer	
Being Loyal And Trustworthy	
Tutor A Subject	
Lift Peoples Spirits	
Repair a wooden object	

Functions I Enjoy (Likes)	**Functions You Enjoy (Likes)**
Having A Good Friend	
Educating Others	
Designing Graphics	
Manipulating A Problem	
Being Recognized	
Good Music	
Painting A Picture	
Watching A Good Movie	
Being Appreciated	
Planning Ahead	
Making Money	
Doing A Good Gym Routine	
Writing A Blog	
Satisfying A Customer	
Dancing	
Dressing Well	
Understanding Another's Feelings	
Having A Computer Program Work	
Swimming	

Very good! You are on your way to completing your goals. The next step is to number each of your strengths and likes. Here is how you do it. Figure out if each strength or like is a financial goal, personal growth goal, or relationship goal. When you know what it is, number the strength or like with (1) for financial, (2) for personal growth and (3) for relationship. One strength or like could help fulfill all three goals.

Your Advantages

The first thing we want to discover are your strengths. For this, you will need to look at the exercise you filled out on strengths and likes. You did do it, didn't you? Now you will decide which steps you are going to take to reach your goals. Before using this chart, however, we must first put together another one. In this chart, you should list *every resource and advantage you have.* The following is an example of writing out your *resources and advantages.*

Later in this book I have a surprise for you. It is a business plan with full instructions on how to start it. It is for you to use. Use your business plan, but if you don't know what business or project you want to hedge your goals on, just use my real estate business plan. You can use it to make money even if you have no money. It is an excellent real estate business plan in this book that you can complete easily.

Resources and Advantages

People:

- Uncle Ted: He owns a printing shop.
- Dad: He could guide me and help me financially.
- Tom Philip: A good friend and sales manager of a car dealership.
- Aunt Lucy: She runs a small motel.
- My wife: She has office experience.

Money

- I have $3,408   in savings.
- I have $45,000 equity in my house.
- I have a job that pays $720 a week.
- I have rare coins valued at $1,610.
- I have collectables worth $330.
- I have furniture worth $2,530.
- The equity on my car is $4,360.

Other

- I have some office equipment and supplies.
- I could use my uncle's office
- I could use my aptitude for work

Your Resources And Advantages

People

_____
_____
_____
_____
_____
_____
_____
_____

_____
_____
_____

Money

_____
_____
_____
_____
_____
_____
_____
_____

Other

_____
_____
_____
_____
_____
_____
_____
_____
_____

At a glance, you now can survey your resources and strengths. This is the information you will need to make decisions concerning your future. The next step will be to compile this information and decide which project(s) will be the most successful. By analyzing yourself, you will know how to take advantage of your strengths and preferences so that you can pursue your goals most efficiently. I want you to use the chapter of this book on problem-solving to decide your future. It is a very good, but effortless method of solving problems. Use it to better yourself.

Your Success-Oriented Machine

Your subconscious mind is a strong success-oriented machine. If you give it a task, it will strive to fulfill that task. It has the ability to undertake many projects. If you don't work for any goals, however, your mind will lay unused. Giving your mind nothing to work on is like letting go of the steering wheel in your car while you are driving. You could be lucky and just travel in circles. But it is more likely that you will run off the road and harm yourself. The same thing happens with your mind. Give your mind a goal and let the gears in your mind work for you.

Defining your goals tells your subconscious mind exactly what to aim for. Failure to define a task will confuse your subconscious mind. You must tell that part of your mind what to do so that it can use its powerful resources to work for you.

Programming Your Mind

A computer program needs information to work. Without information, a computer program will not compute answers. You mind is the same way. Your mind needs information, so give it what it wants. To give your mind information, I want you to begin by writing out a list of everything you want. You can first review the list of items you may want in the next few pages. I want you to write down reasonable items, no matter what they cost or what they are. Write them down. If another person possesses such a thing, write it down. Don't limit yourself. If you desire it, then you have the capacity to get it. .

With your written desires, you are sending signals to your mind to awaken your hidden ability to achieve. Knowing this, just use the full capacity of your imagination. If you desire it, then include this item on your list. Let me tell you what stemmed from one man's desire.

He Wanted A City

When Milton Hershey was young, he wanted a city. Can you imagine wanting a city? He wanted a city when he had little. He had a burning desire to build a city. He didn't want it built just anywhere; he wanted his city built on the Pennsylvania farmland that his parents had lost to foreclosure years earlier. When he began to plan his building, people thought he was crazy for wanting to sink so much money into an area that was literally in the middle of nowhere.

But Hershey built his city. His goal was fulfilled. If he had limited his goals and told himself that he couldn't build a city, his city would have never been built. Hershey's dream city was made out of one-story limestone buildings covering multiple acres. This town now provides good living conditions for thousands of employees. In the town he built, Hershey now operates the largest chocolate factory in the country. You should go up to Pennsylvania to see the results of one man's impossible goal. It's called Hershey, Pennsylvania. When you see it, you will see the city he founded.

I have used Hershey to illustrate one point; even goals that seem farfetched can be met. If a goal, within reason, can be imagined, it could be

(1) Financial/Career Needs and Wants

- ❏ A new, large home.
- ❏ A new luxury car.
- ❏ A 30 foot sailboat.
- ❏ A log cabin in the woods.
- ❏ New furniture.
- ❏ My own manufacturing factory.
- ❏ A house in California.
- ❏ A house in New York City
- ❏ My bills paid.
- ❏ My own office building.

accomplished. Your mind can help you complete a goal that is if you try to achieve a goal. It takes raw courage and determination to set goals and fulfill them. Don't limit yourself.

Steps For Getting What You Want

It is very important that you know exactly where you are going in your life and how you plan to get there. That is why I have devised these five steps for achieving your goals. Follow these simple steps and; see what they can do for you. You may recognize these steps as ones that have already proven unsuccessful for you, but believe me, you will be surprised by the successful results you will achieve once you've completed this exercise. This same exercise has been used to make millions for many of this nation's leading citizens. Try it. You'll be surprised.

What Do You Need Or Want?

The next thing I want you to do is to make a list of all the things that you want or need. Look at the strengths and likes that you have chosen and pick goals that you would enjoy fulfilling. Don't limit yourself to only the things that you *think* you can have. Remember Hershey's city. He didn't limit himself. Choose anything you desire, whether or not you feel you are worthy of those things or those qualities. I want you to let yourself go, use your imagination. Go after things and qualities that you have always had an urge to possess. For the following step, I wrote more goals than I actually wanted. You can use my list as an example when making your goals. Remember, make your list reflect *your* desires.

- ❑ A new recreation vehicle.
- ❑ A trip around the world.
- ❑ A 10 carat diamond.
- ❑ My own jet.
- ❑ My private deserted island.
- ❑ A microwave oven.
- ❑ My own maid.
- ❑ A new wardrobe.
- ❑ A law degree.

(2)   Personal Growth Needs and Wants

- ❑ Self-Control.
- ❑ Decisiveness.
- ❑ Openness and honesty.
- ❑ An accomplished conversationalist.
- ❑ Concentration.
- ❑ The ability to solve problems.
- ❑ Stronger awareness.
- ❑ Becoming more persistent.
- ❑ Lack of procrastination.
- ❑ Better organization.

(3)   Relationship Needs and Wants

- ❑ Good relations with my mother-in-law.
- ❑ A stronger commitment.
- ❑ A stronger sense of loyalty.
- ❑ More empathy for others.
- ❑ Children I can be proud of.
- ❑ Closer business ties.
- ❑ Friendships with influential people.
- ❑ Good, reliable friends.

Excellent! We are moving right along.   We are now going to modify your goals. If you give yourself a vague goal, such as needing money, you won't get as much out of your efforts.   We are going to give you specific goals, such as needing exactly $74,000, not just needing money.   This technique will allow you to become very successful at attaining your goals.

There is a reason we must do this.   Your mind has a hard time completing vague requests. When you are given instructions that are vague, you don't know exactly what to do, and because of this, it is likely that you will wind up not doing anything.   When you are given specific instructions, you can go right to work.   Your mind is the same way.   To get results, tell your subconscious mind exactly what to do.

Due Dates & Times Required.

All goals can't be completed overnight.   It takes time to be successful.   It takes time for a seedling to become a tall tree.   A small plant grows and grows until it becomes a sturdy tree. You must do the same with yourself.   Give yourself time to grow into sturdy successful person.   We will go into detail in the next few chapters as to a time frame to complete your goals. You can vaguely write in the time frame you want to reach in a rough notes.   Just become familiar with a time frame to reach your goals.   In a later chapter we will write down definite times.   Think about five year goals, one year goals, 90 day goals, and one week goals or a combination of these time limits to reach your goals.   Just jot down the due date that you wish to complete your goals.   You could write down vague goals like, "*I want $74,000 in one year*." In a later chapter we will write in goals, due dates and time required.

Keep A Book For Your Notes

Buy a lined journal with blank pages and use this for your notes. Write down your progress, needs and desires as a to-do list. This will be a list of things you will have to do to complete your goals. Keep all of your important items that you will need to complete in a journal note book. Date your entries on a regular basis and cross out any item on your lists that you have completed. Make sure that your book filled with notes and dates is confidential. I think this is a good idea. The only person that should read some of your notes is someone who supports you. In this way you have support. Make sure others cannot read your book and criticize your activities and your "to do" notes. Some people will unintentional be non supportive and sometimes tend to be negative towards your goals. Other people tend to copy other people's plans and tend to be competitive and sometimes jealous. This will de-motivate you, so keep all of your personal notes confidential.

Make Your Goals Specific

We must make your goal specific and put it into the present tense. Instead of saying "1 need money," say, "I have in my possession $200,000." Notice, I quoted an exact sum of money and made the statement as if I already had the money. Make sure your goal is realistic. By that, I mean that another person has completed the same goal as you are contemplating. Let me take some of my nonspecific goals and change them so that you will understand what I mean.

In a later chapter I have a surprise for you. It is an excellent startup business plan that you could use to complete your goals. Use your own business plan or consider using my fabulous "no money down" real estate business plan to complete your goals.

1) **Automobile**: I have in my possession a new, silver luxury Mercedes Benz sports car.

2) **Home**: 1 now live in a $500,000, 1,500-square-foot home by the beach.

3) **Concentration**: I can now devote my full energy and concentration to a subject of my choice. I can devote my full attention to any activity or subject without being distracted.

4) **Persistence**: I always get what I want because I am the persistent type. I keep striving for what I want until I have it or until I no longer desire it.

5) **Closer ties**: I am now a good friend of Bob Fields, the manager of the bank with which I conduct all of my business affairs.

6) **Health**: I have lost 45 pounds and I am thinner and full of energy.

7) **Relationships**: I am developing a more loving and meaningful relationship with my wife and my two-year-old son. I will spend more time with them because I want to grow with them.

8) **Travel**: I would like to visit the country of India. I will visit Bombay, Calcutta and New Delhi. I feel that I can travel to that country on a budget since the hotel and food is cheaper. I would like to look at products that are manufactured there.

Your Completed List of Goals

Look over your list of realistic, specific goals in the present tense. Make sure that these goals are exactly what you want. If you are unhappy with a goal or you think it will conflict with your life, remove it from your list. Make sure your goal is something that you want. As you read each goal which you have decided to undertake, visualize it as if it were completed. See yourself driving down the street in a new Mercedes Benz sports car or a new Porsche sports car.

See yourself sitting on the porch of your new home. Visualize the sound of the ocean as you relax. Visualize the kitchen, dining room, bedrooms and bathrooms. Visualize these thoughts in your mind.

Get posters of pictures of your goals and put them on the wall. You can even get toy models of your goals and put the models on your desk. If you want a new car, put a picture of the new car poster on your wall. You could even buy a new car toy model and put that model on your desk. If you want a new home, put a picture of the home on your wall or get a toy model of your home and put it on your desk.

Sit down and imagine what life will be like after you have completed your goals. Believe that the items that you want will be yours. It is up to you to dream about what life will be like when you are extremely successful and prosperous. Remember, think positively about reaching your goals. If you don't believe in yourself, no one else will. Believe in yourself and have a positive, achievement-oriented attitude.

Repeat Your Goals

Repeating your goals is important. You must do this in order to succeed. Out of all the things that I will relate to you, this one step is a very important key for your success. You must do

this in order to succeed. Repeat your goals to yourself at least three times every day with enthusiasm and visualize their completion. Three times a day, repeat every goal at least 10 times. So, at least three times a day, repeat each goal to yourself 10 times with enthusiasm. I can't emphasize this point strongly enough. You do want to become successful, don't you? Well then, you must repeat each goal to yourself ten times in a row, at least three times a day, with enthusiasm and visualize their completion. You absolutely must. If you can manage repeating your goals (ten times), five times a day then repeat your goals five times a day to yourself and work toward getting better. Carry a copy of your goals with you, so you can repeat them to yourself.

You can repeat them more often, but make sure you repeat them at least three times a day. Don't let a day go by in which you don't repeat your goals to yourself and visualize their completion. You absolutely must do this, I repeat, *it is essential that you repeat your goals to yourself at least three times a day and then visualize the completion of your goals and become enthusiastic about your goals.* This paragraph contains the magic key to success. What do I mean by magic? I mean, a process with information that will benefit you the rest of your life.

When You Should Repeat Your Goals

There are two great opportunities for you to repeat your goals to yourself. One time is just before you go to sleep, when you are feeling drowsy. The other good time is just when you wake up. You should repeat your goals at other times also, but you should repeat them, particularly at these two times because they are the best times of the day. Take advantage of these times.

Why? At these times your subconscious mind is more susceptible to your commands. Studies show that your mind accepts your instructions more *readily* at these times. If you want your mind to take advantage of what you tell it to do, take advantage of these times.

Repeating your goals to yourself traps them in your subconscious mind and imprints your commands. Your mind responds immediately when you repeat your goals. It starts to work on them right away, as soon as it hears your goals. The key is to imprint your commands in your subconscious mind. That is what this powerful technique does. This technique, alone, can make you invincible. Remember: Repeat your goals to yourself ten times each, at least three times a day, become enthusiastic and visualize the completion of your goals.

Your subconscious mind is filled with explosive power that in most people goes largely untapped. Your mind is a goldmine of wealth; give it a task and watch it work for you. Give your subconscious mind instructions. Once it has your instructions firmly imprinted, it will follow them. To your amazement, it will follow your instructions step by step. Make a commitment to follow this step of repeating your goals faithfully. This step is the key to reaching your powerful, subconscious mind. It is essential that you follow this step.

Mike Did It

Mike had a hard time concentrating on his projects at work. He didn't know what to do. He used this system. Four times a day he repeated his goal of being able to focus on a single object without being distracted. Every day he felt an improvement in his concentration. He gave himself three weeks to complete his goal. His due date was March 1st. By the end of one month his concentration had improved so much that he was able to concentrate effortlessly on his projects at work. He was later promoted. This is just one example of what repeating goals, becoming enthusiastic and "visualizing success" can do for a person. Try it and see what it will do for you. Try it.

The Essential Step

I found in my many years of experience that if you repeat the following steps with your other goals, your whole program will benefit. Add these to the list of goals that you will repeat to yourself on a daily basis. Repeat these goals every day; they will really make a difference in your life. Here they are:

1) I will follow this program on a daily basis so that I can fully realize my goals. I will repeat my goals ten times each to myself, three

SUMMARY

- There are two things that you must do to get what you want. First, you must know exactly what you want. Second, you must work faithfully for what you want.
- Like computers use software, goals will be used to program the mind.
- Create and write down obtainable goals that you want to achieve.
- In choosing your goals, you must not limit yourself to what you think you can have. Aim for the sky within reason.
- Write notes in a book, but make sure your notes are confidential.
- Make your goals specific and write them down and give yourself a time frame and due date to reach your goals.
- Repeat, visualize and become enthusiastic about your goals.
- Repeat your goals, ten times to yourself at least three times a day; once before you sleep, once when you wake up and once during the day.
- Make your goal reciting a habit.

times a day. I will follow through with this program until I have accomplished what I have set out to do.

2) I will visualize the completion of my goals as I repeat them to myself.

3) I will become enthusiastic with the completion of my goals.

4) I have a strong belief in myself. I have the potential and the ability to succeed. I can see myself as a success now. I have no thoughts of failure; I have no negative thoughts to ruin my success.

Repeat these goals (and your actual goals) daily to yourself and you will come closer to your dreams.

Chapter Five

Making Your Wealth Dreams Come To Life

I am going to introduce you to one of the most important elements involved in being successful. It is very powerful and surprisingly simple. What is it? Knowing how to use your imagination is the answer. It can get you many things that you wanted in your life. Whether it is a lot of money or better relationships, you can achieve them through dreaming, visualizing and imagining. Your ability to dream will make you more successful than you ever thought possible.

Your subconscious mind can't tell the difference between a dream and the real thing. Dreaming or visualizing convinces your subconscious that you are already in possession of the success or wealth that you desire. Your subconscious mind takes action by putting you in a successful frame of mind. Visualizing and dreaming can give you many things that you want.

You Can Bank On Dreams

When you want to borrow money from a bank, you must have collateral. No one will lend you money if you don't have any money, or some other type of collateral. Success is the same way. To be successful, you must feel successful. Dreaming and visualizing your success does that for you. That is why I urge you to dream, to visualize and to fantasize about the things that you want. I want you to see them in your possession. Visualizing and daydreaming will do wonders for the completion of your goals. Dreaming will make your goals come to life.

This is what I would like you to do. Repeat your goals to yourself, just like you have been

doing, three times a day. While you are repeating your goals, visualize them. Actually visualize what you will feel like when you are in possession of that thing or quality. Let's say, for example, you want a $500,000 house. Find a house that looks like the one you want. Look it over. I want you to notice everything about that house, and size of the pool, the type of yard, the shape of the house and everything else about that home. You can put up full color posters on your wall or have toy models to help you visualize. Get both the posters and models. Do this to help you visualize your goals.

Make Your Dream Real

What I want you to do now is "to think", or I should say, dream about this your new house. Visualize walking in and out of the house. Stroll in the yard and enjoy the view. Visualize the living quarters, as well as every single aspect of this house. Have your mind dwell on this house on a daily basis. Believe me, your subconscious mind will help you get that house. I should know because I used this technique to help obtain my house. When I first dreamed of my house, there was no way in the world that I could afford it. I visualized, dreamed and looked at many homes. I bought many houses later. Remember the saying, "*You reap what you sow*" I am going to modify it slightly. "You reap what you dream." You should visualize your goals as being completed. Dreaming about and visualizing your goals will help you to achieve them. Let me tell you what visualizing has done for one man.

One Man Who Dreamed

This man worked in the merchandising field for 25 years. He had a wild idea. He had a dream that he could sell merchandise by mail with a money-back guarantee. He visualized this merchandise concept. He felt that this idea would work, but people who knew of his dreams mocked him. He didn't give up and began to put his dream into effect.

He started his business in 1871. He lost his business and all of his possessions that same year in the Chicago Fire. His dream lived on. He visualized his dream so often, that it became an obsession. He could see people by the thousands ordering from him. He was determined to sell by mail. In 1872, he printed a catalog with 30 items for sale. Every cent he had was used to buy merchandise stock. He also guaranteed all his merchandise. A. Montgomery Ward's dream was fulfilled. He revolutionized mail order; his dreams became reality. Today's giant company began as one man's dream, one man's goal.

A Dream That Created A Blade

The year was 1895. King Gillette was shaving. He was having problems with his straight razor. You see, it needed honing, and strapping and he couldn't put the edge back on. To get a straight razor honed, you had to take it to a barber or a cutler. This frustrated Gillette. He decided that he would do something about this.

Gillette used his imagination to solve his problem. These were Gillette's words: "As I stood there with the razor in my hand, my eye resting on it as lightly as a bird settling down on its nest, the Gillette razor was born. I saw it all in a moment, and in that same moment many unvoiced questions were asked and answered, more with the rapidity of a dream than by the slow process of reasoning." Gillette saw a piece of steel sharpened on both sides. He visualized a blade that could be held in a holder. These were his exact words: "All this came more in a picture than it did by thinking or through a plan. It was as though the razor were already a finished product, right before my own eyes."

"I stood there in a trance, full of complete joy at what I saw. Fool that I was, I knew little about razors and practically nothing about steel, and could not foresee the trials and tribulations that lied ahead. I believed in it, however, and I knew immediately that it would be a success." Gillette's dream became a reality. His story stands as an inspiration to anyone who dares to dream and to achieve. *Do you dare to dream and to achieve?*

Notice The Details

When your mind knows exactly what you want, it will have an easier time getting it. Have you ever driven to someone's house following directions that were vague? You might turn on the wrong streets. You might even end up in a different neighborhood. It takes longer to get where you're going when directions are vague, doesn't it? Your mind is the same way. It wants you to draw a map for it. It has to know precisely what you want. Write down specific goals with time limits, then dream very specific dreams, and don't leave out any details.

To help you make you visualize I have a surprise for you in a later chapter. I have added an excellent "no money down" real estate section with many pictures that you can use to visualize your business start-up plan. Use your own business plan or use this superb business plan, that I wrote it for you, so if you would like to use this business plan, you will find it in the later chapters.

He Wanted To Secure A Position

Ralph wanted to be the financial director of his company. He didn't get the promotion and asked me why. I asked him to tell me how he was visualizing his new position. After listening to him, I told him to imagine his new job very vividly, with all the details. I told him that in his dreams I wanted him to smell his new office. I wanted him to look outside his office window and to appreciate the beautiful view. I told him to imagine the office chatter, the phones ringing, the office personnel walking to their desks. I wanted him to notice every little thing. He did what I instructed him to do. Three months later, he became the financial director. The more vividly you imagine events and things for your subconscious mind, the sooner you will obtain them. Instruct your subconscious mind to give you what you want. Instruct your mind to succeed for you.

A New Person Arises

After following this step for a few days, you will notice changes starting to take place within you. Don't be alarmed if your personality begins to change. It is one of the most mysterious things that you will ever experience. The instructions that you give your subconscious are in many cases, obeyed and followed. You will know what I mean after you start using this method. Don't ask me why it works. I only know that it does. I know that your mind thinks in pictures, not in words. It understands your dreams very vividly. Your new tool, your subconscious mind, will be one of your greatest assets to you. This method isn't new. Believe me, all of the most successful people have used this technique to control their subconscious minds.

Are You Skeptical?

I have described many famous people to you. Now tell me, couldn't you relate to some of them? Weren't they, before they made their fortunes, doing what you are doing right now? Before they made their fortunes, they were just like you and me. You might have noticed that they really didn't make any money until they were about 40 or 50. What happened to them in the early part of their lives that prevented them from being successful? They had the potential, so why didn't they achieve? What is the answer?

They were asleep the early part of their lives. They *didn't know* that they had the potential so they didn't do anything. When they finally realized their potential, they did something about it. It was locked up inside of them and they set it free to let it work for them. Will you let your mind work for you? Now ask yourself, "are you asleep, or awake"? Be honest.

Most of the people who I have discussed here made their fortunes a multitude of years ago. Let me ask you a question. Was it easier to make money back then? What do you think? It's funny, but most people think that it was. Well, it wasn't. Let me tell you why. In those days, you had to find everything out the hard way. Today, you can pick up a book or a video on any subject. Back then, you were lucky if you knew how to read.

Rich Society

Now, we have knowledge at our fingertips; we have the world's accumulated information at our disposal, available through books, videos, computers, and even the smart telephones. In those days, it was very difficult to make money. The good old days were the hard old days. You will find that more people make more money, and at an earlier age, than ever before in history. This is because we live in a rich society where technology has evolved so much, that computers and machines do the work of many people. What do I mean by that? Let's say a company, called Widget Inc in the 50's had an accounting department where people did almost all of the accounting by hand, so they employed 40 accountants. Well, that same company called Widget Inc. in today's age can do the same accounting with 5 accountants and a whole lot of computers. What a difference for that company and what a savings in money. Now, because this company hired 35 less accountants, this company has earned more money. Computers, machines, telephones and electronics has earned all of us more money. We are all rich thanks to the modern age.

It is a lot easier to make money now than it has ever been; but most people are asleep. That is why they don't get far. You must have faith to succeed. Believe in yourself. You have the power to have almost anything that you want. Realize your power and you can have more things in your life. Ignore your power and your dreams will go unrealized.

Dreaming Helped Me

Many years ago I drove a beat-up Fiat and lived on the wrong side of town because it was the only place I could afford. I dreamed of having a $500,000 home that had 4 bedrooms. I wanted to look out my window and see the ocean. I also dreamed of having a new Mercedes Benz sports car. Having this two-seater Mercedes Benz convertible has been a dream of mine, my whole life. When I told people my dreams, they laughed and said that I would have to wait many years to earn those things. It didn't matter what they told me because I still dreamed of having these lavish luxuries.

My faithful work paid off and in only a few

years, these expensive items were mine. I became a millionaire, and it was due in no small measure to the fact that I had the dream. I worked faithfully on making my dream come to life. Everything I have ever dreamed of having, I have gotten. It took time but I eventually got it. The same could happen to you. Visualize almost anything you want, and it may be yours. I absolutely guarantee it.

Dreaming Helped Sam Walton

Sam Moore Walton was born in 1918 in Kingfisher, Oklahoma and constantly dreamed of becoming very successful. A good schooling was very important, so he enrolled in college. In 1940 Walton graduated from the University of Missouri with an Economic degree and joined J.C. Penny as an Iowa management trainee for 18 months, due to his military duty, but that job taught him so many valuable lessons and skills he would use later. In 1945 after leaving the army, the 26 year old Walton managed a variety store, but he dreamed of owning his own store and even a large chain of stores. He knew he would become rich and in 1945 with a $20,000 loan from his father-in-law and $5,000 he had saved, he purchased a Ben Franklin variety store in Newport Arkansas. His dreams had come to life and in the early 60's Walton and his brother owned a regional chain of Ben Franklins. There were many concepts the Walton forged that made him successful. According to Walton, if he offered prices as good or better than stores in cities that were four hours away by car, people would shop at home. Walton made sure the shelves were consistently stocked with a wide range of goods. He founded the first true Wal-Mart in 1962 and by 1990 Wal-Mart had become the largest retail sales chain in the United States, making Samuel Walton who worked so hard, one of the richest men in America.

Coming Even Closer To Your Goals

There is one more thing that you need to do in order to move closer to your goals. I want you to feel your dreams. I want you to involve your emotions in the process. I want you to imagine what success feels like. I want you to imagine and experience every emotion that you will experience when you finally reach your goals. You should feel victorious. If you do, you have won most of

SUMMARY

- Imagining and dreaming will make you more prosperous and successful.
- Visualizing your goals in necessary to make your goals come to life.
- Dreaming or visualizing convinces your subconscious that you are already in possession of the success or wealth that you desire.
- Most people are asleep so they don't use their hidden potential.
- Create the sensations, enthusiasm and feelings of already being successful. This enthusiasm will make you successful.
- Feeling successful will make you successful.

your battle. Rejoice and experience the *high* that wealth will bring you when you achieve it. And remember, just to help out my readers, I have included an excellent "no money down" real estate business plan in later chapters. The plan comes with many pictures, so my readers can use this plan to imagine and visualize their money dreams.

Enthusiasm Made Him A Fortune

I knew a man who felt enthusiastic about his goals. He decided that his fortune was going to be made with brass trinkets that he wanted to import from Korea. He got very excited and was always emotional about his business. At the time, he was struggling, but you would have thought that he was making a million bucks a year. It was as if he were experiencing something that he didn't have, but knew that he would get. He reacted to everything as if it were a million-dollar decision. His enthusiasm for his business was very high. I remember going to his house and watching him and his family ship packages out. They all worked as if they had drunk five cups of coffee. They also had big smiles on their faces. I had never seen such enthusiasm. If there is a secret to motivation, they knew what it was. I believe it was enthusiasm. It was raw joyful enthusiasm.

I'll tell you something, every member of his family has as much enthusiasm for the business now as they had many years ago. There is one difference, however. The company now makes an enormous amount of money each year importing from the Orient. A little enthusiasm can do wonders for you. This man proved it to me.

I am sure that you have noticed a different you. I am sure that you have already noticed this strange, but miraculous change. If you have been repeating your goals to yourself on a daily basis, then that is what will happen. You are going to see yourself get closer and closer to your goals every day. People always ask me, "How does it work?" I always tell them, "I don't know how it works, but thank God that it does." You know, I only included this paragraph, so I could share in the development of the new you. It always excites me to see people becoming successful.

Chapter Six

Securing Your Wealth Goals

I know that you have been looking forward to this chapter. I will show you how you can make your dreams a reality. We will begin to plan the steps necessary for your successful future. We will use your mind to plan and execute those steps. It's what you might call the "*Lazy Man's Method of Becoming Wealthy*." We can also call it, "*Novanetics*". It really doesn't matter what we call it, as long as you get the results that you want. This chapter will get you the results. The first thing that I want to do is to refresh your memory about some of my goals that I described in a previous chapter. I am doing this so that you will have an example to study. I have re-written some of the instructions for you in this chapter.

1) **Automobile:** I have in my possession a new, gray luxury new Mercedes Benz sports car.

2) **Home:** 1 now live in a $500,000, 1,500-square-foot home by the beach.

3) **Concentration:** I can now devote my full energy and concentration to a subject of my choice. I can devote my full attention to any activity or subject without being distracted.

4) **Persistence:** I always get what I want because I am the persistent type. I keep striving for what I want until I have it or until I no longer desire it.

5) **Closer ties:** I am now a good friend of Bob Fields, the manager of the bank with which I conduct all of my business affairs.

6) **Health:** I have lost 45 pounds and I am thinner and full of energy.

7) **Relationships:** I am developing a more loving and meaningful relationship with my wife and my two-year-old son. I will spend more time with them because I want to grow with them.

8) **Travel:** I would like to visit the country of India. I will visit Bombay, Calcutta and New Delhi. I feel that I can travel to that country on a budget since the hotel and food is cheaper. I would like to look at products that are manufactured there.

I just picked out eight achievement goals from my list. Remember, you can pick either more or less than the number of goals that I picked. The choice is yours. You could pick more. Let's start with the first two goals.

You have been repeating your goals to yourself, haven't you? I hope so. How do you achieve your goals? Repeat your goals to yourself on a daily basis. Not only should you repeat your goals to yourself, but you should also visualize their completion. Let me show you. Visualize your new luxury car. You can see yourself driving down the highway in your new luxury Mercedes sports car. You can smell the soft leather and feel the instruments with your fingertips. You will get excited knowing that you own this car.

Visualize your new house. You can see yourself living in a new luxury elegant house. You can walk through the modern kitchen and walk through the living room then run up the stairs to view the upstairs bedrooms, including your huge master bedroom. Look out the window and enjoy a great view of the city. You will even get excited knowing that you own this luxurious house and this fine car. You should have a burning desire to obtain this luxurious house and fine car. If you can conceive of its possession, with some work, the luxurious house and expensive car could be yours.

Your Ultimate Plan

The first thing you must do is plan your success. You must ask yourself some simple questions. The first is: When do I want my luxury new Mercedes Benz sports car or the Porsche sports car? And the answer is: I want it one year from now. I also want a $500,000 luxurious house. When do I want the house? I want the luxurious house in one year. I want both the car and the house in one year. I want you to put a due date on each of your goals.

Don't worry about underestimating the amount of time that you will need to acquire your goal. You can revise your goal any time that you want. You don't have to stick with the figure that you have right now. But it is important that you put due dates on everything which you desire. This is the case for all your needs and wants: financial, personal, growth and relationship goals. We'll talk more about this later.

What I Need To Achieve These Goals

You must ask yourself, "What do I need to achieve my goals?" This is a very important question, one which you must be able to answer in order to fulfill your goals. Also, you must have a plan. Your subconscious mind will help carry out your plan of action. If you have any problems relating to your plan of action, use the problem-solving technique listed in the previous chapter.

Use A Worksheet

The use of a worksheet will make this step easier for you. Let me explain. As an example, I am working on two goals right now. They are obtaining a car and a house. I know that to get these items, I must earn a certain amount of money. Because of that, I will add a third goal. The third goal is: "I have $200,000 in my possession. I will use this money to pay for my car and to make a down payment on my house." To get my car and house I need the money. I should now start to concentrate on the money.

My next question should be, *what do I need in order to produce $200,000?* I need a source of income. I have decided to add income rentals on my property with no money down. I will divide sections of my property to raise rental income in order to raise enough capital to buy my house and car. Use your plan but if you don't have a plan, then use the business plan in this book. As a favor to readers, I have included details of this "no money down" income property plan. Refer to the real estate "apartment addition" section of this book.

What Did He Need?

Lunsford Richardson started out as a school teacher. He later became a druggist with his own wholesale drug business. The year was 1898. Back then, druggists created their own home remedies. Richardson created 19 home remedies that he planned to sell in Greensboro, New York. Richardson wanted to make more money with his products; he had a dream of becoming wealthy. He wanted success. At the age of 55, Richardson decided to fulfill his dream. He planned his destiny. He had to concentrate his effort on manufacturing his 19 new remedies. Richardson planned out his new venture very carefully. In 1905, Richardson sold his wholesale business for $8,000. He then rented out a factory to manufacture his 19 remedies. Only one of Richardson's products was selling; it was called the *"Croup and Pneumonia Salve."* The new manufacturing business was not doing well and Richardson knew that he had to make another plan.

He had a dream and he was determined to

succeed. He studied his business and decided that what was needed was a name change for his one successful product. He named this product after his brother-in-law, Dr. Joshua Vick. He called his new product VICK'S VAPORUB. This new name helped his product do much better. Richardson concentrated on this one product and did very well with it. Today, this same company Richardson founded is a billion dollar corporation. I am sure that you have heard of VICK'S VAPORUB.

Your Needs

You must have certain requirements. These are things that you need, in order to achieve your goals. Use these sheets for every goal that you have. Fill in this chart so that you will know exactly what you need to complete your desired goal. Filling in "My goal requirements" chart will help you fill in the second chart called "My Goal Chart." For each section, write in what you need.

Planning Your Goal

You should use one of these sheets for each goal you have. Write the goal that you want to complete in the first column; in the second column, fill out the appropriate due date for each goal, i.e., the day that you will achieve that particular goal. I will go over the rest of the worksheet in the following paragraphs.

My Goal Requirements

Your Goal	
Monetary	
Time	
Physical	
Educational	
Personality	

Skill	

My Goal Chart

Your Goal(s)	
Monetary	
Due Dates	
Obstacles	
Solutions	
Rewards	

Any Obstacles

To achieve your goals, you need money. To obtain money, you must have a plan. Money will come to you through a plan that you create and successfully carry out. I am going to show you a simple system that will allow you to look for any hidden obstacles.

First, visualize that you have already completed your goal. I want you to think backwards, think of all of the things that you had to do to complete your goal.

My goals are to have a new car and a house. I need $200,000 to achieve those goals. I need a source of income in order to get $200,000. You can use your business plan. If you don't have a business plan, use the business plan, I have written for you.

1) Starting capital
2) Lack of education
3) Time
4) An office
5) Office equipment and supplies
6) Transportation
7) Employees
8) The right attitude

Just to show you how to do it, I will list the solutions to all of these obstacles. I am using the resource and advantage worksheet to help me arrive at the solutions. Make sure that you have your strengths, likes, resources and advantages worksheet in front of you before you start this exercise. They can be found in the chapter titled: "*How To Get The Wealth You Want.*" You will have to do the same exercise, so pay close attention to the way that I do it.

1) **Starting Capital**: I have $3,408 in my savings account that I can use. I also have rare coins and collectables that I will sell if I have to. I also make $720 a week at my regular job. I will budget that money to allow for capital expansion.

2) **Lack Of Education**: It is important that I specialize in a field before I enter it. That is why I must educate myself in the income property field. I need more education in adding income rentals on my property with no money down. I will divide sections of my property to raise rental income in order to raise enough capital. I have decided to go to the public library and get books that I can on the subject. I

Business Plan: I have decided to add income rentals on my property with no money down. I will divide sections of my property into apartments to raise rental income in order to raise enough capital. What obstacles do I face? Let me list all of my obstacles. (As a favor to readers, I have included details of this "no money down" income property plan. Refer to the real estate "apartment addition" section of this book.)

will also sign up for a business class once a week at the local college and I will talk to anyone who can help me. I will also go to the local bookstore and buy books on starting an income property business with no money down. (The bookstore usually has more up-to-date books than does the library. (As a favor to readers, I have included details and pictures of this "no money down" income property plan. Refer to the real estate "apartment addition" section of this book.)

3) **My Time**: I work days, so I can only work nights and weekends on this project. My wife is home during the day, so she can help with this new business. My kids can help during the weekends.

4) **An Office**: My business is still small, so at this point I don't need an office. I will use my home. I can set up my business in the living room. If I have to, I can always use my uncle's office. I will put up a website and rent a P.O. Box for my incoming business mail.

5) **Office Equipment & Supplies**: I have some office equipment and supplies in my home right now, I can use them. I can also use office equipment at my uncle's office. For any other equipment or supplies that I need I will buy them out of my budget.

6) **Transportation**: I have a car that I can use for transportation. My wife has a car so she can use her car for the business while I am at work. If a van is needed for the business to load and unload large items, I can sell my car and/or budget for a van.

7) **Employees**: I will not hire any employees now because I can't afford any. My wife and my kids can help me for now. I can hire out, for any specialized duties that have to be performed.

8) **My Attitude**: I am going to be very positive about my new business. I will also be persistent. I will work hard to achieve my goals. If any obstacles gets in my way, I will overcome them. I will talk to business people and also read many self-improvement and business books so that I can be the best that I can be.

Putting Together Your Dreams

You have given yourself one year to achieve your goals, one full year to reach your objectives. It is now time to work out the game plan for reaching your goals. By now, you should have a plan of action. You can work your plan out alone or you can get some help from others. In this regard, two heads are always better than one.

Frank Set Out To Do It

The subject of setting and achieving goals reminds me of someone who has inspired me. Frank, a 32-year-old restaurant cook, told me that he had dreams of becoming wealthy one day. He just didn't know what to do. I asked him to fill in the exercise that would pinpoint his strengths and weaknesses. He went through that example and

then, before going to sleep one night, he asked his

A PLAN FOR GOAL SETTING

1) Create and write down obtainable goals that you want to achieve.
2) Set up a time limit for each of your goals so that you can achieve your goals.
3) Have five year, one year, 90 day and one week goals or a combination of these time limits for your goals.
4) Divide your goals into segments and chart the progress of the segments of your goals.
5) Create rewards for yourself when you have completed segments of your goal. You should get a large reward when you have completed your full goal.
6) With a plan understand what you have to do to achieve your goals.
7) Make a schedule of everything you have to do to complete your goals.
8) Make it a habit to take notes in a book on your progress and needs.
9) Find any obstacles in your path and find creative solutions for them.
10) Repeat, visualize and become enthusiastic about your goals.
11) You have to sow the seeds before you reap the harvest, so set your goals, for your life.

subconscious mind to tell him what direction to follow. The next morning, as he woke up, it hit him. A sudden thought came into his mind. From that day on he knew what he wanted.

He came to me and said, "You know, Dave I am really a good cook. People come from all over to eat what I have cooked. Two weeks ago, I tried your exercises. I decided to have my own restaurant. I know I can make it work. Every day I can see myself in my own restaurant talking to my customers, and in the kitchen, overseeing the cooks who work for me. I walk outside my restaurant and I can see the sign with my name on it. It's not a dream, because I know that what I see will be mine." He told me these words with an urgent seriousness. "Have you planned out what you are going to do?" I asked him. "Yes," he said, in a confident voice. I looked over his plans. I was so proud of Frank. I told him, "Frank, you are an inspiration. You did your homework. Do your financial research, so that there is little doubt in your mind that you will succeed."

Two years later, I heard from him. He told me then that he owned the restaurant of his dreams. He wanted to serve me a dinner personally. I asked him what he had done in the past two years, and he told me he had left the task up to his mind. He dreamed and dreamed about the restaurant that he knew he would own; that he was determined to own. In a sincere voice, he told me that he worked very hard as a cook to save up for this venture. He worked so hard that he was promoted twice, once to head cook and a second time to restaurant manager. With the experience and extra money that he made in his managerial position, he was able to obtain the restaurant of his dreams.

Creating Your Ultimate Plans

The main task now is to put your plan of action into some kind of a time frame. Make yourself responsible for certain tasks every month. Break your ten-year goals into yearly goals. Then, break your one-year goals into 90-day goals and then break your 90-day goals into weekly goals. If you do a lot of work, break it down into daily goals. You can break down your goals whichever way you want. Do whatever you feel comfortable with. Let me give you an example of a one-year goal that has been broken down into 90-day goals.

My One-Year Goal: To buy a new Mercedes Benz sports car and buy a $500,000 house; to create an income property business, with no money down, and to have a more loving relationship with my wife and son.

Ninety-Day Goals

Every 90 days, new 90-day goals should be created. The reason for this is that you won't know what has to be done until the time comes. I have listed here the first two 90-day goals of the year. I can't do a full year of 90-day goals because I don't know what will happen in a year's time. The things listed are necessary to reach my ultimate goal.

SUMMARY

- Use a worksheet with the goals and time frame that you plan to complete.
- Repeat Visualize and become enthusiastic about your goals.
- Understand what you have to do to achieve your goals; find any obstacles in your path and create solutions for them.
- Create rewards for yourself when you have completed segments of your goal.
- You should give yourself a large reward when you complete your goal and small rewards when you have completed a segment of your goal.
- It is easier to achieve your goals if you place them in a set time frame with due dates.
- Have a five year, one year, 90 day and one week goals or some combination of these times.
- You will have to sow seeds before you can reap success.

January - March goals: Form the income property business, get the rough blueprints to add income property to the home; find the plan that is most suitable to myself; My goal is to add income rentals on my property with no money down. I will divide sections of my property to apartments to raise enough capital. I will sign up for a business class; obtain self-improvement books and design a budget for conserving capital. Take out one week from work to spend more time with my wife and son. (As a favor to readers, I have included details of this "no money down" income property plan. Refer to the real estate "apartment addition" section of this book.)

April - June goals: Maintain income property business, find new books on doing the rough blue prints. Find licensed professionals that can give advice. Study books on income property or apartment rentals and business. Study hard and get good grades in my business classes and study my self-improvement books. Look over the budget and look for ways of raising income. Find ways of lowering expenses. Take my wife on our second honeymoon so that we can experience more loving, meaningful moments together.

One-Week Goals

To plan your weekly goals, you will break down your 90-day goals into workable parts. Let me show you what I mean by breaking down 90-day goals into weekly goals. You can also think of this as planning ahead.

January 1 - January 7 goals: Register my business name; be firm on the blueprint plan, get estimates for future rental income. This way I don't use my money, pick up books at the library on, adding rental units to your property, and self-improvement, and see what my local bookstore has as well. (As a favor to readers, I have included details of this "no money down" income property plan. Refer to the real estate "apartment addition" section of this book.) Get a class schedule from the local college for classes. Begin to create my budget. Take my whole family to Disneyland on Sunday afternoon.

Do you see how everything can be organized and set up neatly? When something is organized, it is carried out properly. I want you to venture out and be a big success. That is why I am showing you the best possible way of planning your goals.

Get a monthly, or preferably a weekly planner. You can use any calendar that you can write on. On this planner, write down all of the things that you plan to do. In this way, you will get everything done on a weekly basis.

Rewards

It would be asking a lot of yourself to complete all of the steps necessary to achieve your goals without pausing to enjoy an occasional reward. We all need rewards. Yes, we do. I have left a section on the chart for listing your rewards. Whenever you accomplish something, give yourself a reward. When I speak of an accomplishment, I am referring to the completion of one of the goals that you have listed on your weekly or 90-day goal chart. When you finish a weekly goal, go for a walk in the park, or to a movie, or go bowling or go out with a friend. When you finish your 90-day goal, take yourself out to a steak dinner, or to a theater play, or on a small fun vacation. You name the reward.

Make sure that the reward fits the task. If you do something large, give yourself a large reward. If you do something small, give yourself a small reward. Write the reward out on the chart and enjoy it only after you have completed your task.

Fun Things You Can Do For Rewards

- Watch a movie in a movie theater.
- Go to a bowling alley and bowl.
- Go to a rink and ice skate.
- Go to a sidewalk or a rink and roller skate.
- Ride a bicycle.
- Have a barbeque in your backyard.
- Have a picnic on the beach.
- Go to an amusement park on go on the rides.
- Go to a theater and watch a theater play.
- Play basketball, baseball or football in a park.
- Go to a professional sports event.
- Go out and get ice cream, frozen yogurt, or a milk shake.
- Go to a park and go camping with tents or a rented recreational vehicle.
- Eat at a dine-in restaurant.
- Go shopping in a mall.

Achieve Your Goal

The most important goal that you must set for yourself is to fulfill all of your other goals. Make sure that you have a plan of action. You will then know what you will need to complete your goals and how you are going to complete your goals. Stick by your plan of action or your plans will never be realized. I know that you want to succeed.

Success is around the corner. The price is some hard and faithful work. The reward? Wealth. If you follow my methods of carrying out your plans, you can be wealthy. I am showing you how to unleash the power of your mind. Realize all of your potential and victory will be yours; back away from your opportunity and failure is all that you may know.

Chapter Seven

Laugh Your Way To Wealth.

In this chapter I will show you how to develop a great funny personality. There is a secret makes a person funny in all situations. This chapter will disclose this secret to you. With this chapter you master the technique of being funny and likable. This comedy secret is guarded in a lock box by the best people in the world. Now, it is available to you. You can be a hilarious and funny person who is the life of the party. Being funny and having good spirits will definitely, help you be a likable and lovable person. As you read this chapter, you will read the secret methods funny and likable people all over the world, use to win friends over and earn their love.

Smiling.

The first steps to being funnier is you have to smile. That's right smile. Get a mirror and put it in front of you. Now, make a big smile as you stare into the mirror. Round your lips and make a big smile. Keep practicing smiling. Smiling alone will make you a funnier person. Keep practicing to smile in the morning, in the afternoon and in the evening. Make sure your smile is a heavy smile. Tense your whole face for long periods of time, using your big heavy smile. This is an exercise to get you used to smiling. You might try practicing smiling about twenty minutes every day. When you practice, imagine being in bad situations and difficult situations, then put on a very big smile. I have provided smiling exercises in this section. Smile and act joyful, as you say each statement.

1) A person hits you with an umbrella. Smile cheerfully as you say, "*You hit me. I might have a bump. I don't have insurance.*"

2) You taste your food and there is too much salt on it. Smile cheerfully as you say, "*What's in this? There is too much salt. It isn't good for my diet.*"

3) Money from your pocket falls on the floor. Smile cheerfully as you say, "*It my money. I need it to make my car payment.*"

4) The coffee at work spills on your shirt. Smile cheerfully as you say, "*You stained my shirt. My dry cleaner have to clean it.*"

5) It started to rain on your newly styled hair. Smile cheerfully as you say, "*My hair is ruined. I should have used hairspray.*"

6) As you are walking, you trip and fall, then stand up. Smile cheerfully as you say, "*I must have slipped. I'm up again. My clothes are fine.*"

Laugh Out Loud

The first step to being funny is smiling and the second step to being funnier is to laugh well. When you laugh out loud, situations are better and you actually do better due to your laughter. Practice laughing out loud. Just let out a loud ha ha and keep laughing out loud. As you practice laughing practice a loud bellowing laugh that makes the room shake. You know the type of laughter. Practice very loud, ha, ha, ha ha ha, loud bellowing deep laugher. You must keep practicing this loud deep laughter and don't forget your heavy smiles. You could try laughing bouts that add up to twenty minutes a day. Keep practicing the loud bellowing laughter and you will find that you are starting to become a funnier person. Funny people are liked by other people. Practice this type of loud laughter with difficult and unpleasant situations. Here are some situations, that I want you to practice laughing, so that you are calm and collect during difficult and tough situations. FIRST EXCERCISE: To do this exercise right, imagine and do the act on this list, then just burst out and laugh loudly for one full minute. SECOND EXCERCISE: Imagine that the bad thing happens to you then, laugh as you say the reply. Keep going through this list and laugh loudly so you are used to being funny. You can add other examples to this laughter list. Keep practicing laughing loudly for bad or difficult situations. You want to be funny don't you? Yes, so start the list.

Practice laughing and being funny.

1) Your car just broke down and you have no ride. (use a loud bellowing laughter) *Laugh as you say*, "I'm going to call the Auto Club. My car isn't completely broken."
2) You find out you have no money in the bank and as you leave the bank a pick-pocket steals your cash filled wallet. (use a loud bellowing laughter) *Laugh as you say*, "Return my money. I need the cash more than you."
3) Your wife has packed her things and is going to leave you. (use a loud bellowing laughter) *Laugh as you say*, "You can't leave me. We're not apart yet."
4) A tow truck is towing your car because you didn't make car payments. (use a loud bellowing laughter) *Laugh as you say*, "You can't tow my car. I need it to go to the doctor."
5) Your boss fires you from your job for wrecking the office. (use a loud bellowing laugher) *Laugh as you say*, "I'm a good employee. You didn't give me a thirty day notice."
6) You are camping and a large bear chases you in the woods. (use a loud bellowing laughter) *Laugh as you say*, "I'm being chased by a bear. I better find a tree to climb."
7) You just fell as you walked and hurt your leg. (use loud bellowing laughter) *Laugh as you say*, "If this gets any worse. I will need a wheelchair."
8) Someone threw a whole red cherry pie on your white shirt and face. (use a loud bellowing laughter) *Laugh as you say*, "My shirt is ruined. I prefer apple pie. It would taste better on my shirt."
9) A person hit your hand with a hammer as they worked. (use a loud bellowing laughter) *Laugh as you say*, "Don't hit me. I need my hands. My medical insurance has a deductible."

If you continue these exercises you will be able to act cool and pleasant in bad or difficult situations. Do this and you can logically think in bad situations and other people will like you more. Don't forget when practicing these laughter exercises; use a loud hearty bellowing laughter. Keep practicing and you will become funnier and funnier.

VOICE TONE

Change The Tone Of Your Voice

We talk when we want to communicate with another person. This way we can communicate ideas and knowledge. Changes in your voice tone create more interest in your talk. As you talk make a high pitch with your voice then make a low pitch. Practice using your funny voice with the following six different techniques. These techniques are like musical notes for singing.

The six funny vocal techniques.

1) Say, "Hi dear. It's me. I'm home." (Say it in a high pitched voice, with a cheerful smile)
2) Say, "Hi dear. It's me. I'm home." (Say it in a loud whisper voice, with a cheerful smile)
3) Say, "Hi dear. It's me. I'm home." (Say it

in a loud whining voice, with a cheerful smile)

4) Say, "Hi dear. It's me. I'm home." (Say it in a low pitched voice, with a cheerful smile)

5) Say, "Hi dear. It's me. I'm home." (Say it in a medium humming pitched voice, with a cheerful smile)

6) Say, "Hi dear. It's me. I'm home." (Say it in a fast pitched voice, with a cheerful smile)

Now we are going to take the following six sentences and change the way you say them.

1) I went to the garage. (Say it in a high pitched voice, with a cheerful smile)

2) The door was open. (Say it in a loud whisper voice, with a cheerful smile)

3) I walked into the garage slowly and carefully. (Say it in a loud whining voice, with a cheerful smile)

4) Then all of a sudden it came out. (Say it in a low pitched voice, with a cheerful smile)

5) A large raccoon ran in circles. (Say it in a medium humming voice, with a cheerful smile)

6) Then the large rodent ran out the door. (Say it in a fast pitched voice, with a cheerful smile)

When you sing out one to six, you will sound funny. You can change the order of the tones. Change your talk so you are loud and times and quieter at other times. An example is that you are loud when something is good or exciting and quite when something is secretive or sad. This way other people are interested in what you say and you will sound funny.

Comically Singing Criticism

If you have something to say that may sound awful, then sing it, instead of yelling. Do this and you will sound funny. Singing makes everything you say, sound so much better. If you smile as you sing, the criticism sounds a lot better. Try singing these examples of critical things you might say to other people. You could end your song by singing out the last word three times longer than the other words. Pick you favorite singer, to sing to people.

1) Try talking in a normal voice, because you yell too much. (Sing it with a cheerful smile then laugh at the end)

2) Find out in your own way. I am not telling you. (Sing it with a cheerful smile then laugh at the end)

3) I don't like your attitude. Change it and go in the other room. (Sing it with a cheerful smile then laugh at the end)

4) You took my money. Give it back to me and we'll be fine. (Sing it with a cheerful smile then laugh at the end)

5) I don't like the way you are dressed, your clothes do not match. (Sing it with a cheerful smile then laugh at the end)

Begin Humor With Positive Traits Then Be Critical

Begin your humor with positive feedback of their strong points then end off your funny lines with criticism of their faults. So when we say this to other people we will start off defining their strengths by giving them positive feedback, like you are good, great or smart, then you would criticize them. So despite their positive traits, you feel there are behaviors they could change. After discussing their unfavorable trait, you could begin another sentence with more admirable positive strengths. Here are some examples of these funny statements.

EXAMPLES OF CRITICAL HUMOR:

First Person

1) You're a great person to work with, but you just lose your temper and get angry a lot. (smile and laugh as you talk and you could change voice tones)

2) You are so much fun to be with, but I can't stand all of the things you break. It's shattering. (smile and laugh as you talk and you could change voice tones)

3) I have this great feeling around you, but you are so irresponsible. (smile and laugh as you talk and you could change voice tones)

4) You are so smart and you are witty, but you're. How do I say it? Oh boring. (smile and laugh as you talk and you could

51

change voice tones)

5) You are so dependable and you get the job done right, but I never get paid what I am owed. (smile and laugh as you talk and you could change voice tones)

6) You are so adult like and mature, but lately you have been acting like a child.. (smile and laugh as you talk and you could change voice tones)

7) You do a good quick job, but you broke my equipment and it will cost you $200. Two hundred. (smile and laugh as you talk and you could change voice tones)

Third Person

1) She is a great person to be with, but if you do the wrong thing she loses her temper and yells. (smile and laugh as you talk and you could change voice tones)

2) He is such a pleasure to work with, but if you make one mistake he will take the files away from you. He will. (smile and laugh as you talk and you could change voice tones)

3) He has a heart of gold, but push him the wrong way and you'll hear the door slam after he throws you out. (smile and laugh as you talk and you could change voice tones)

4) This partnership with him is great, but he shortchanged me twice. No once but twice. (smile and laugh as you talk and you could change voice tones)

5) He is so good at counting the money that it is exact to the penny, but sometimes you don't get your 30% share. It's less. (smile and laugh as you talk and you could change voice tones)

6) She looks pretty, but after you get to know her, she gets conceited. (smile or laugh as you talk and you could change voice tones)

7) He is so smart and knows what he is talking about, but if you won't listen he will point his finger at you and lecture you. (smile or laugh as you talk and you could change voice tones)

USING BODY LANGUAGE

We can make hand signals, face signals, and body signals when we want to communicate with another person. This is body language. Another method of improving your communication is body language. It can make you funnier. You could use hand signals or face signals instead of words. Don't forget to laugh. That is using your body to talk. You must move your arms, hands, head and other parts of your body to gain interest. Move your body and arms in such a way as to get more interest in what you have to say, but don't forget to laugh. Do these exercises and others excercises that you "make up" to practice good funny body language?

1) When you say "me" or "I", you could point to yourself. (Smile cheerfully and laugh)

2) When you talk about another person point to that person or point away. (Smile cheerfully and laugh)

3) When you say "NO" use body language to say no. When you say yes, use body language to say yes. (Smile cheerfully and laugh)

4) When you seem upset you could put your hands out. (Smile cheerfully and laugh)

5) When you want walk or go in a direction you could point to that direction. (Smile cheerfully and laugh)

6) When you talk about something good then you could put on a big smile and you could put out your hands. (Smile cheerfully and laugh)

7) When you talk about something sad or unpleasant, you throw our arms down and could look sad or frown or gasp. (Smile cheerfully and laugh)

8) When you talk about something funny then you could laugh. (Smile cheerfully and laugh)

9) When you talk about something unpleasant you could laugh as you say it. (Smile cheerfully and laugh)

10) When you don't know something, you could shrug your shoulders. (Smile cheerfully and laugh)

11) When you are happy or your team won, you could clench your fists and put your arms up. (Smile cheerfully and laugh)

12) When you don't like someone you could hold your palms out acting to hold that person back. (Smile cheerfully and laugh)

Funny Dancing

Sometimes you have to do something peculiar in public or to other people, like sneaking away, hitting someone or taking something away. The best thing to do is to dance out what you are doing. Dancing out the act will make you seem funny. One of the best dances to do to be funny is ballet with a cheerful smile. You know, the dance where they dance on their toes, and they twirl around. When you do ballet with a cheerful smile, people will laugh. You can use another dance like rapping or waltzing, but with a cheerful smile. When you dance to these examples, take steps that make you twirl, prance, move back and forth and even move side to side, with a cheerful smile. To practice being funny when you dance, try the following exercises while you dance. You could try another dance, but ballet is one of the better funny dances.

1) Take something away from someone with your hands. (Dance as you laugh or cheerfully smile. Make your fingers dance with this example)

2) Sneaking away from a room or house. (Laugh or cheerfully smile as you dance).

3) Slowly walking into a tense room or tense house. (Laugh or cheerfully smile as you dance).

4) Pushing or hitting someone lightly. (Laugh or cheerfully smile as you dance).

5) Taking an object away from a person. (Laugh or cheerfully smile as you dance).

6) Picking something up and holding it as you walk away. (Laugh or cheerfully smile as you dance).

7) Doing work that you don't like for someone like, sweeping the floor or washing the dishes. (Laugh or cheerfully smile as you dance).

8) Slowly take some of your clothes off. (Laugh or cheerfully smile as you dance and remove your clothes).

9) Changing the channel on the television if others are watching television. (Laugh or cheerfully smile as you dance with your hands)

10) Telling someone you don't like them, after they did something awful. (Laugh or cheerfully smile as you dance)

Use Funny Items To Make People Laugh

Funny clothes, gag props and other funny items always make people laugh. You never know when you will have to make the mood funny. Bad situations need funny items. I have seen many people wear and use funny items and I have laughed. I personally have funny shirts, funny glasses, funny hats, plastic bunnies and funny slippers, that other people think are funny. Buy funny gags, props or items and use them for those special occasions or whenever the mood is gloomy. Good funny items are:

- ❖ Funny shoes, pants, ties and socks.
- ❖ Funny hats, glasses, masks and wigs.
- ❖ Funny clothes, garments, attire and costumes.
- ❖ Funny gags, tricks, jokes and stunts.
- ❖ Birthday, Christmas, Halloween and Holiday party, gags, props and favors.

Funny Words

How do you use awful words and still be funny. To continue to be funny, change the word to a different word to say awful and disturbing words. You could have the words rhyme with other words. You could also repeat words to be funny. (Instead of saying, "You broke my car." You would say, "You somehow rearranged my ride and now it is worse). You can even switch around some words in sentences so they don't get angry from your angry statements.

Three Ways To Make An Awful Word Funnier

Change the word to a different word, with similar meaning . Instead of "broke" use "rearranged." Instead of "arrest" use "took away." Instead of "insulted" say "said." Instead of "stole" say "took."

Use a rhyming words that sounds like that word. Examples: Instead of "dumb" use "crumb." Instead of "fight" use "trite." Instead of "cash" use "stash."

You could repeat a dull word. Examples: He took took took. It is night night night. I was beaten beaten beaten

How To Make Bad Things Funny

There are times when you want to explain an unpleasant or bad situation. It could be a difficult or foolish situation. To be funny you must use more words, remove and change or repeat some of the words to describe the situation. In other words you must be wordy but "non insulting" to be funny. Increase the description of the statement by adding words. You can even repeat words. This way the foolish act is clear and easy to understand. Don't say angrily, "You hit the window and broke the glass." As you laugh and sing funny tones, do say "You threw that baseball at my window from your yard, to my yard. You broke my new glass window. It's broken. Try the following exercise with your own sentences at home.

FIRST EXAMPLE

FIRST SENTENCE *(laugh and cheerfully smile as you say this and you might sing different vocal tones and use body language)*

SUMMARY

- Creating a funny and cheerful personality will make you more likable and have more friends.
- Being a funny person will help you keep your job, keep your marriage and help you communicate with others.
- Practice putting a big heavy smile on your face on a daily basis.
- Practice a loud bellowing "laughing out loud" laugh every day.
- Change the tone of your voice to sound interesting and funny.
- Try to comically sing criticism to others, so they hear your concerns.
- You can begin humorous statements with positive traits.
- Use body language to appear funnier and to communicate better with others..
- Use funny props, items and gags to create a positive funny tone in a bad situation.
- Use funny dancing like ballet when trying to use objectionable body language.
- Make awful words sound funny. Add details to statements to make them funny.
- In emergency or important situations you must yell with a harshness in your voice.
- Being funny will make you a better and more likable person.

You bumped the dish and broke it.

FUNNY SENTENCE *(laugh and cheerfully smile as you say this and you might sing different vocal tones and use body language)*

You bumped bumped, bumped the white saucer and broke it.

FUNNIER SENTENCE *(laugh and cheerfully smile as you say this and you might sing different vocal tones and use body language)*

You bumped the porcelain dish with your

leg.   Yeah you did.   You did.   You did.   The dish fell and broke.   Its in little pieces.   Little tiny pieces.

SECOND EXAMPLE

FIRST SENTENCE   (*laugh and cheerfully smile as you say this and you might sing different vocal tones and use body language*)

You hit my car and put a big dent in it.

FUNNY SENTENCE   (*laugh and cheerfully smile as you say this and you might sing different vocal tones and use body language*)

You hit my car.   It was my car.   My car. There's a big dent on the side.

FUNNIER SENTENCE   (*laugh and cheerfully smile as you say this and you might sing different vocal tones and use body language*)

You hit my car with your front bumper.   I heard it smack. It smacked on the side.   There is a big dent.   And I mean it is big.   Do you have insurance?

Combining Comical Techniques

Sometimes you want to say something rude or annoying and you want to say it funny so the other person will not get offended.   Sometimes you just want to say, "You are stupid" or "You are foolish."   For these cases you should be funny when you talk to other people.   It is better to use humor in these cases.   If you must criticize a person's faults then follow two steps.   First, laugh as you talk and you could change your voice tone as you laugh and talk.   You could be using body like moving your hands and smirking your face. Do these things while you criticize the person's faults.   Practice doing this when saying difficult statements or when acting peculiar (like taking

something, or pushing something).   It may seem to others that you are making fun of them or joking about their faults.   If this happens it is better to be silent or to say less and being funny.   If you are not funny you will not be liked and you will not be able to communicate with other people in difficult situations.   Use humor to be funny to help your life and other people's lives and be the life of the party.   If you need help with any topic, call my office and I will try to help you with any questions that you have.

Yell Your Way To Success

Laughing and smiling create a likable funny personally.   What about using a serious disciplined and authority personality that makes people jump and act quickly.   People will only act if there is harshness in your words and actions. Yelling with some anger will get people to act.   In an emergency situation, or important situations, you would have to be loud and harsh instead of funny and happy.

Try yelling with some anger in those situations where you need immediate action. You will be surprised at how quickly people do what you want.   Yell at others with anger in your words if you want to command the situation.

Final Comedy Words

David Bendah hopes that the readers enjoyed and laughed through this chapter.   All humor aside, the purpose of this chapter is to help the reader in their life.   If the reader wants to be successful, they must have a jolly side and a good sense of humor.   If you would like to be on David Bendah's mailing list to receive more information, or you would like to send him a story about yourself in regards to *"Novanetics"*, please write him.   David Bendah, PO Box 152808, Dept. DD2, San Diego, CA   92195.

Chapter Eight

Wealth Apartment Additions To Pay Your Mortgage Payments (Part One)

You are in luck. I will provide you with ten methods of reducing your monthly mortgage payments up to 100%. All ten methods of reducing your monthly mortgage payments are explained in the book *"NOVANETICS"* in the real estate chapters. You must read the four real estate chapters contained in this book. In the REAL ESTATE chapters I give you real examples and real situations that will help you reduce your monthly mortgage payments up to 75% or more. Almost every single person with a mortgage payment can reduce their monthly payments. There are limitation for condominium mortgage payments and certain commercial mortgages, but even these monthly mortgage payments can be reduced. Please write me with any stories or testimonials you might have after you have lowered your monthly mortgage payment up to 75% or more. This chapter will begin with Wealth Apartment Additions.

The Ten Methods Of Mortgage Assistance

1) Refinance your home and take the equity.
2) Refinance your home at a lower interest rate.
3) Get a "reverse paper" or a reverse mortgage.
4) Build an apartment in your basement
5) Build a studio apartment in your garage and an attic apartment above your garage.
6) Build a cottage or separate apartment dwelling in your backyard.
7) Build a studio apartment in your large attic. This includes the room above your garage.
8) Build an apartment addition attached to the walls of your home.
9) Convert your house into two or more different apartments.
10) Contact a government agency or your bank or your mortgage company for financial assistance to pay your mortgage.

Wealth Apartment Additions

Congratulations. Welcome to the first chapter of the Real Estate Course. I am going to provide you with many business startup plans to reduce your mortgage payments up to 75% or more. You can start with this rental income "business startup plan" that you can use in certain situations with no money down. These plans could pay up to 100% of your mortgage payments. They are very good and I am sure they will help pay your mortgage payments. Take the time to read this chapter and the other real estate chapters, if you want a lower monthly mortgage payment. After you read it, I am sure you will be very grateful you read it.

In earlier chapters I have given you examples

on setting your goals. I used income property rentals as a business startup plan. This is the goal that was used in the example. *I have decided to add income rentals on my property with no money down. I will divide sections of my property to raise rental income in order to raise enough capital to buy my house and car.* Just as a favor to my readers, I have added the details of this income property "startup plan", that can be used by any of my readers. The startup plan can pay up to 75% or more of your monthly mortgage payments. It is extremely good, so I advise you to read it. It is a great method of earning rental income that you should consider. If you own a home and are having problems paying your mortgage, then use this plan. If you don't own any real estate property you can still use this method. This method can show you how you can buy real estate with little or no money and still make a large profit. For examples in this chapter you would have to get a construction permit from your local city building department before starting construction. If you require a construction permit contact your local city building department

Adding Income Property To Your Home And Lot

Some homeowners can't pay their mortgage payments, but still want to live in their house. If the mortgage payment is $1,800 a month and the homeowner can only afford $500 a month then this route is a good way to lower monthly mortgage payments. If the homeowner has a $1,100 mortgage payment a month and the homeowner wants to stay in the home, but wants someone else

to pay the mortgage and also needs an extra $800 a month in income, then this is a good way to earn an income, live in your home and have others pay your mortgage payments. In this chapter, I will give you all of the information you will need to commit to this type of a real estate business plan. I am sure you will love the business plan, that I have written for you.

Partition Your Home

You could build walls in your home to convert it into two to three apartments and still live in your home. You could build an apartment in your garage. You could build two apartments with a private entrance, in your basement. You could even build rental cottages in your backyard.

You could even divide your home into sections and collect rent. The options are endless. You should do these modifications to your home, since the rental income, will increase the value of your home, when you sell it. What do I mean by that? Your home will go up in value since it produces rental income.

An Example Of A Home Value Increase With Rental Income.

That is what would happen if you have rental income units on your property. Your $300,000 home would have mortgage payment of about $1,300 a month (mortgage payments for 3% for 30 years would be $1,300 a month). Explain to the prospective buyer that their mortgage payments would be $1,300 and the rental income would be $1,400, so the buyer is buying your home for $100 in positive income every month. That is a great selling line.

Rental Income Example

Mortgage Payment = $1,300 a month
Rental Income = $1,400 a month

Monthly Profit For Buyer After Paying The Mortgage And Living Rent Free = $100 a month profit.

FIRST PARTITION EXAMPLE

An example of an inexpensive home partition is illustrated on the picture on this page. In this picture the home owner gives up one bedroom and one bathroom in their home for a rental. In this example "Bedroom One" and "Bathroom One" are partitioned into a studio apartment. The owner of the house puts a lock on the door of "Bedroom One" and another lock on the door of "Bathroom One." These locked doors are black in the picture. The homeowner could also put four two inch nails in each door to make sure they stay locked. The owner of the house then would put an exterior pre-hung 36 inch door in "Bedroom One." When you go to the hardware store ask for a 36" "pre-hung door (This type of door with hinges and frame is ready to install). With an exterior door the people renting "Bedroom One" would have their own outside door exit that they can use to leave their apartment. The outside door is shown in the picture on this page. The total cost of locking two doors and adding one exterior door to create a studio apartment is about **$975** (without complications and using inexpensive material and labor). As far as the electricity, water, sewer, heating and air-conditioning expense. It is too expensive to have a separate electric service, water service, a second furnace and a second air conditioning unit for the new apartment. It is easier to share the utilities with your tenants. In this example, I think between $75 to $200 a month should cover electricity, hot and cold water, heating, and air conditioning. It is simple to estimate your new tenant's utility costs.

After this simple construction, the owner of this house could collect $600 to $1,000 a month in rent. For this example, the 1,235 square foot, three bedroom house in the picture on this page, has mortgage payments that are $759.00 a month (That is $180,000 over 30 years at 3%). The rent that would be collected is $650 a month (plus $75-$200 utility expenses).

The mortgage payment is $759 a month and the tenant would pay the home owner $650 a month.

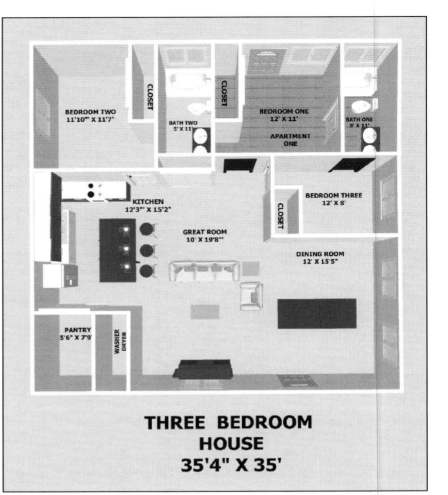

THREE BEDROOM HOUSE 35'4" X 35'

After the rental income the homeowner is out of pocket every month only $159.00 to pay the mortgage. Anyone who is unemployed or on social security income can do type of construction and end up with a profit.

SECOND PARTITION EXAMPLE

In the second picture of the three bedroom house, that home owner decided that he wanted to earn more rental income. The home owner wanted a larger positive cash flow. The home owner was paying $159 for his home mortgage after subtracting his rental income $650 from his mortgage payments.

For the second apartment addition, the home owner partitioned off "Bedroom Three" by adding a door lock to the door and adding four two inch nails. The "Bedroom Three" door that was sealed off is colored black. The three bedroom home owner has decided to partition off his dining room by building a new wall and he also built a third bathroom we will call "Bathroom Three." in his old dining room. The homeowner has built a "pre-hung" interior door in "Bedroom Three." The homeowner has also built a separate pre-hung exterior door in his "Great Room." He contacted the city building department and got a building permit. The cost of this construction to the three bedroom house to the homeowner is about $8,500 (without complications and using inexpensive material and labor). The homeowner could refinance his home and add the $8,500 cost to his new mortgage. The monthly cost of the new apartment addition on his mortgage is $35.84 a month ($8,500 for 30 years at 3% interest).

"Bedroom Three" and the "Dining Room" will be a second apartment with a full bathroom, that the home owner will rent for $850 a month (plus $75 - $200 utilities a month). The construction cost of the addition to his new mortgage is $35.84 a month. The mortgage cost for the three bedroom homeowner is $759.00 + $35.84. That is $794.84 a month in mortgage payments.

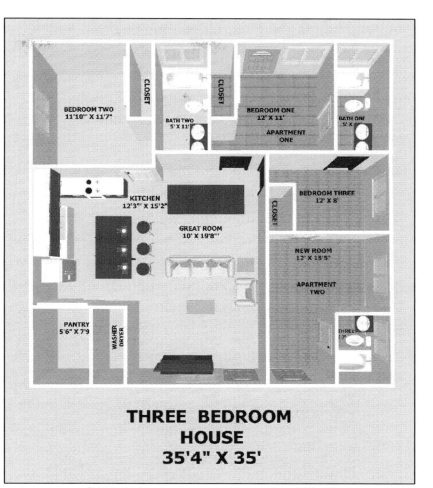

THREE BEDROOM HOUSE 35'4" X 35'

Rental Income Calculations

The rental income for both apartments is $650 for apartment one and $850 for apartment two. That is a total of $1,500 income from two apartments. $1,500 a month is $18,000 a year. If you had this rental income for ten years you could end up with $180,000 in rental income, before expenses. This homeowner also has a total of

$794.84 in mortgage payments and $1,500 in rental income. The homeowner will earn $705.16 a month after mortgage expenses. The means the homeowner will earn $705.16 a month and live rent free. That's right you heard me rent free, with a profit every month. The following example will show you how much you will earn after the apartment additions.

Rental Calculations

Mortgage Payment = 794.84 a month
Rental Income = $1,500 a month

Monthly Profit For Buyer After Paying The Mortgage And Living Rent Free = $705.16 a month profit.

A Profit Of $8,461.92 A Year or
A Profit Of $84,619.20 Over Ten Years.

You will be glad you bought a house, when you study this rental income plan. As I said in the previous example, it is much cheaper to share utilities with your tenants then have to have separate electrical, plumbing and air vent system. For both of these examples, a cost of between $75 to $200 a month should cover electricity, hot and cold water, heating, and air conditioning. It should not be hard to estimate your new tenant's utility costs. This project is great for an unemployed person or a couple on social security that want a positive cash flow, while they are on social security. It is a great program for any homeowner that wants a positive cash flow every month.

Hiring A Contractor

Make sure to pay as little as possible when constructing your apartment addition. You must cut costs to be profitable. Try to do some of the work yourself, or work with family and friends. Licensed professionals are not difficult to find. Beware of using contractors that overcharge. If you use a licensed contract, you must get three estimates from three different contractors. Some contractors overcharge by large amounts of money. You may end up with no profit and a huge debt, if you hire an expensive contractor that will take you to the grinder. Many contractors charge for extra payments for work not on their contract. I have seen contractors charge their clients $25,000 for a $4,000 job. Don't overspend and don't pay an expensive contractor a heap of money, when you can get the work done cheaper. Use professionals but budget yourself and negotiate a very low price for all work done on your home.

Have an architect look at your home plans and get the architect's advice on how to divide your home so you can still live in it. An architect may be able to recommend a very inexpensive construction company. After you get a building permit from the city, you could build studios, one bedroom apartments or even a two bedroom apartment. A studio could have a separate entrance, a kitchen and a bathroom. If you need any assistance with the construction of apartment units, please call my office and I will try to help you. You could refinance your home or get a second mortgage, and use the money; you get to renovate your home. Make sure to use a good bank.

A TYPICAL BUILDING REGULATION FOR A CALIFORNIA CITY

Accessory Dwelling Units / ADUs and JADUs An accessory dwelling unit (ADU), also known as a "mother-in-law" or "granny flat," are attached or detached residential dwelling units, on the same lot as an existing single-family dwelling unit which is zoned for single-family or multifamily use, that provides complete independent living facilities for one or more persons. This includes permanent provisions for living, sleeping, eating, cooking, and sanitation, all on the same parcel as the primary, single-family dwelling. An ADU can be an efficiency unit, as defined in Section 17958.1 of Health and Safety Code, or a manufactured home, as defined in Section 18007 of the Health and Safety Code.

A junior accessory dwelling unit (JADU) is a residential dwelling unit that is no more than 500 square feet in area, contained entirely within an existing single-family residence, and can have separate sanitation facilities from, or shared sanitation facilities with, the existing residence.

ADUs and JADUs provide housing opportunities within existing neighborhoods, creating housing that is already connected to the local character and infrastructure. The additional units help diversify the market for renters while proving supplemental income for homeowners, and thus increasing affordability throughout the city.

The Market Price Of Your Home Will Go Up

Rental income will drastically increase the value of your home. Building a rental income property on your property is a great investment, because your home will be worth more money. If your home is worth $250,000 and you paid $50,000 to build rental income property on your home. With the rental units built on your home, your home might be worth an extra $150,000. This is great for you when you sell your home for more money then you paid for it.

Building A New Home

If you are building a new home, you absolutely should add construction accessories to the construction to accommodate adding livable units to your home at a later date. If you do this, then the value of your home will go up in value. Let's say that a regular 2,000 square foot home is worth $200,000. If during the construction, you add the bathrooms, outside stairways and multiple exits, then that 2,000 square foot house could be worth $300,000, due to that added construction that will earn you rental income. The newly designed home that could be divided into separate apartments should have:

- Build a basement below the house.
- Basements could include multiple bathrooms and multiple exterior doors to the outside.
- Extend the concrete foundation of the house, but be sure to include sewer, water, cable and electricity hookups. The extended concrete foundation can be used at a later date when that part of the house is included in a construction that includes a unit with walls and a roof.
- Multiple exterior doors on each level. Floor one and floor two may have many exterior exit doors in areas where you may partition an apartment at a later date.
- Smaller windows in certain bedrooms to allow room for exterior doors and other modifications.
- Outside stairways to exterior doors on the second and third floors, so those floors can be built into separate apartments.
- Kitchen plumbing and sewer hookups in different parts of the home including the basements.
- If the attic is large enough, then a plumbing and sewer lines should be installed.
- The garage and the level above the garage with electricity, bathroom plumbing and sewer lines.
- Have a bathroom installed in any building constructed in your yard.

Electricity, Water, Heating and Air Conditioning

When dividing your home into apartment units, you may be tempted to separate all of your utilities between you and your new tenants, by installing separate plumbing, electrical, heating etc. Don't do it. It is too expensive. Separating utilities for just one studio could cost you many thousands of dollars. For water service, you would need a separate water meter for your tenant, but besides that, it is expensive to re-pipe your house.

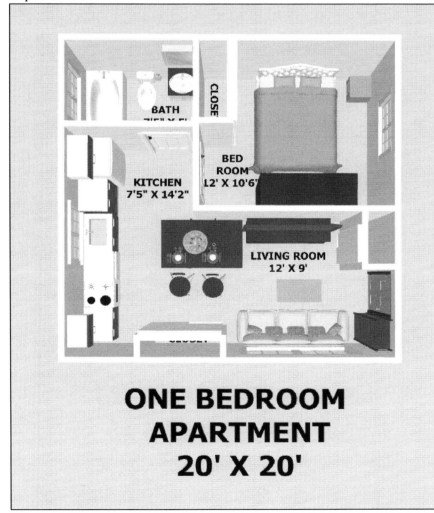

ONE BEDROOM APARTMENT 20' X 20'

Don't install separate plumbing. Having separate hot water plumbing, means having a second water heater with costly plumbing expenses.

Don't buy a separate water heater. It is too expensive. Share your cold water and your hot water with your tenant. To separate electricity, you would need a separate meter and electrical box. This doesn't include all of the costly cable rewiring. Don't separate your electrical system. Share your electrical bill with your tenant. To separate your heating you would have to buy a second furnace and then you would have to build a separate air duct system. Keep the same heating system but share your heating system with your tenant. You could also install a portable heater for your tenant. To separate air conditioning, (if you have central air conditioning) you would have to

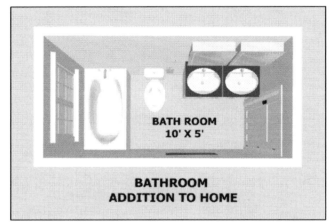

BATH ROOM
10' X 5'

BATHROOM
ADDITION TO HOME

buy a separate air conditioner and you would have to build a separate air duct system. This is too expensive. Some homes don't really need air conditioning. If air conditioning is important, you could share your air conditioning system with your tenant, and your tenant might possibly have a portable air conditioning system.

There is an easy solution to this utility expense problem. Share your utilities with your tenant and charge your tenant a monthly charge between $75 to $200 a month for electricity, hot and cold water, heating and air conditioning and you could give your tenants free Wi-Fi. Buy a good monthly internet provider like AT&T and provide free internet Wi-Fi for all of your tenants.

Building A Kitchen

In order for a section of your home to become an apartment, you will need a kitchen. You can

KITCHEN
10'10" X 10'

create a kitchen area by bringing in water, sewer and electricity to an area. You would need to bring in electricity for your refrigerator, dishwasher, garbage disposal unit and oven. Bringing in gas for your stove is an expensive option, but can be done. You would need hot and cold water and a sewer pipes for your kitchen sink and your dish washer. You could convert a bathroom to a kitchen, or a kitchen to a bathroom since water, sewer electricity is available in both. To save some costs you can build a bathroom next to a kitchen, this way both of these rooms can use the same plumbing, sewer and electricity lines.

Range hood fans installed above the stove could be vented to the outside. You would have to cut a hole in the wall or ceiling that leads to the outside. This is expensive. You can buy a vent-less range hood fan for about $50 that just circulates air in the kitchen.

Building An Apartment Unit With A Partial Kitchen

If you want to save costs, you don't have to build a full kitchen. You could buy a microwave combo with two hot plate burners on the top. The microwave unit with two burners and a refrigerator could be the kitchen.

The renter supplies the refrigerator. You could install one cabinet stainless steel sink next to the refrigerator that could be used for preparing food and washing dishes. Kitchens have stainless steel sinks to prevent breakage from dishes and pans.

A kitchen could consist of one 30 inch wide appliance. This compact appliance includes one stainless steel sink with a kitchen faucet, a compact refrigerator and freezer, a small storage compartment and two hot plate burners.

Building Bathrooms

All separate apartment units need at least one bathroom. The minimum amount of space you would need to build a bathroom with a bathtub, toilet and sink is seven feet by five feet or 35 square feet, but be sure to follow building codes, with specifications when building a bathroom. Do not

SMALL BATHROOM ADDITION TO HOME

make a bathroom less than five feet wide if you want to include a bathtub. Almost all bathtubs are five feet wide, but there are some models that are 4'6." If you install a shower in the bathroom, you will save on water bills. Standard shower stalls are 32" X 32" you can buy larger shower stalls. If you are paying the water costs, you might want to install a shower instead of a bathtub. If you already have two to three bathrooms, in your home then you can easily divide your home into different sections. Any room with a bathroom could be

BATH ROOM WITH SHOWER 6' X 5'5"

partitioned off (walls added and/or doors locked) and could be an apartment. If you are constructing a new home make sure the water and sewer pipes and electrical wires to build a bathroom are installed in an area that you might build a bathroom in a future date. Have bathroom plumbing, sewer and electricity installed in the garage, attic (if it is large), extra rooms and especially the basement. Bathrooms are essential for all apartment additions. If you want to plan a unit addition in the future, you could always go to the city planning department and get a permit for building an extra bathroom in

your garage, basement, and many parts of your house. If you do this work now, you can always do the apartment conversions later. If you build a small cottage, cabana or other dwelling in your yard, it needs a bathroom to become a separate apartment.

Adding A Outside Stairway And A Separate Entrance.

If you plan to convert a second floor of your house or the second floor of your garage into a apartment, then you will need a stairway and a separate entrance to this unit on the second floor of your home or garage. This type of a home addition can be done inexpensively, by just building a stairway, then building a separate outside door. If you are considering a new home construction, you may consider the addition of this type of stairway to your new home, so that at a later date you can convert a second floor of your home into a rent earning apartment. See the picture of the stairway addition on the previous page.

Getting A Bank Loan For The Construction

A one bedroom apartment in your large home would have a separate entrance, a kitchen, a bathroom and a bedroom. A two bedroom apartment in your large home would need a separate entrance, a kitchen, a bathroom and bedrooms. You could get a second mortgage or refinance your home construction. When going to the bank, do tell the banker that you plan to add additions to your home and you plan to collect rent. If you can get an architect to draw up rough plans, then bring a copy of the modified house plans and to the bank. Your bank should be more than happy to help you with a loan since you will have rental income to pay off any bank loans.

An Example Of Home Construction

In this home construction example we would assume that the $235,000 mortgaged house was refinanced for

64

NEW YORK CITY BASEMENT APARTMENT CONVERSION PILOT PROGRAM

Administered by the New York City Department of Housing Preservation and Development (HPD), in partnership with Cypress Hills Local Development Corporation, a local non-profit, the **Basement Apartment Conversion Pilot Program (BACPP)** provides eligible low- and middle-income homeowners living in one- to three-family homes in East New York and Cypress Hills, Brooklyn (Community District 5) with low or no-interest, or possible forgivable, loans to convert their basement or cellar into a safe, legal, and rentable apartment, based on altered building code legislation passed in February 2019, Intro. 1004. The homeowner is also provided with technical assistance needed to close on a loan and complete the construction project.
This pilot program will help to create safe housing for tenants or occupants, while providing homeowners an opportunity to earn rental income.

For information on loan terms and the program, see the BACPP term sheet. It is also available in Spanish: Hoja de condiciones del Programa Piloto de Conversión de Sótanos en Apartamentos.

PROCESS

Eligible homeowners are provided with financial assistance in the form of a loan to convert their basement or cellar into a safe, livable apartment by providing low - or no-interest loans, with a maximum loan amount of $120,000, and the technical assistance necessary for completing a construction project

$300,000 (to take out a $65,000 construction loan). At a 3% interest rate, the $300,000 - 30 year home mortgage has payments of $1,264.81 a month. After the construction and in the example the house would earn $2,200 a month from a studio apartment and two one bedroom apartments and you would get free rent.

The cost per month of financing the $65,000 construction loan is $274.04 a month (which is part of the $1,264.81 mortgage payment) but the income would be $2,200 a month from the construction.

To Begin Construction

Decide on what construction you plan on your property and then contact a licensed architect who can advise you of local city building department rules and regulations and also advice you of costs and city permits to begin your construction.
Following this construction plan will streamline your construction plans to build income producing units on your home property.

Income Calculations For Building Four Units

A studio apartment rental:	$600
A one bedroom apartment	$800
A one bedroom apartment	$800
One two bedroom apartment (Free rent home)	$0
Total income after construction.	$2,200
Monthly mortgage payments	$1,265
Profit after mortgage payments & free rent.	$935

BOOKS TO PURCHASE ON HOME ADDITIONS

● *Black & Decker The Complete Guide to Room Additions (Black & Decker Complete Guide) By Chris Peterson* *Covers, home construction details, additions and bump-outs, garage conversions, attic conversions and room expansions.*

- *Converting Garages, Attics & Basements Sunset Books -* *Covers, home construction details, garage conversions, attic conversions, and basement conversions.*
- *In-laws, Outlaws, and Granny Flats: Your Guide to Turning One House into Two Homes By Michael Litchfield.* *Covers, basement units, garage conversions, backyard home, attics and bump-out additions.*
- *Builder's Guide to Room Additions By Jack P. Jones.* *Covers, home construction details, bathroom construction, basement construction and attic conversions,*

Build Apartments In Your Basement

Some basements in homes are not used for living spaces. If that is the case then you could remodel your basement by installing a bathroom, kitchen and walls. Make sure to water proof your basement for outside water. If the basement is already developed, then you will only need some walls, a bathroom and possibly a kitchen. If the basement has a separate entrance then, that could be used as two possible basement apartments. When I was growing up in Toronto, Canada part of our basement (in Bathurst Manor) was converted into a large one bedroom apartment unit. It had a separate entrance and a bathroom and kitchen. Many families rented this apartment and the apartment money was used by my parents to help pay the mortgage payment. Anyone could do this kind of construction, cheaply, and it could pay much of the mortgage payment. See the list of books or a licensed architect for more information on basement apartments.

Build a studio in your garage and above your garage.

Garages are great for building small studio units. You can easily convert the garage into a small apartment. You can also convert your garage and the room above your garage into two separate units. If you are building a garage build a attic apartment above your garage. You should put bathroom hookups in the garage and in the room above the garage, if the upper garage attic room is large enough for an apartment. A bathroom hookup would be plumbing, sewer and electricity. Get the building permits for a bathroom installation in your garage and a possible

SUMMMARY

- Homeowners with rental units in their home can get a monthly income without paying their mortgage payments.
- Building a rental income property on your property is a great investment, because the market price of your home will go up in value.
- Homeowners can build walls in their home to create two to three apartments to get rental income.
- Hire a good contractor or good work men, but don't overpay for building services.
- A kitchen and bathroom plumbing and wiring for water, sewer and electricity can be added to different parts of the home.
- When building a new home add more bathrooms, exterior doors, upper floor stairways, and extra plumbing, electricity and sewer hookups.
- Electricity, water, air conditioning and heating can be shared and a utility bill is added to the rent.
- Separate entrances can be added to the first floor. On the upper floors separate entrances would need outside stairways.
- Adding apartments in your basement, in your garage, in your backyard, or your attic will earn you money.

bathroom installation for the room above your garage, that is if you want to covert both of these spaces into apartments. In the Milwaukee, television series "*Happy Days*", Fonzie rented an apartment above the garage from the Cunninghams, that had a separate stairway and an entrance, above the garage.

Build a cottage or separate dwelling in your backyard.

Backyard cottages and houses are private dwellings that are not attached to your home and have separate electricity, plumbing and sewer hookup. You could build a cabana, modular dwelling, tiny home or cottage in your backyard. In some cases you could buy the building prefabricated and have a crane drop the small building in your back yard on the concrete footing you have built. You would still need city building permits, sewer, electricity, water plumbing and cable hook-up for your backyard apartment. You could get a city permit for a cabana (pool house) with a bathroom in your back yard. I know many people that have cabanas (pool houses) with bathrooms in their backyard.

If you build a small building in your backyard and you only have 400 square feet of yard space to build, consider building a two story building in your backyard. If you do this you will have an 800 square foot cottage or two separate dwellings in your back yard. If you build a stairway and a separate entrance, you could have two apartments in your backyard. Contact an architect about these building plans.

Build a studio apartment in your attic.

Attics could make good living quarters, but almost all attics lack bathrooms. If your attic is large enough, you could build a small bathroom in the attic, and convert your attic into a living space. Your attic would need a full bathroom to make it an apartment unit. To make it a separate apartment, you would have to build a separate entrance with a stairway from the outside.

Build an apartment addition attached to your home.

A room addition that is added to your house is called a bump out. This would be achieved by building a room and a bathroom in your backyard that is attached to your home and would have a separate entrance. A trench would have to be dug and concrete would be poured to create a footing. The wood frame would be attached to the footing. The water, sewer, electricity and cable can be attached to this unit from the main house. This type of construction is popular because you would be using electricity, phone, water, sewer, heating and air conditioning utilities from your home and you would also be using at least one wall of your home.

I would like to extend my assistance to your home or apartment project. If you have any stories you would like to share with the readers, please send details of your story with pictures if applicable. Sending any success stories would be greatly appreciated. If you would like help from the author please write him. David Bendah, PO Box 152808, Dept. DD2, San Diego, CA 92195.

Chapter Nine

Wealth Apartment Additions To Pay Your Mortgage Payments (Part Two)

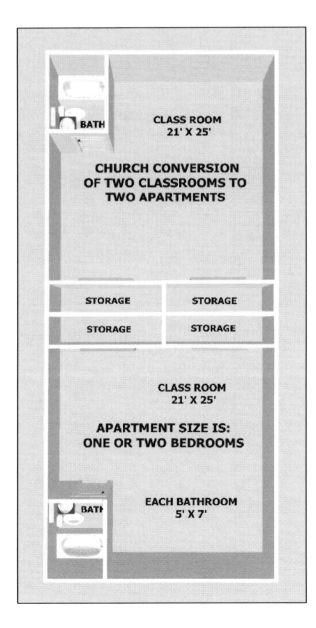

CLASS ROOM
21' X 25'

CHURCH CONVERSION
OF TWO CLASSROOMS TO
TWO APARTMENTS

STORAGE   STORAGE

STORAGE   STORAGE

CLASS ROOM
21' X 25'

APARTMENT SIZE IS:
ONE OR TWO BEDROOMS

EACH BATHROOM
5' X 7'

BATH

Convert A Building Into Two Or More Different Apartments.

You can subdivide a building into different parts, by building walls, bathrooms, kitchens (optional) and separate entrances. This way the building could be three different apartments. You could add a two bedroom apartment, a one bedroom apartment and a studio apartment to a building. You could always build rooms that would have one bathroom, and maybe a kitchen and a separate entrance to the outside. These rooms would make excellent apartments with separate entrances. You would need the commercial property rezoned to residential property from your local city building department. Do contact the local city building department for zoning and construction permits before starting construction.

A large empty building, warehouse or school could be converted into apartment buildings. A 128-year-old Cincinnati, Walnut Hills School was converted into a 41 unit luxury apartment building called Windsor Flats. Rents range between $900 to $2,059. These types of apartment conversions take place all of the time in every part of the country. Convert your home to apartments, now and start to earn apartment rental income.

2020 was a year of financial hardship for many churches, synagogues, and other houses of worship. Many have lost needed funds in 2020 and do need additional financial support. Let me

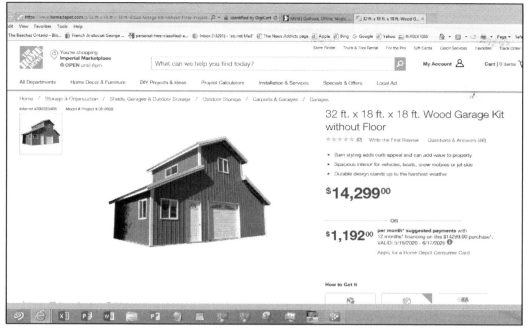

Some farms have experienced financial difficulties, due to lack of income. Many buildings on a farm could be used as rental units. With a construction fund and permits from the city planning department, these buildings could become rental units that produce needed cash for the family on the farm. It is a matter of bringing plumbing, sewer and

start this chapter with Church and Synagogue conversions. Then later we will discuss adding rental units to farms who are also in need of financial support.

Adding Rental Units To A Churches Or Synagogues.

Some churches have fallen on hard times and need a method of raising money. Churches can increase their monthly income by adding rental units to their building. Many people would prefer rent apartments on the church property, so it is a good idea for everyone.

With the addition of bathrooms, the classrooms that are not being used could be converted to rental units. See the diagram of two church class rooms that were converted to apartments on previous page. Doing this conversation is just a matter of going to the city and getting building permits to start the construction. The city can advise on zoning rules for rental apartments within that city. A construction fund could be raised to build apartments on the church lot. These apartments could be built at a modest cost to increase church revenues.

electricity to these buildings. Home Depot, Lowes, Ace Hardware, Dixieline and other hardware stores sell readymade buildings that are garage kits and barns kits. Pictures of these garages kits and barns kits are located in this chapter. These garage kits and barns kits cost from $3,000 to $20,000. The garages and barns kits these stores sell, includes much of the lumber and fixtures needed to build the building. You may have to upgrade these buildings to the building code. You can ask the retailer, what these buildings will need to meet the city building code for residential housing. You can also go to the city building department with specifications of these buildings and ask the city, what these

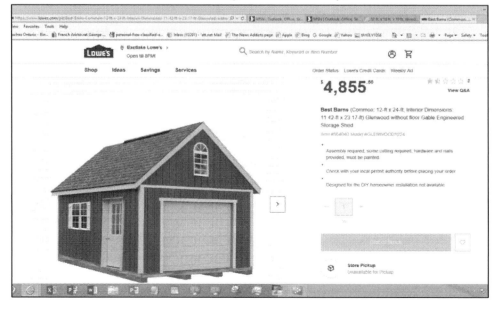

buildings will need to meet the city building code.

Some buildings are purchased as a kit with blueprint instructions and construction parts, ready for you to build. Refer to their advertising to determine if these buildings are suitable for your farm. These buildings include everything you see in the picture or description, but usually do not include the concrete foundation, plumbing, sewer, electricity and other features. It is advisable to pour a concrete foundation before installing these garages kits and barns kits, but check with your local building department but. Before construction, check with your local building, zoning or neighborhood association to obtain all applicable permits.

Manufactured homes

Manufactured homes are homes that are completely built in a factory or can be purchased used. Manufactured homes can be delivered and installed on your property, sometimes with a crane, but they require a building permit. Contact your local city or county building department with specifications before purchasing a manufactured home and installing it on your property.

Mobile Home Parks

You can live in a mobile home park in a manufactured home for thrifty living. You can buy a new manufactured home and place it in a mobile home park but there are so many used manufactured homes on the market that you can just buy a used manufactured or mobile home that only requires a monthly rental charge. Depending on the age, used manufactured homes are inexpensive. You can buy a manufactured home then pay the monthly rent in a mobile home park or you can even move a manufactured home to the mobile park of your choice. Consider living in a manufactured home or mobile home in a mobile park to keep your housing costs low.

Rooming Houses

Rooming houses are houses where many people share bathroom, living rooms and kitchens. It is a very affordable type of housing for many people on a limited income. Some rooms could

---

BUILDING REGULATIONS FROM A LARGE WEST COAST CITY

Accessory dwelling units — also called ADUs, secondary units, or granny flats — are small living units, including a kitchen and bathroom, on properties zoned residential with a single-family home, duplex home, or multifamily building in place. Junior Accessory Dwelling Units (JADUs) are small (less than 500 square feet) that must be converted existing square footage of a single-family home. JADU information and requirements can be found on the JADU Zoning Ordinance. Tiny homes on wheels (THOWs) are a type of ADU; they are allowed only on single-family properties and have different requirements and a simpler, lower-cost permit process.

There are many benefits to ADUs, including that they:...
◆ Create more affordable housing for our community and families;
◆ Provide an income opportunity for homeowners;
◆ Promote infill development; and Encourage the use of public transportation.
◆ A tiny home on wheels (THOW) may be a more affordable approach to an ADU. Please read Bulletin 291-Tiny Home on Wheels Permit Checklist.

If you're exploring how to finance or save money on an ADU, please be sure to check out these additional resources:

---

have bunk beds in a single bedroom which could accommodate several people. I have included one city's regulations concerning rooming houses.

I ran a small rooming house when I attended San Diego State University in San Diego. Since I was attending college and I worked every day I wanted to conserve expenses. I bought a three bedroom condominium on the second floor of a building. I lived in one bedroom and I placed ads

TORONTO, CANADA REGULATIONS FOR MULTI-TENANT HOMES (ROOMING HOUSES)

Rooming houses are where you rent a room and share a kitchen and/or washroom with four or more unrelated people who pay rent. Rooming houses can also include some self-contained units/bachelor apartments.

The City of Toronto permits rooming houses in some parts of the city and licenses some rooming houses. The following buildings do not need to be licensed as rooming houses:
•dwellings licensed and inspected by the provincial or federal government, such as group homes or retirement homes
•cooperative student residences that have more than three bedrooms.

Due to a recent amendment to the rooming house by-law, fraternity and sorority houses may need to be licensed as rooming houses if they meet the definition of a rooming house.

Current Rules and Regulations

Rooming houses are only permitted in certain parts of the City.

in the local newspaper for roommates for the other bedrooms. I got two male roommates and they each rented one room in my condominium apartment, similar to the television show "Three's Company." It was a good living arrangement that drastically lowered my mortgage payment.

A Concrete Foundation

A foundation is the load bearing part of the house where the house sits. Trenches are dug and concrete is poured in a square pad where your new unit, addition or building will rest. Rebar which is long bars of steel, are placed in the concrete mold before the concrete is poured. Before the concrete is poured into the foundation, sewer pipes and other conduit pipes are laid out in the foundation trenches, before the concrete is poured. Conduit pipes are hollow pipes that will make hollow channels (after the concrete hardens), in the concrete for your utilities.

GETTING A BUILDING PERMIT FROM THE CITY BUILDING DEPARTMENT.

There has been a lot of legislation for rent control and affordable housing. A regular homeowner renting out spaces in their home, would help their city with rent control and their affordable housing goals. What is the point of a city enacting rent control, when the homeowners in the city could help develop more affordable apartment units? Do your share of apartment conversions to help your city beat rent control.

Building Permits

You must get building permit from your local city, building department before you can start construction on your new apartment, studio or house division. You don't need a building permit for minor repairs or painting. Building permits are for structural changes to the building. There could be substantial red tape before you can begin construction. Many cities have allowed split homes and apartment conversations in their city. The government is supportive of helping people support their families. 2020 is a year of trying times for some people, who may lose their homes because they can't pay their mortgage payments. I am sure your city wants to help them. One of the largest city to allow "apartment home conversations" is Toronto, Canada. Toronto, Canada has at least one television show on the topic of home conversions. Another large city to be supportive of people making apartment conversions is New York City.

If you can't get your real estate building permit to start construction from your local city, you can try moving to another city that will give you building permits.

It would be unfortunate if you couldn't pay your mortgage payments and you need this "apartment construction" to pay your mortgage and support your family. Many cities can give you a

71

building permit, which could earn you real estate income and get you out of debt. If I can help you in anyway, please don't hesitate to write me. If your city still will not allow you a building permit, you could write the Department Of Housing and Urban Development, at 451 7th St, SW, Washington DC 20410. Tell them you need the "building permit" to make your monthly home mortgage. They may be able to help you.

Subdividing Land

You might be considering dividing your land into many different properties. This is called subdividing land and this is something building contractors may do, because it is very expensive and requires extensive engineering. You don't have to subdivide your land. The reason a company or person would want to subdivide land is to sell land. You can contact your local city planning department and ask them about subdividing your land. Some cities can give you the information on their website or you can go to see them and ask them about the subdividing city planning process. The cost for subdividing your land could cost you from $12,000 to $35,000.

REAL ESTATE TAXES

Tax Points To Remember

1. The cost of your property, for tax purposes, includes all costs incurred in obtaining title to the property; also, use this amount for figuring out your depreciation deduction and your interest payment deduction.

2. To the cost of your property, add expenditures you make to improve the property.

3. The more your expenses cost you, the less that you will own the IRS and other tax departments, while you own property and when you sell property.

4. A good way to save on taxes is to exchange property instead of selling it. This is done through a 1031 tax deferred exchange. 1031 exchanges defer taxes by exchanging a property and not selling a property, so they are for the most part, not taxable. Under Section 1031 of the United States Internal Revenue Code (26 U.S.C. § 1031), a taxpayer may defer recognition of capital gains and related federal income tax liability on the exchange of certain types of property, a process known as a 1031 exchange.

5. You pay less taxes on the sale of a property (if your profit is substantial) if it is an installment sale. In an installment sale, the income is paid over many years for the seller, this allows the sale to be taxed over a period of many years and not immediately after the sale.

6. Time your sale. If you want the tax break available when your profit is classified as "long term," you must hold on to the property for at least a year.

7. Improvements made by your tenants are can be a tax deductible expense as long as you get an invoice and pay your tenants for the work they do.

8. There are good tax breaks available for substantial property improvements made in the last few years; familiarize yourself with the most recent tax law because it allows you more advantages on property you buy or improve. Contact a licensed tax professional for information on these tax breaks

Capital Gain Taxes

Profits for the sale of certain "assets" are called capital gains. Assets that can be taxed for capital gains are shares of stock, bonds, a piece of land, real estate (usually not your home), other investments etc. The tax rates for these items are lower than the regular tax rate. Ordinary income is taxed at a higher rate. The reason for the capital gain tax rate is to encourage investment in real estate, stocks and other investments.

In 2019 and 2020 the capital gains tax rates for the IRS are either 0%, 15% or 20% for most assets held for more than a year. Capital gains tax rates on most assets held for less than a year correspond to ordinary income tax brackets (10%, 12%, 22%, 24%, 32%, 35% or 37%). Each state charges a separate capital gain tax.

CONCLUSION

Anyone that owns a home or wants to buy a home can earn rent income from their property. Making your home income property is a matter of getting a permit from the city, then starting construction. Rental properties will increase the value of your home. With the correct instructions anyone can make money from rental properties and also increase the value of their home. Invest in your own home or buy a home and have people that rent your property pay your mortgage and give you the rental income that you need. An additional word of thanks for purchasing this book and it's contents. The author, David Bendah does extend his hand out to offer assistance to readers. Please write with any rental stories you have, that pertain to this book. If you would like to be on David Bendah's mailing list please send your name and address to the author. Thank you again for purchasing this book. Write David Bendah at:

SUMMARY

● Adding apartment rentals to a church, synagogue or a farm will increase their income.
● Do it yourself garage barn and house kits can be purchased from hardware retailers.
● Manufactured homes can be purchased already built and can be set on your property but do require a building permit.
● Rooming houses are where you rent a room and share a kitchen and/or washroom with four or more unrelated people who pay rent
● Before any construction, check with your local building, zoning and neighborhood association to obtain all applicable permits.
● Dividing your land into many different properties is called subdividing.
● There are many ways to reduce taxes from your real estate property ownership.
● You can deduct property taxes, title and closing costs, property improvements and other costs on your tax return.
● Profits for the sale of certain "assets" like real estate and stocks are called capital gains.
● To quality for long term capital gain tax benefits you must hold on to your property at least one year.

David Bendah, PO Box 152808, Dept. DD2, San Diego, CA 92195.

73

TAX RATES FOR LONG TERM CAPITAL GAINS

Filing Status	0%	15%	20%
Single	Up to $39,375	$39,376 to $434,550	Over $434,550
Head of Household	Up to $52,750	$$52,751 to $461,700	Over $461,700
Married filing jointly and surviving spouse	Up to $78,750	$78,751 to $488,850	Over $488,850
Married filing separately	Up to $39,375	$39,376 to $244,425	Over $244,425

USING A PROPERTY MANAGEMENT COMPANY

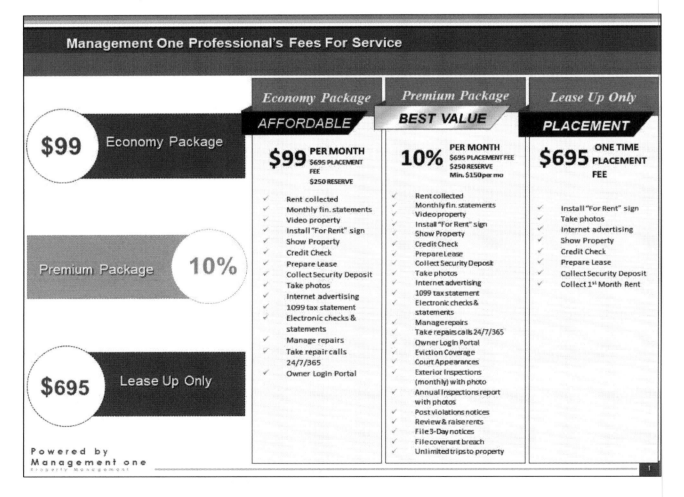

Chapter Ten

Making A Fortune With Real Estate

One of the biggest myths about real estate is that you need money to buy property and make big profits. As this book will show you, anyone with no money and the right instructions can become a millionaire from real estate.

Few millionaires get rich by working and getting paid by an employer -- virtually all millionaires get their money through investing, and most of them through wise investments in real estate. Real estate is the surest bet because the banks where you deposit your money in savings accounts, only give a low percentage rate and banks invest their own money in real estate.

Advantages Of Real Estate

1. Most of your real estate ventures can be financed with other people's money.
2. Real estate provides a lucrative tax write-off.
3. Real estate is the one of the best protection against inflation, and often increases in value at a greater rate than inflation.

Ideally, The Property You Buy Should Have Some Or All Of These Features:

1. **Good location.** Real Estate appraisals can vary by 200% or more, just on location.
2. **Relatively good condition.** If the condition is bad, just ask for a much lower purchase price.
3. **Priced below market value.** A good bargain is always welcome. You should buy low and sell high.
4. **Owner is anxious to sell.** If the owner is motivated to sell, you can get a bargain.
5. **Low or no down payment.** Try to get "*no money*" terms, so you can easily purchase real estate with no money.
6. **Can be resold, rented or improved easily.** The income potential is based on these factors.
7. **Good finance terms.** Always insist on good financial terms, so you can make more profit.
8. **Quick possession.** This is very good, because then you quickly hold title to the real estate.

The Four Major Real Estate Factors.

The four major factors are location, condition of the market, the attitude of the seller (how desperately he wants to sell), and the terms of the buy.

1) **Location**
2) **Condition of the market,**
3) **Terms of the real estate purchase.**
4) **Attitude of the seller (how desperately he wants to sell)**

Location

No matter how appealing the terms of the deal, nothing will make up for a poor location. If the building is in a run-down neighborhood with little new construction planned, attractive terms will not make up for the costs in both monetary and psychological costs. You can lose money from a bad location due to, the low rents that you will earn, low profit resale potential when you sell and bad tenants in a low income area. If your location attracts the worst and/or poorest tenants, you're in for problems.

The rule of thumb is to purchase the worst property in the best area, rather than the best property in the worst area. In a bad area, your property value will only fall, as the value of the neighborhood declines in value. In a good location, you can upgrade your property to the same level of surrounding properties and your property value will jump up.

It's easy to find out which areas to avoid. Just drive through and take note of such things as run-down buildings, un-kept yards, broken windows, trash, higher crime rate, and the quality of people who live there. Also, check with the city planning department (or the county equivalent if the area you're interested in is unincorporated) to see what construction is planned in the area, such as new roads, schools, shopping centers, churches, etc. The city planning department can also tell you what services are available there now, and you need to know this because apartments, homes and commercial buildings all need adequate traffic flow and nearby amenities, such as stores, restaurants and parks.

You can also get opinions about the area from a local property management firm, local real estate agents and the tenants themselves. You should also analyze the area by gauging the competition. Is the area already saturated with apartments, making low rents the norm and leaving little immediate chance for rent increases? Would the rents be high enough to cover your mortgage? What is the area's apartment vacancy rate?

Condition Of The Market

The most important factor for you is if the property you are interested in will be available for less than the market price. This way you can get a bargain. To know this, you must know what the market price is. You can find approximate values of the homes or apartment buildings in a neighborhood simply by finding out what properties in that area have sold for. You can use the internet for property sales information. For a good estimate, keep track of all sales in the area, listing each according to price per property, local amenities, terms, condition of building, etc. You could also ask people who live there, what the properties in the area are worth. For a professional opinion, hire an appraiser to make an appraisal.

Terms Of The Real Estate Purchase

The best terms lead to the lowest monthly mortgage payments. When purchasing real estate always pay the lowest price possible. Paying a price below the market value is always a great idea. When financing your real estate make sure to get the lowest interest rate possible.

Seller Motivation To Sell

Owners desperate to sell are usually easy to deal with, flexible and open to negotiation. They are the type you should seek out.

Owners become anxious to sell for many reasons:

a. Tenants who are always late with rent, or who refuse to pay.
b. A high vacancy rate.
c. Competition from nicer neighboring apartments.
d. Condition of the building, such termite infestation, aging plumbing etc.
e. A deteriorating neighborhood.
f. The property has been left to several heirs, who just want their share and not the property.

g. The owner retires or is in poor health.

h. The partners who own the building dissolve their partnership.

Whatever the reasons an owner is anxious to sell their property, make sure that you don't simply inherit those problems, that are unsolvable, or you also will soon be anxious to sell the property. You should know how to recognize a bargain (I will explain favorable purchase terms later); now you need to know how to find a bargain.

FINDING A BARGAIN PROPERTY

Professional Help

Your first stop, if your feel you need professional help, is a real estate agent. An agent can be a great help -- he knows what price properties sell for, what the sales terms are, how fast properties sell and where the best areas to buy are. But for this you pay, and remember that he works for and is paid by the seller. Just hire your own real estate agent and both real estate agents can split the commission. Commission rates range from 3% to 6%. Shop around and get the lowest real estate commission possible.

Other professionals to turn to are attorneys, who charge a lot but can save you thousands by spotting, for example, a faulty closing document. Accountants are also helpful -- they can instruct you how to keep the income for your major purchase out of the taxman's hands. Appraisers can give you a certified property value which can be used to obtain financing. Title companies assure you that the seller is actually the legal owner of the property up for sale. Title insurance is costly but absolutely necessary; in some states, the seller must pay for it, and so you should insist that he does.

Advertising & Publications

Look under the "Real Estate For Sale" classified ad section of your local paper or the internet -- many of the listings are from people anxious to sell. Call all the phone numbers just to see what terms sellers will accept. Make an all-cash offer at least 20 to 30 percent lower than the advertised price, just to hear the response. Probably one out of every 15 or 20 sellers will jump at the offer. Of course, you don't really plan to buy the properties, but now you know that an intensive search for financing and for just the right property will pay off. You could put up signs or billboards to advertise your business.

You can even run an ad yourself: "Cash to buy home. Fair price with small down; fast closing. Call David, 555-4444." Every time you see a "For Sale By Owner" sign, stop and check out the details; check out the property and ask lots of questions.

Your Local Courthouse

You can find out a good deal of information at your local county courthouse. Legal notices on display or records open to the public list companies and people who have had properties foreclosed, who are behind on their payments, who have filed bankruptcy, who have judgments against them, or who are way behind on property taxes. Most of these individuals and companies are anxious to sell. Get their names and addresses from the courthouse or county building.

Also at the courthouse and county building, you can find properties that have recently gone to heirs; the heirs may be looking for a quick sale. Also, look up recent divorce filings. Property owned jointly by both parties in the divorce may be a prime target for you. Make a list of all recent divorce filings (addresses of the parties are listed) and send each a tactful letter stating that you understand they may have a desire to sell their property and that you buy property; ask them to call you at their convenience for an offer on the property.

BORROWING MONEY

Let's say you've found a great deal, but you need a fair amount of money fast. Once you're sure you can make a very good profit on the deal and after you 've exhausted all other sources of income, go to a either a credit union, commercial bank, cash-by-internet company or finance company. Loans from these institutions will be at a relatively high interest rate with a short-term payback time; your monthly payments will be high. It is not unheard of for a person with a good credit history built up over many years to borrow $250,000, from a single bank. The same person could probably borrow this amount from, say, four banks, giving him virtually instant $1,000,000 cash. More than likely, the bank will insist on securing your loan against any property you have.

Credit Unions

If you already belong to a credit union, your chances of getting a loan for a property investment are good. If you don't belong to one, join now so you have this option in the future. Credit union loans are generally a similar deal in comparison to commercial bank loans.

Commercial Banks

Commercial banks are plentiful and can offer loans for your real estate venture. Commercial banks offer many different products and usually have many branches. Consider using a commercial bank for your real estate loan.

Cash By Mail Or By The Internet

To qualify for these unsecured, high-interest, short-term loans, this loan-by-internet service requires that you work for an employer and earn a high salary. Internet loan companies usually have a higher interest rate. If borrowing money from an internet company, it is advisable to research the loan terms and the interest rate.

Finance Company

Unless you get remarkably good terms, avoid finance companies, also known as thrift companies. They charge a high interest which is frequently up to 18 percent and sometimes more than 30 percent, they require secured loans and monthly payments. Before signing up with a finance company find out how much the interest rate is.

Buying Property Insurance

In order to purchase a property all banks make it mandatory to have property insurance. Property insurance is protection from fire, theft, weather and other property losses. This is important to the bank to protect their investment. If your house or building had fire then the insurance could pay for the damage. Make sure to get property insurance to cover the full value of your real estate or you may end up with property losses. Many a property owner has lost money in real estate due to fire and floods and other catastrophes because they didn't have adequate insurance coverage on their property.

Add renters insurance to all leases agreements you have with renters. If you have renters make sure they have renters insurance that covers the value of their property.

FIVE KINDS OF PROFIT RETURNS FROM REAL ESTATE:

1) **Cash Flow:** This is your profit after expenses. This is the amount left over after you've paid all expenses, including mortgage payment expenses.

2) **Equity**: It is your real estate profits that you can borrow against. The value of your property after the deduction of the amounts owed on the property.

3) **Depreciation:** Depreciation can be deducted on your tax return as a legitimate tax deduction, to lower your tax debt.

4) **Appreciation**: Appreciation is the increase in the value of real estate, which can be converted into a cash profit. When a property goes up in value, financial tools are available to capture the equity or raise money.

5) **Interest Payments:** Interest expenses are a legitimate tax expense. The monthly interest expense

you pay for your house payments can be deducted on your tax return.

Refinancing Your Mortgage And Getting Cash Out

Often, refinancing your mortgage is a great way to lower your monthly mortgage payments or a good way to raise money for real estate investment. Make sure to use a good bank. Here is an example of a refinancing.

Say Mr. Smith's house cost him $150,000. He financed $140,000 and put $10,000 down to buy the home.

Mr. Smith's house cost	$150,000
Down payment	$10,000
Amount Financed	$140,000

Over the years, Mr. Smith's made mortgage payments to his property, which included principal (principal payments lowered the amount owed). His property was also worth more than he paid for it because it went up in value. He now only owes $125,000 on his home. Mr. Smith's home has also gone up in value and is now worth $225,000. The equity on his home is now $100,000.

Value of Mr. Smith's home.	$225,000
Amount financed (after payments)	$125,000
Equity on home.	$100,000

Mr. Smith wants to borrow $50,000 from the equity in his home. He then refinances the $125,000 he owes on his home and takes out $50,000 that he needs.

Old Amount Financed (after payments)	$125,000
Equity removed from home	$50,000
New amount financed	$175,000

An Example Of Refinancing

Mr. Smith pays off his existing mortgage of $125,000, by taking out a new, bigger mortgage at $175,000, probably at a lower interest rate of 3.5 percent. Mr. Smith has refinanced his mortgage and has gotten $50,000 in cash from the refinance. With this $50,000, Mr. Smith could do some many things like build an apartment in his garage or renovate his basement into a large apartment. If he does this Mr. Smith will have monthly rental income. Is this route of getting refinanced, removing equity and building apartments worth it? It absolutely is, but make sure to use a good bank. The rental income alone will bring much joy to everyone in the household. If you have a rental income investment which can cover your repayment costs and make you a hefty profit that would be good.

Refinancing Your Home For A Better Interest Rate

You could refinance your home for a better interest rate and the closing costs and financing costs will be well worth the expense, due to the savings in monthly payments. Let's say you bought a property and you needed to get a mortgage for $200,000. Use the following table to determine your monthly payments.

SECOND MORTGAGE

Instead of refinancing your mortgage, consider a second mortgage, also called a junior mortgage. The reason for a second mortgage is that bank lenders will not loan you the money.

When primary lenders refuse to fund up to 85% of the value of a home, a second mortgage can be used. When getting a second mortgage use a good bank. A rate for a second mortgage varies from 4.99% to 14.99%, and depends on factors like credit risks and market values.

House Worth	$200,000
Mortgage	$150,000
---	---
Second Mortgage	$25,000

For example, Mr. Jones owns a house worth $200,000; he has a mortgage of $150,000. He takes out a second mortgage of $25,000 at 8 percent interest with a 10-year payback period. Mr. Jones' monthly payments for the second mortgage are $303.32 a month.

INTEREST RATE FINANCIAL TABLE				
Principal Amount	Term Of Loan in Years	Interest Rate	Monthly Payment	Monthly Savings From 6.5% Interest
$200,000	30	2.50%	$790.24	$473.89
$200,000	30	3.00%	$843.21	$420.93
$200,000	30	3.50%	$898.09	$366.05
$200,000	30	4.00%	$954.83	$309.31
$200,000	30	4.50%	$1,013.37	$250.77
$200,000	30	5.00%	$1,073.64	$190.49
$200,000	30	5.50%	$1,135.58	$128.56
$200,000	30	6.00%	$1,199.10	$65.03
$200,000	30	6.50%	$1,264.14	$0.00

REVERSE MORTGAGE

A financial agreement in which a homeowner uses the equity in their home in exchange for regular payments is called a reverse mortgage. A reverse mortgage generally requires no payments, and uses a homeowner's equity to make house payments. Using a reverse mortgage the home owner draws on the equity in their real estate, in monthly increments.

REVERSE "PAPERS"

A reverse "papers" could be any mortgage payment where the home owner, who owes a set amount of money, pays less than the agreed payment. Let's say a home owner is required to pay $1,500 a month for thirty years. If maybe

through a financial hardship, the homeowner cannot pay the obligated $1,500, where $1000 is the principal and $500 is the interest. Let's say the home owner can pay $950 a month. Then a new mortgage is drawn up and the term is increased to 35 years and if applicable interest is tacked on to the payments.

DEPRECIATION

According to the IRS, and only the IRS, the value of the apartment buildings (not the land) is divided by many years (arranged by an accountant) and is used as a yearly tax deduction. This is called depreciation. The costs that incur for the purchasing and improving of a real estate property can be deducted for depreciation. Residential rental property and residential property can be depreciated over a 27.5 year period and the commercial property rate is 39 years. Depreciation can be deducted on your tax return, this is great news for you because it will let you pay less taxes. This results in a tax savings, allowed because the government encourages investment in real estate. Depreciation recapture tax is a required payment if you decide to sell your real estate for a higher price than its current depreciation amounts. Contact an accountant for the exact tax deduction and recapture amounts.

Depreciation Calculation Examples

Let's say you invest $300,000 in a building and land. Then only part of the $300,000 investment is for the building, the rest is for the land itself. Say that according to the county tax assessment, 20 percent, or $60,000, of the $300,000 investment is for the land, and 80 percent, or $240,000, is for the building. The time limit varies year to year, but let's say the IRS allows the apartment investor to appreciate his whole investment over a 27.5-year period; this means that after 27.5 years, the building has been completely depreciated.

Dividing 27.5 years into $240,000 (the cost of the actual building) shows that the building loses $8,727,27 in depreciation, each year. The owner can now deduct this $8,727,27 depreciation as a loss from his income from the apartments. He can also deduct the amount of interest paid on the mortgage (but not on the principal amounts). The depreciation deductions have to be paid back with a depreciation recapture tax, when the property is sold (based on it's current depreciation value). Contact a tax professional for these amounts.

APPRECIATION

Property values always keep pace with inflation, but it is impossible to say exactly by how much properties will rise because that depends on inflation and demand. Real estate could fall in price, but over a period of time it goes up. From 1968 to 2009, according to the *National Association Of Realtors*", the price of existing

SUMMARY

- Anyone with little money and the right instructions can become a millionaire from real estate.
- The property that you buy should have a good location, relatively good condition, priced below market, an owner who is anxious to sell, little or no down payment, can be resold or rented easily, has favorable finance terms and quick possession.
- You can find a bargain property from professionals, from advertisements and from your local court house.
- There are many good sources for borrowing money.
- The five kinds of returns on real estate are cash flow profit, equity, depreciation write-off, appreciation profit, and interest payment write-offs.
- Refinancing your mortgage is a great way to lower your monthly mortgage payments or a good way to raise money for real estate investment.
- From 1968 to 2009, according to the *"National Association Of Realtors"*, the price of existing homes increased by 5.4% annually.

homes increased by 5.4% annually. Appreciation is the increase in the value of real estate, that can be converted into a cash profit. So when your property goes up in value you can use financial tools to capture the equity. Let's say that the property that you paid $200,000, appreciates at a rate of 5 percent a year and let's say, your down payment was $20,000. Five percent of the $200,000 purchase price is $10,000.

Return On Investment For The First Year

Five percent of $200,000 is (appreciation profit): $10,000

Down payment is (your investment): $20,000

Five percent of $200,000 is $10,000   (Your appreciation profit)

$10,000 divided by the $20,000 is a 50 percent.   50% is the return on investment in one year.

A 5% Increase In Value For Ten Years

If a $200,000 real estate parcel were to appreciate or increase by 5% every year for a period of ten years then the real estate would become more valuable over time.   The following table shows you how much the real estate would be worth at the end of ten years.   In ten years you have earned in $110,265.64 appreciation value.   This is a lot of money.   Much of this money can be converted into cash by refinancing the house.

REAL ESTATE APPRECIATION TABLE

Years	Market Value Of Real Estate
Year 1	$200,000.00
Year 2 - 5% Increase	$210,000.00
Year 3 - 5% Increase	$220,500.00
Year 4 - 5% Increase	$231,525.00
Year 5 - 5% Increase	$243,101.25
Year 6 - 5% Increase	$255,256.31
Year 7 - 5% Increase	$268,019.13
Year 8 - 5% Increase	$281,420.08
Year 9 - 5% Increase	$295,491.09
Year 10 - 5% Increase	$310,265.64

Chapter Eleven

Income Property Wealth

Income property is property that can earn you an income. If you own apartments or retail stores that produce rent income, this is income property. For this section on income property we will use a six unit apartment building as our example. Apart from such obvious expenses as the down payment and repayment of mortgages and other loans, income properties, such as rental units, have other expenses. Income producing real estate can be a good profit maker for you.

There are five types of profit returns from income properties:

1) **Cash Flow:** This is the rental income and other property incomes you will earn after expenses..
2) **Equity:** The value of your property after the deduction of the amounts owed on the property.
3) **Depreciation:** Depreciation can be deducted on your tax return, to lower your tax debt.
4) **Appreciation:** Appreciation is the increase in the value of real estate, which is your profit.
5) **Interest Payments:** Interest expenses can be deducted on your tax return.

Six Unit, $300,000 Income Property

For this example, let's consider a six-unit apartment building in good condition and location. Each unit has one large bedroom, one bathroom, and rents for $600 a month. The renter pays utilities. The purchase price is $300,000, and the down payment is $25,000. The total amount you would have to finance is $275,000. If you got a 3%, (30 year) loan to finance $275,000, for the sales price of the six apartment units, your monthly payments would be $1,159.41 a month.

Let's use the six-unit apartment building for the example.

If fully rented year round, you would gross: $600 x 6 = $3,600 monthly income. $3,600 x 12 = $43,200 yearly income. In addition, you may have income from vending machines, water and washing machines.

Gross income from the six apartment units	$3,600.00
Payments from $250,000 financed:	$1,159.41
--	
Income before operating expenses (monthly)	$2,440.59

STUDIO APARTMENTS
41'9" X 29'
1,209 SQ FT

Appreciation Profit If 5%

Appreciation is the amount of money you earn from your real estate when the real estate goes up in value. From 1968 to 2009, according to the "*National Association Of Realtors*", the price of existing homes increased by 5.4% annually. Is this a good deal? Of course it is. Let's say that the ($300,000) six unit apartment complex appreciates at 5 percent a year for the next 10 years – it will be worth $465,398.46. At the end of 10 years and Mr. Jones will have made $165,398.46. That is an average of $16,539.85 a year, in appreciation income.

Market value at year 10:	$487,832.05
Purchase price	$300,000.00
--	
Profit (Appreciation)	$165,398.46

Depreciation Tax Deduction

For this example you can depreciation the building value and not the land value. Let's say the land value is 20% of the buying price and the building value is 80% of the total buying price of $300,000. Eighty percent of the building is $240,000. For this example let's say we use a 27.5 year depreciation period for the $240,000 (building value). The monthly depreciation tax deduction is $8,727.27 a year. That means you can write off $8,727.27 each year from this property. Let's say you keep the property for twenty years and you also write-off depreciation for twenty years, when you sell the building you must pay back a depreciation recapture tax.

Vacancy and credit losses

A vacancy rate is the rate at which the apartment rentals are empty. Expect at least a 3 to 12 percent vacancy rate, which means that your gross income will be cut by 3% to 12% each year. The vacancy rate would be higher in depressed areas. Make sure to research the vacancy rate in an area that you are interested in purchasing income property.

Operating expenses

Operating expenses include all of the expenses except for mortgage expenses. Subtract all the expenses you will have in one year from the gross income. The operating expenses are as a rule about 35 percent or more of the gross operating income (GOI). They don't include the mortgage payments but do include:

1) Accounting services and legal fees
2) Advertising

3) All services and supplies
4) Insurance
5) Legal fees
6) Licenses and permits
7) Maintenance and repair
8) Miscellaneous (This includes all expenses not included)
9) Office Expenses
10) Property management (including payroll for resident manager)
11) Property Taxes
12) Travel & Vehicle Expenses
13) Utilities

EXAMPLE (OPERATING EXPENSES ARE 34% OF GROSS INCOME)

$43,200 (yearly gross income)
$3,800 (property management fees)
$2,400 (maintenance)
$2,500 (property taxes)
$2,800 (insurance)
$3,200 (misc)

$28,500 (Net income)

Net Income ($28,500)

------------------------------------- = Capitalization Rate (11.4%)

Seller Asking Price ($250,000)

Capitalization Rate Or Cap Rate

You may consider buying income property, and you want to know a method of rating for the income property. One of the most popular methods of rating real estate is the cap rate. You can ask a real estate agent for a cap rate to be able to determine profitability of real estate. If the cap rate of the property has a rate of 10% or higher then you have a good property. If the cap rate of the property has a rate of 5% or less then the property has some problems. The following is three reasons for a lower cap rate.

1) The rents are too low.
2) The expenses are too high.
3) The price of the property is too high.

Net Income

------------------------------ = Capitalization Rate

Seller Asking Price

EXAMPLE (OPERATING EXPENSES ARE 36.5% OF GROSS INCOME

$20,000 (yearly gross income)
$1,700 (property management fees)
$1,200 (maintenance)
$1,500 (property taxes)
$1,400 (insurance)
$1,500 (misc)

$14,400 (net income)

Net Income ($14,400)
-- = Capitalization Rate (7.06%)
Seller Asking Price ($180,000)

Cash Flow Before-Taxes

This the amount left after all mortgage payments and expenses have been paid. If your gross yearly income is $50,000, and your yearly expenses are $20,000, and your mortgage payment is $12,000, then your cash flow before taxes is $18,000.

FIVE KINDS OF PROFIT RETURNS FROM REAL ESTATE:

Please refer to a previous chapter or this chapter for the five kinds of real estate profits. There are five types of profit return from most income properties:

1) Cash Flow:
2) Equity:
3) Depreciation Deduction:
4) Appreciation:
5) Interest Payment Deduction:

GET UP TO 100% ASSISTANCE WITH MORTGAGE PAYMENTS

Due to financial hardships, you may not be able to pay your mortgage payments. Many people lose their homes because they cannot afford their mortgage payments. The following list contains ten methods of reducing or eliminating your mortgage payments up to 100% of the payment. Use these methods to pay up to 100% of the mortgage payments and keep your home. The previous chapter, shown in the table of contents, has details on building apartments in or outside your home, to lower your mortgage payments.

The Ten Methods Of Mortgage Assistance

11) Refinance your home and remove the equity.
12) Refinance your home at a lower interest rate.
13) Get a "reverse paper" or a reverse mortgage.
14) Build an apartment in your basement (see previous chapter).
15) Build a studio apartment in your garage and an attic apartment above your garage (see previous chapter).
16) Build a cottage or separate apartment dwelling in your backyard (see previous chapter).
17) Build a studio apartment in your large attic. This includes the room above your garage. (see previous chapter)..
18) Build an apartment addition attached to your home (see previous chapter).
19) Convert your house into two or more different apartments (see previous chapter).
20) Contact A Government Agency Or Your Bank Or Your Mortgage Company For Financial Help.

Refinance your home and remove the equity and refinance your home at a lower interest rate.

You could refinance your home and get a better interest rate which will lower your monthly mortgage payments. If your interest rate is 5.5% and your mortgage is a 30 year $250,000 mortgage and your monthly mortgage is $1,419.47 and if you refinance to a 2.5% 30 year mortgage then your monthly savings is $431.67 a month or a 30.5% reduction in your mortgage payment. You could save up to 40% by refinancing, but make sure you use a good bank.

To top it off you could take out the equity cash you have built up in your home. Let's say your property is worth $200,000 and you have a mortgage on your home of $100,000. The $100,000 for a 30 year loan and with a 5.5% interest rate would cost you $567.79 a month. If you refinanced your home and got a new mortgage for $125,000 for 30 years, at a 3% interest rate, you could take the $25,000 equity and your new house payments (for $125,000 at 3%) is just $527.01 a month, which is less then you paid with the $100,000 mortgage. If you didn't take $25,000 from the home equity, and financed $100,000 at 3% for thirty years, the new payments would be $421.60 a month. When financing a property use a good bank.

Get "reverse paper." And Reverse Mortgage

If you are having a difficult time making home payments, you may choose "reverse papers" to reduce your mortgage payment. Let's say your monthly payments on your home are $1,500. With this payment, $1,000 is the principal and $500 is the interest. For this example, you cannot afford the $1,500 a month amount but you can afford $950 a month. The term is increased to 35 years to lower payments and interest if applicable, is tacked on to the payments.

A reverse mortgage is a financial agreement in which a homeowner uses the equity in their

home in exchange for regular payments. A reverse mortgage generally requires no payments, and uses a homeowner's equity to make house payments. Using a reverse mortgage home owner draws on the equity in their real estate, in monthly increments.

Contact A Government Agency Or Your Bank Or Your Mortgage Company For Financial Help.

You can get mortgage assistance from government agencies. To find out about current government home assistance programs contact, Department Of Housing & Urban Development (HUD). You may qualify for a Federal Housing Administration (FHA) home loan. For assistance in rural areas contact: Farmers Home Administration, Department Of Agriculture. You can also contact the Department Of Veteran Affairs, to see what housing benefits they have available to eligible veterans.

You can get most of the mortgage assistance programs that are available from your bank or mortgage company. They have a large list of mortgage programs that you are eligible for. Contact your bank or mortgage company and tell them that you cannot pay your mortgage payments or that you need mortgage assistance. Your financial institution would be more than happy to help you the monthly mortgage reduction you need.

How To Negotiate A Good Deal

The first rule of negotiations is: Don't be too eager or act uninterested. If the

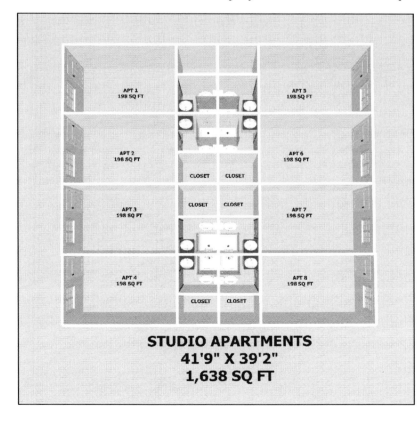

STUDIO APARTMENTS
41'9" X 39'2"
1,638 SQ FT

seller "can tell" you are desperate and you want his property, he immediately has the upper hand in the negotiations.

Know before the negotiations start, exactly what price you will not exceed and what terms you must have. If during the course of negotiations, it becomes obvious that you won't get what you want, leave negotiations with no bad feelings. Knowing that you aren't bluffing about your refusal, the seller may back down and give you what you want.

Act uninterested. Tell the seller that his property is only one of several you are looking at and that there are several others equally attractive and competitive properties. Point out all negative features (the living rooms in this complex are not as large as those in other complexes you've just checked out, the pool is small, the laundry room needs repair, there is termite damage, the carpet needs replacing, the lot is too small etc.) -- This will lower his price expectations and may even convince you that the property is not worth the money and effort. You must convey to the seller that the only reason his property has been on the market for a while is because it priced too high.

If, however, the seller is inflexible on his

Ask Questions About The Property

price, you must strive for flexible terms of payment. If the seller is inflexible in his terms (probably meaning he wants all cash), then you must strive for the lowest price. Ideally, you should choose both price and terms.

Insurance Protection

It is important to have a good property insurance policy on your property. Banks and financial institutions make a property insurance policy a condition of the property financing. Property insurance includes protection from fire, theft, flood weather and other causes of property damage. Contact a good insurance company when getting property insurance, since if you house burns down or has a flood you will need an insurance coverage to cover the cost of all repair of damages. Make sure your insurance coverage is complete and your insurance coverage covers the complete cost of the repairs.

Questions For Property Purchase

Don't hesitate to ask questions; make a list of questions before your see the seller. For example:

1. How many offers have you had on this property?
2. Why did you turn down the offers?
3. When did you buy this property?
4. From whom did you buy the property?
5. What did you pay for this property?
6. What capital improvements did you make on this property?
7. How long has the property been listed for sale?

When you have all the information you need, leave the negotiations, go home and study all the data you have and then you can prepare a formal offer of purchase.

In your offer, make ample use of the weasel clause, better known as the "subject-to" clause. Put it in your "Offer To Purchase", it limits your liability by stating your offer to buy is subject to certain conditions being met. For example:

1) Subject to all specified repairs being done. List repairs that are needed to bring the property to standard, such as foundations or wall cracks, new stairs, etc. Also, you could insist the seller paint the interior and exterior of the property.

2) Subject to the seller getting a building-code inspection of the property, or termite, roof, foundation or any kind of inspection you want.

3) Subject to the seller proving the property is legally his.

4) Subject to the seller paying all closing costs.

The list can go on and on, but there will be a point where the seller refuses to meet any additional "subject-to" clauses.

HOW TO BUY WITH NO MONEY DOWN

You may decide to pay a large down payment, which would probably lower the total selling price and cut your monthly payments. However, you may not have the cash, or have a better use for the money, so you will want to purchase real estate with "no money" down payment. The real estate agent handling the sale (concerned about his commission) will probably try to advice you against it, but he has to tell the seller about your offer. The seller may be willing to deal, especially if the property has been up for sale for a while. Try these buying techniques:

1) Offer to pay a higher total selling price. In this example if the buyer is asking for $200,000 then you could offer the buyer $225,000, but with financial terms that you need.

2) Offer to pay a higher interest rate. If the buyer is carrying the loan, you could offer the buyer a better interest rate then the buyer could get from conventional sources. The rate of return for investments could be 3% to 5%. You could offer the buyer 7% and try to get the financial terms that you need.

3) Offer a faster payoff of the total price. A regular term for a home mortgage is 30 years. Some mortgages are 15 years. You could offer to pay off the total price of the real estate within one year and get the financial terms that you need.

4) Offer a personal note which he can use as security for a loan, instead of a down payment. By doing this you don't have to put any money down and you could buy properties with no cash.

5) Offer to assume the seller's financial obligations. If the seller is selling to relieve himself of debts, you could offer to transfer some of those debt obligations to your name. Contact the seller s creditors to

SUMMARY

- There are five ways to earn money from income property.
- One: Cash Flow: This is the rental income and other incomes you will earn after expenses..
- Two: Equity: The value of your property after the deduction of the amounts owed on the property.
- Three: Depreciation: Depreciation can be deducted on your tax return, to lower your tax debt.
- Four: Appreciation: Appreciation is the increase in the value of real estate, which is your profit.
- Five: Interest Payments: Interest expenses can be deducted on your tax return.
- Operating expenses include all of the expenses except for mortgage expenses.
- One of the most popular methods of rating real estate is a cap rate, which is net income divided by the real estate selling price.
- You could refinance your home and with a better interest rate and get a lower mortgage payment.
- Contact a government agency for mortgage assistance.
- Reverse papers and reverse mortgage can lower or eliminate your mortgage payment.
- The first rule of real estate negotiations is: Don't be too eager and seem uninterested.
- Ask questions and find out everything you can about the property, you want to buy.
- There are eight ways to buy real estate with no money down.

see if the payback time can be extended or if a discount is possible by paying cash.

6) Suggest that, before he sells you the property, he refinance it -- he would get the cash with no immediate tax liability.

7) Offer the seller free rent in lieu of a down payment. If the seller needs a place to live (say he lives in the apartment building you are buying), offer him free rent, the total rent saved going toward the down payment.

8) Buy the property, refinance it, and with that cash, pay the down payment. This is an excellent method of making money with real estate. To do this you must buy the property far below the appraised value. Get the property appraised before you buy it so that there is little risk when refinancing the property.

"No Money Down" Duplex Example

Let's say Mr. Jones uses $0 as a down payment on a duplex which is two apartment units. The owner of the duplex wants $150,000. Mr. Jones puts no money down and gets the buyer to agree to carry the, $150,000 balance with $795.00 monthly payments for the next 25 years. The buyer charges Jones a higher interest rate then the bank, but Jones didn't have excellent credit so he chose to have the buyer finance the duplex. Jones will cover these monthly payments by charging $800 monthly rent for each apartment, which is $1,600 a month in gross income. This $1,600 amount is income before expenses. Of course, after expenses your income will be less. Doing this Jones ends up with $805 a month, before expenses.

Gross Income from the two apartment units	$1,600.00
Payments from $150,000 financed:	$795.00

Monthly Income (before expenses)	$805.00

"No Money Down" Fourplex Example

Let's say Mr. Paul wants to buy a four unit apartment building with no money down. The owner of the fourplex wants $275,000 for the four apartment units. Mr. Paul has the property appraised and the appraiser tells Mr. Paul that the fourplex apartment unit is appraised for $350,000. Mr. Paul refinances the property for $300,000 and with the cash pays off the property and in ends up with $25,000 in cash from the deal. The four apartments earn $800 each. All four apartments earn $3,200 a month.

Gross Income from the four apartment units	$3,200.00
Payments from $300,000 financed (30 years at 3%):	$1,264.81
--	
Monthly Income (before expenses)	$1,935.19

If you give a little, the seller may give a little, too; and, for a good property with no down payment, you can afford a reasonable concession. Remember, if a seller doesn't need cash, or must sell quickly, he is ripe for a no-money down payment deal. Contact my office and I will try to help you with any questions that you have.

CONCLUSION

You don't need money when making money in real estate. Making a fortune in real estate could be easy, if you do all of the right things. With the right instructions anyone with no money, can become a millionaire through real estate acquisition. Invest in real estate and you too can become a Real Estate

Chapter Twelve

The Super Influencing Wealth Technique

I am going to show you how to progress at a powerful rate. In a quick period, you will feel like a different person. How am I going to do all of this? I am going to show you how you can tap directly into your subconscious mind. You will be able to unleash part of that valuable energy locked inside of you, any time that you want. We are going to tap into the source that has made fortunes for many men.

I want you to try this technique and find out what you are capable of doing. I am sure that this technique will amaze you as it has the thousands who have tried it. It all sounds so easy, and it is, but it really does work.

This technique involves direct communication with the deep powers that lie within your mind. This is similar to a different technique that I showed you, but with one exception, it is much more powerful. There are a few rules that I must point out when using this super-influencing technique. You should use it at least once a day, preferably at a time when you are relaxed. It is important not to miss a day. Make sure that this is a daily priority. Using this powerful technique on a daily basis will give you astounding results.

The Technique Is Too Powerful

You could use this technique to alter or improve your personality. Pick qualities or characteristics that you would like to incorporate into your life. Don't use this technique to acquire material possessions, because you would have to fine tune your goals into segments. Use it to perfect your personality. This method works well to improve qualities like persistence, honesty, deepness, concentration, and decisiveness. Virtually any trait can be improved using this method. There is one point to remember: The more you fine tune the quality, the better able you will be to achieve your goals. Let me give you an example. Let's say that you want to be more persistent, in fine tuning this quality, you would say, "I am very persistent with my rental income property project."

I Used It To Concentrate Better

I had my own business. I was doing pretty well, but I was having trouble concentrating on my work. I just couldn't get my mind on what I had to do. I'd sit and waste my time. It was terrible. My profits weren't growing and my business was going downhill. I knew that I had to do something. It was then that a friend of mine with a Doctorate Degree in Psychology showed me this fabulous technique. He told me to use it every day. At first I couldn't believe that his technique would work. It seemed so elementary. A month passed before I decided to try it, probably because I really didn't want to. One Sunday morning, out of desperation, I tried it, and then once again that same night.

It was as if a miracle had taken place. I got to the office on Monday, as usual, but I was already

91

a different person. I was no longer the person who stared out into space and got nothing done. I had started to become productive. As the weeks went by, my concentration increased tremendously. It improved so much that I was reading journals that I could never have comprehended before. My mind no longer wandered. When people talked to me, I understood and remembered every word they said.

I have gained so much by using this technique that I want you to get as much out of it as I have. Just use it for a few weeks and see what it does for you. I am sure that after you use it, you will want to use the technique every day. Do you know of any qualities that you want to possess? Do you? That's great, you do. Now you have some reason to use this technique. Use it and see what the hidden power of your subconscious can do for you.

HOW TO PERFORM
SUPER-INFLUENCING

This powerful technique involves going into another *state of being.* You will need to be in a state of relaxation. Your mind will be tranquil and so will your body. You will feel very relaxed and refreshed. This relaxation will rid you of stress and other mind-centered, harmful influences. This relaxation will create harmony between your emotional and your physical centers. When you are in this state of relaxation, your powerful subconscious mind is easily influenced. This is what you want.

Relaxing The Mind

The following exercise will acquaint you with this state of deep relaxation. It will create a refreshed and peaceful feeling in your body and mind. Only in this state will you be able to make positive changes to your personality. You are now in control of yourself. Whatever changes you want to make in yourself, you can make. If you tend to fall asleep while using this technique, sit up while you perform it.

Step One

Lie flat on your back or a mat or a soft surface. I will refer to this surface as the floor. Be comfortable. As you lay on your back, place your feet about 18 inches apart. Your hands should rest slightly away from your trunk with your palms up. Close your eyes and gently move all parts of your body so that you experience a gentle feeling of relaxation.

Step Two

Start by relaxing your body, part by part. First, concentrate on relaxing your right leg. Inhale and raise your leg about one foot off the floor. Hold it fully tensed. After five seconds, exhale quickly and relax the muscles of the right leg. Allow your leg to fall to the ground on it's own. Shake the leg gently from right to left, relax it completely and forget about it. Repeat this process with the left leg.

Step Three

Concentrate on the muscles of the buttocks and pelvis. Tense them and then relax. Once again, tense them and relax. Next, concentrate on the abdomen. Raise your abdomen, inhale deeply through the nose and hold your breath. Hold your breath for five seconds, then let the air burst out through your mouth. At the same time, relax all of the muscles of the abdomen and the diaphragm. Now, concentrate on your chest region. Inhale deeply through your nose, expanding your chest. Again, hold your breath for five seconds and suddenly let all of the air out through your mouth while relaxing the chest area.

Step Four

Concentrate on your shoulders. Without lifting your forearms off the floor, try to make your shoulders meet in front of your body. After doing this, relax them and let them fall gently to the floor. Concentrate on your arms. Lift your right arm up. Inhale and raise your arm about one foot off the floor. Hold it fully tensed. After five seconds, exhale quickly and relax the muscles of the right arm. Allow your arm to fall to the ground on its own. Do the same relaxation exercise with your left arm. Now slowly, gently, turn your neck right and left, right and left, and then back to center. Then, relax your neck muscles.

Step Five

Now, concentrate on your facial muscles.

Move your jaw up and down, then right to left a few times, then relax. Squeeze your lips together in a pout and suck your cheek muscles in, then relax again. Tense the tip of your nose and wrinkle your forehead muscles, then relax.

Step Six

You now have relaxed all the muscles of your body. To make sure of this, search for any tension spots by allowing your mind to wander over your entire body, from the tips of your toes to the top of your head. If you come across any tension, concentrate on those spots and they will relax. If you do this mentally without moving any muscles, you will notice that any part of you that you want relaxed, can relax.

Beginners must go through all of the steps to use the super-influencing technique. If you feel very confident with this technique, you can take this small shortcut: Start with step six. The only change is that instead of physically flexing your muscles, you just relax your muscles with the use of your mind. Have your mind relax your body as shown in step six but start there only if you are comfortable with this method.

Step Seven

Tell yourself that you are going deeper and deeper into a state of relaxation. Count to ten. Say this to yourself as you count: "One, I am going deeper and deeper into a state of relaxation. I feel very peaceful and perfectly relaxed. As I count to ten, I will feel more and more relaxed, more and more relaxed. Two, I am going deeper and deeper into a state of relaxation. I am going deeper and deeper. I feel very peaceful and perfectly relaxed. As I count nearer to ten, I will feel more and more relaxed, more and more relaxed. Three, I am going deeper and deeper into a state of relaxation. I am going deeper and deeper. I feel very peaceful and perfectly relaxed. As I count nearer to ten, I will feel more and more relaxed, more and more relaxed. Four, etc." Say the same thing for numbers, 4 - 10 as you count to ten. When you are finished counting, you will be in a complete state of relaxation.

Using Super-Influencing To Get What You Want

What you will experience is complete relaxation. Even your mind will be at rest now. Observe your thoughts without trying to take your mind anywhere. Remain in this condition at least five minutes. You are now at the point of high suggestibility. Any suggestion that you give yourself at this point will be readily accepted by your mind, such as, *I am able to concentrate on my class instructions,* or *I want to express my loving feelings to Nancy.* Give yourself the suggestions in a repetitive, but calm manner. Say them to yourself over and over again while you are in your relaxed state. This is one of the best times to give yourself suggestions. Don't miss out on this opportunity. The Super Influencing Technique will do wonders for you, but only if you make the suggestions at this time. Make use of this golden opportunity. Give yourself good constructive suggestions.

Waking Up

When you decide to wake up from this relaxed condition, do so slowly. Imagine fresh energy entering every part of your body. Give yourself the suggestion, "Ten, when I wake up I will be fully relaxed and refreshed, when I count to ten. Nine, when I wake up I will be fully relaxed and refreshed, when I count to ten. Eight, when I wake up I will be fully relaxed and refreshed, when I count to ten. Seven etc." At this point, begin counting to 10 backwards. Keep counting until you reach one. At one, you will wake up fully refreshed and relaxed. Tell yourself that when you finish counting you will be fully relaxed and refreshed and wide awake. When you finish, *you will be* fully relaxed, refreshed and wide awake.

This technique will leave you very relaxed and will also imprint anything in your mind that you want. Create an outgoing personality. Make yourself a more loving person. Stop putting off those things that are important. You can create any positive qualities that you want. Many things that you want for yourself can be yours if you employ this simple technique. Do it on a daily basis and watch the amazing things that it will do for your life. I know that it will astound you, just as it has me. Many of the most powerful men and woman use this exact, incredible technique to get the kind of personality that they want. You can do the same. Get in the luxury boat for a cruise with the winners and use the super influencing techniques that could change your life forever.

How To Relieve Stress

I am going to show you how you can use the super-influencing method to relieve stress. I urge you to use it because it will do wonders for your complete well-being. I want you to relax just as you did in the previous exercise. The suggestion I want you to give yourself is: *I will feel very relaxed and refreshed. All stress and anxiety will be removed from my body.* Just as before, count to ten backwards and wake yourself up when you reach *one.*

You should stay in this state for ten to fifteen minutes. I caution you to do this just once. If you go into this state for a second time, you will not get the full benefit of this treatment. You may have the tendency to fall asleep while in this state. If that is a problem, do the prescribed steps sitting up.

How To Deal With Aggression

We all need to deal with our aggression. We need a method to *blow off steam.* If this aggression is allowed to stay in our bodies, it will cause frustration. We may even explode if we let aggression build up inside of us for too long. We must find a harmless release for all of this energy.

First, let me point out that aggression is good. It is not a bad quality. Aggression can be very useful in completing our goals. A strong, persistent, aggressive attitude will allow you to fulfill your goals and to hit your target. Aggression, if used negatively, for resentment, envy, hate, etc. - will hurt ourselves more than others. We must be willing to use aggression positively and constructively, not negatively and destructively. There is one simple secret for directing aggression properly and that is to act out your feelings and emotions. I will discuss acting out your feelings and emotions in a later chapter. Expressing your aggressive feelings will help you to understand yourself. You may want to do this privately or with supportive people. Scream, yell, shout if you have to, but express your aggressive feelings.

The Aggressive Person

Every one of us has found ourselves in

SUMMARY

- Super-Influencing is a very powerful technique and could be used for all sorts of things including altering your personality.
- Completely relax your whole body, part by part at a time.
- Your subconscious mind is open to suggestions in this state.
- To get what you want, repeat positive suggestions to yourself in a calm and repetitive manner.
- Use this technique every day to imprint suggestions on your mind.
- The technique will relax and refresh your body and can relieve stress.
- An aggressive person could relieve stress with the super-influencing technique, or with laugher and humor, or with exercise or by thinking about something pleasant.
- If you are upset or angry, count from one to five before losing your cool.

situations where we are so stressed that we lose control. This is a time when you don't care about anything except your feelings. If you ever slip into this state, you must learn how to relax. Relaxation will calm your nerves and make you a more pleasant person. Use the above method for relaxing when you need to let off some steam. Being relaxed will make you feel a whole lot better.

Exercise can work wonders for you. Exercise does a great job of burning up all your excess stress. Join an exercise club or exercise in your home. Buy a treadmill or an exercise bike. I know a woman who has a punching bag in her garage. If she has a rough day at work, she lets her bag have it. She tells me that she always feels good after using this method. Have you ever considered buying a punching bag?

Think About Something Relaxing

Another good method for relieving aggression is to think about something relaxing. Think about fishing in a quiet lake or walking in the park. To keep you calm and cheerful and relieve your stress use the laughter chapter in this book.

Whatever it is, think about something pleasant and relaxing. I am sure that it will make you feel a lot better. Doing this should put your mind in a calm state.

A friend of mind told me that when he is very upset or angry he counts to five before doing anything. This method helps him clear his mind so that he can think rationally. Try this method, it works too. If you get angry could from one to five. That is one, two, three, four and five. Count from one to five when you get angry. The most important thing to remember is to keep your cool. If you can keep your cool, you will be able to get along better with yourself and with all of the people around you. You want that, don't you? Of course you do, then use this method and count from one to five, when you get angry. If you count to five whenever you get angry, you will do better with your life.

Chapter Thirteen

Using Your Hidden Computer To Solve Complicated Problems.

I am going to show you how you can use the powerful ability of your mind to make accurate and precise decisions. I will share with you the same problem-solving techniques are used to make important decisions. It is by far I will show you the most powerful methods for finding simple solutions to complicated problems. The ability to solve problems is a very strong asset. I am sure you want to be a great problem solver. Don't you? When you start to increase your wealth, you will have to make important decisions. These are decisions that will affect you the rest of your life. That is why it is important that you make the best possible decisions.

Making Accurate Decisions

Let me show you how to be an effective decision-maker. Before I do this, I want to tell you the qualities that a good decision-maker possesses. The wealthiest and most powerful men have these problem-solving qualities. First, they come to a routine decision very quickly. Second, they are very slow at changing their minds on firm decisions. How many decisions do you deal with in this way?

All of your decisions from routine situations should come to you quickly, and they should be changed slowly. Even if you are not sure of the solution, make your judgment quickly. If you are wrong, you will know what to do the next time that such a situation arises. Taking a long time to make a decision may slow you down. There is

one situation in which you may have to take time to make a decision; that is when it is a particularly difficult decision to make, because the situation is unfamiliar to you. If this is the case, use the subconscious decision-making technique which will be explained later.

Borden Had To Make A Decision

Gail Borden was a very compassionate person. While on a boat trip from London, he heard the cry of hungry babies. In those days, cows had to be taken along on such journeys in order to supply milk for the babies. On this voyage, the cows were seasick, which made the milk bad. He felt so badly for the babies that he decided to solve the problem. He knew he could do it and he was determined to create and sell sweet condensed milk. Anyone could condense milk, but it had always tasted bad. Borden wanted to create sweet-tasting condensed milk. He was too poor to support his family while he worked on the milk, so he sent his family to his relatives.

Nothing was going to stop Borden from developing his milk. He was determined to succeed. Two years later, he created sweet, condensed milk. He then went to apply for patents. He was denied a patent and told that there was nothing new about condensed milk. Borden, however, was a determined man. He applied for a patent again. He was rejected again. Even his third attempt was rejected, but Borden was persistent. Finally, Borden got a scientist to approve his patent. The scientist claimed that condensed milk wasn't being patented, but the process to condense the milk was. Borden finally got his patent on the fourth try. We all know the end of the story and of Borden's overwhelming success. Borden's milk is still for sale today. Borden's is the story of one man's decision to accomplish something, and the will and determination that it took to see the dream realized.

Henry Ford's Decision Making

There are times when it is necessary to change decisions quickly. Henry Ford was known to make quick decisions and stick by them. His dream of making an eight-cylinder car was considered impossible by his engineers but he stuck by his decision and demanded that his engineers produce the car. This decision to stick to his guns made Ford's company one of the richest and most powerful in the world. There were times when he stuck by decisions that could have changed. For example, Ford would say, "I will sell you a car in any color you want as long' as it's black." This policy helped Ford's competitors who sold cars in different colors. Usually, it is to your advantage to change your firm decisions slowly.

I have just told you a great deal about the problem-solving attitude. I am now going to tell you about the problem-solving process. I know unique and effective methods of making excellent decisions. Many of the most famous and wealthy men of this age use this method or a similar one, to make their decisions. You will be astounded by your results. Follow these simple steps to become an excellent decision-maker.

PROBLEM SOLVING USING THE SUBCONSCIOUS MIND

Have you ever acted on a hunch or emotions and found that you made the right decision? Has the answer to a problem ever appeared to you in your dreams or your head? Has your mind ever solved a difficult problem for you when you weren't looking for the answer? I am sure that you have experienced one of these situations. They have one thing in common. They all involve the subconscious mind solving the problem. I am going to show you a method for solving difficult problems effortlessly. You will be able to join the ranks of the wealthy and rich and solve difficult problems just like they do. Your reasoning ability will be on par with theirs. It is all possible with this advanced problem-solving technique.

This problem-solving technique is very powerful; so powerful that it should only be used to solve important problems. For the best results, you should use this technique as I have prescribed, only when the solution to problem is not obvious.

Deciding On Your Future

In a previous chapter, you have just gone through an exercise where I asked you to list your strengths, likes, and advantages. This exercise gave you the opportunity to see yourself as you are. We are now going to use all of this information to determine your best possible future. Follow the steps outlined in this chapter. If you follow my directions, you will have a very clear idea about how you can make your life better. Your powerful subconscious mind holds the answer. All you have to do is practice this simple exercise and the valuable answer-solving technique will be yours.

Know Your Problem

The first thing you must know is what problem you are solving. This may sound basic, but it is important. Make sure that you are deciding the right situation. *Decisions are only good if they solve the right problem.* I am going to pick a sample situation to help you to understand what I am talking about. What about deciding how you are going to make money? Will that interest you? I am sure it will.

Get All The Facts

It is important to understand exactly what you are dealing with. To do this you must gather information from all angles. It is important when making a decision that you understand all of the variables related to the problem before coming to any conclusion. Get all of the facts.

Make sure that you know as much as you can about the problem. You will need this information to decide how you will become more successful or make money. *You have already completed this step in a previous chapter.* You may be wondering where you completed it. The results of the exercises that asked you to name your strengths, likes and resources contain this information. You did do this exercise, didn't you? That should be all the information needed to decide how you will make your money.

Create Some Alternatives

The next thing we are going to do is have your subconscious mind answer the problem. When you type numbers on a calculator, you don't see crunching of numbers, but you do see the final answer. You mind will do the same thing for you. We are going to use the programs in your mind to do the complicated calculations for you. You won't have to do any actual thinking because your subconscious mind will do all the computing and provide you with the right answer. You are going to be astounded by the ability of your subconscious mind to solve your problems. Let me tell you more about it.

This is the simplest step. It is not only the simplest, but it is the step where most of the work is done. For this step, I want you to create some solutions to your problem. Write down about four or five possible solutions. I don't want you to write down *the* solution that you are going to use. Remember, if the solution were apparent, you wouldn't need this exercise. I want you to write *down four to five possible solutions.* Just write them down on a piece of paper or your note book.

Have you finished writing down your four to five solutions to the problem? This procedure is very important. Now, become familiar with each solution. I want you to become so familiar that you will be able to recall all of them without looking at your piece of paper. You don't have to memorize them, you just have to know what the solutions are.

Solve Your Problem

I want you to put away those four to five possible solutions now. The next thing I want you to do is to relax. It is important that you relax so that you can communicate to your subconscious mind. In a relaxed state, your subconscious mind easily obeys your instructions. Remember, a good time to give instructions to your subconscious mind is just before you go to sleep and after you wake up in the morning. At these times, you are the most relaxed and your mind is easily influenced by your suggestions.

Your Mind Will Do The Computing

When you are in a relaxed state, tell your mind to solve your problem. Ask it to give you an accurate answer to the problem which you are working on. Tell your mind to solve your problem and it will. At this point, there is no need to remind your mind what the possible solutions are. Your mind has already stored them for future reference.

Trust your mind, it will find an answer to your problem. Like a calculator crunches numbers and gives you the numeric solution. Your powerful mind can solve problems that you thought were hopeless. Leave your problems in its hands, and your mind will come up with an accurate and effortless decisions. Let your mind take care of the solution while you do something else. Do what all of the rich and the powerful do? Trust your mind.

The Answer Just Comes To You

It is very important not to try to think out a solution; just let it happen. If you try to extract a solution from your mind, you may not be successful. After you have given your mind its instructions, wait for it to give you an answer. When your mind has finished computing the answer will come to you in the form of a hunch or emotions.

In other words, while you are involved in doing something else, and not even thinking about your problem, the answer will come to you. Don't force it out, it will come. It may take hours or even days, but you can be sure that your mind is working on the problem and will eventually give you an accurate answer.

Visualize Being Happy With A Solution

I want you to visualize how happy you will be with the correct solution: Act out and think about how overjoyed you will be when the correct answer comes to you; try and sense the feeling that you will have when you get the right answer. Keep these feelings in your mind all day and just before you fall asleep. If you do this, the answer will come to you.

It will just pop into your mind, from out of nowhere. When the answer comes to you, it will come in the form of a strong emotional hunch. You will know it is the correct answer because of the force with which it hits you. If you try to force it out, it won't come. It will only come to you when you are relaxed and, usually, when you are doing something else.

The Answer Came To Gillette

Many of the world's great problem-solvers and inventors use this method. Gillette used this method to create the razor blade. He garnered as much information as he could on shaving and then let his subconscious mind solve the problem. The answer to his razor-blade problem came to him one day as a strong hunch. *"Sharpen two sides of a piece of steel."* Through this method, Gillette discovered the razor blade.

Many people tell me how wonderful and amazing this method of problem solving is. They tell me how they are astonished by the ability of the mind to solve difficult problems. I know that every time I use this method, I am surprised by the results. I am sure that you have solved problems in the past using this technique and that you weren't aware of the process that was taking place. This system is nothing new. Empires were created with the help of this technique. Use this method to create your own empire.

Hunches and Intuition

Modern science tells us to listen to our emotions, hunches and to our intuition. A hunch and emotions is the method our subconscious mind communicates with us. Give your hunches more respect; your first feeling about a problem is probably your best. Emotions are also messages from your subconscious mind to explain a situation. Pay attention to your emotions and hunches. That first feeling is an answer that is sent by your subconscious mind. I am sure that you have had a hunch or a feeling that has turned out to be extremely accurate. I am sure that you will agree that paying attention to feelings, hunches and intuition will pay off for you. Good, then we have agreed.

ALTERNATE FORM OF PROBLEM SOLVING

We will now go over one method of problem solving and one method of decision making. Both of these calculating methods can help you make great decisions. They are complex and mind numbing. Some people say they are boring. You can read them now and then possibly use them at a later date. Decision-making has to do with knowing how to handle many problems efficiently. Problem-solving is the method of handling each individual problem. We will start with a method of problem solving.

Identify Your Problem

Understand exactly what you are dealing with, and then gather information from all angles. It is important when making a decision that you understand all of variables related to the problem. Even minute bits of information may be important. All of the information and variables relative to the problem must be analyzed. Recognize a need to look for information from all sources before coming to a conclusion. Get all of the information related to your problem written down. **An example is that we we need more clients and cash accounts for our business.**

Study The Reasons Or Causes For Your Problem

You must study the causes of the problem -- this will help you solve it. What causes your problem? **An examples of the cause of our problem is the lack of funds for our business.**

What Are Your Resources?

You only have a limited amount of resources to use to solve your problem. You must be aware of your limitations. Make a list of people, money, time, equipment, supplies, etc., that you can use to solve your problem.

PROBLEM SOLVING MODEL

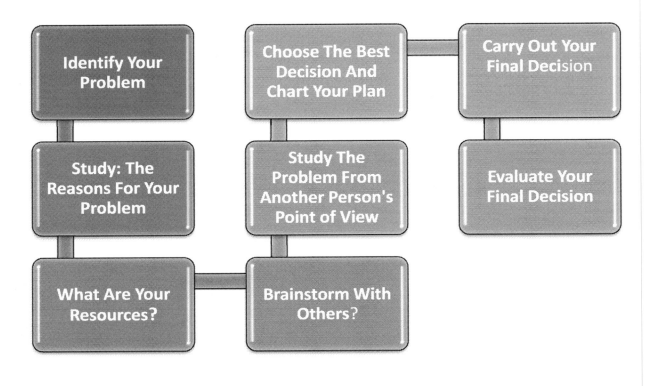

Brainstorm With Others

When solving a problem let others help. There are things other people can see that you can't. Get together with other people to discuss the solution to your problem. Explain the problem to them and get possible solutions from these people.

Study The Problem From Another Person's Point of View

When we use empathy that is putting ourselves in another person's place, we can visualize what another person would do to make a decision. You will find that looking at a problem from a different angle gives you more insight into the problem. Try using empathy to achieve great solutions to your complicated programs.

Choose The Best Decision And Chart Your Plan

Write down a list of solutions you think will solve your problem. Write down three to four good solutions that you think will solve your problem. Put a rating from one to ten by each solution. Then choose the best solution to solve your problem.

After you have picked the best solution, start off visualizing the end results and think backward to an activity you can do tomorrow. In this way you can pick out a fault in a solution. An example is: "I want to place a website on the internet tomorrow." You must then review things like: Do I have to pay now, or will they bill me later? Which company should design my website? Will I be ready when the responses come in? Don't make your plan of action too complicated. Try to make it as simple as possible or it will never be carried out.

Carry Out Your Final Decision

The final stage that you must complete is carrying out your final decision. Act according to a plan of action that you have drawn out. If you want some incentive to act right away, think about what penalties or losses you will pay if you don't act now.

Evaluate Your Final Decision

Make sure you have carried out the correct solution to your problem. Go over your solution just to make sure it was wise. The only time you fail is when you stop trying. If you have not made a good enough decision, then keep on trying. For problems that occur often, keep a record of how you solved them. You never know when these problems may occur again.

MASTER THE ART OF DECISION-MAKING

Decision making involves the handling many problems, while problem solving is the art of handling individual problems. Decision-making is an important element of every day of our lives. If we always made the right decision, our lives would be a great deal better. We will try to make the best decisions possible. Here are steps you can take to improve your decision-making:

Organize Your Work

There are two ways to organize your work: on the basis of the people involved; or by the nature of the problems. Use one of these methods to organize your work.

Prioritize Your Work

When you organize your work, one of the fundamentals to remember is priority. Do the most important things first. Leave the less important things for later. Do not do tasks in the order they are given to you -- do them in order of importance.

DECISION MAKING MODEL

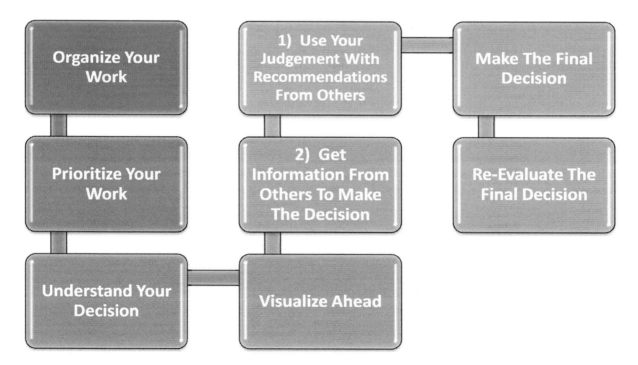

Understand Your Decision

Understand exactly what you are dealing with, then gather information from all angles. It is important when making a decision that you understand all the variables related to the decision. Even minute bits of information may be important. All of the variables relative to the decision must be read and analyzed. Look for information from all sources before coming to a conclusion.

Let Others Aid You In Decision-Making

When making a decision, let others help you. There are two ways to make a decision with the help of others:

1) Make the decision with your own judgment and knowledge, but get opinions from others.
2) Get all of the information that you can get from others, and with their recommendations and your judgment and your knowledge make the decision.
3) Option 2 is always the best. Remember, there are sometimes things that others see but you don't. It's old but true: Two heads are better than one.

Visualize Ahead

Before making a decision, imagine the situation that will occur with your decision. You must be able to look ahead and see what the outcome of the decision you make will be. Visualizing ahead is one of the best methods you can use to make intelligent and wise decisions.

Make The Final Decision

This is the last stage that must be completed when carrying out your final decision. Prepare to carry out your final decision with your plan of action that you have written out. Understand the plan of action knowing what losses you will take if you don't act know. Knowing these losses will give you the profit incentive to carry out the final plan.

SUMMARY

- Routine decisions are made quickly. Changing your mind with firm decisions should be done slowly.
- More complicated problems and problems that are unfamiliar to you, must be thought out.
- Problem-solving is the method of handling each individual problem.
- The steps to problem solving are: First: Know the problem. Second: Study reasons for your problem. Third: What are your resources? Fourth: Brainstorm with others. Fifth: Study the problem from another person's point of view. Sixth: Choose the best decision and chart your plan. Seventh: Carry out your final decision. Eighth: Evaluate your final decision.
- Decision-making is similar to problem solving and has to do with knowing how to handle many problems efficiently.
- An alternate form of problem solving is to use your subconscious mind for the correct answer.
- The answer will come to you in the form of a hunch, emotions or intuition.
- Hunches, emotions and intuition should be given close attention.

Re-evaluate The Final Decision.

It is important that you have the best solution to the problem. Re-evaluate the final solution, making sure it is the best solution. If you feel the solution isn't good enough then keep trying to develop a better solution. You should keep records of any problems that occur and the methods you used to solve these problems. This is important because these problems may occur again.

Chapter Fourteen

How To Achieve Happiness With Success

You can be a happier person with the information in this chapter. No matter what you are doing you can use the secrets that make a person a happier person. The secret of being more cheerful and happy will be revealed to you. The happiest people in the world know the secrets of being happy. But now the secrets of happiness can be yours. Likable people all over the world use these secret methods to spread love, win cheer and become happier. Now you can do the same.

Create Happiness In Your Life

The goal of all of us is to be happy. How could you enjoy life if you weren't happy? A joyful existence will only lead to the creation of love. To love and to be loved is what we all want. Make happiness your goal and you will find much love in your life. Though a truly happy person will not be happy all the time, they will be happy much of the time. Life is not perfect, so not everything in life will be a pleasant experience. Make the best of your life and read this book and your life can be happier. That is what is so exciting about we humans and our lives on earth is that, *"Your life will be what you make of it."* Your happiness is a state of mind that you create. Let me tell you more about happiness.

What is happiness? It is a state of mind, one that any of us can choose to feel. Happiness does not depend on what you have. It depends on how you feel about what you have. You could have all the friends or all the money in the world and still not be happy. Appreciating what you have will make you happy. Being with a certain person or having a certain item can make you happy, but will not necessarily guarantee your happiness. You have to appreciate what you have before it will bring you joy. Happiness can be equated to certain types of activities and functions. Doing something that is supposed to bring you joy usually brings joy but will not necessarily bring you joy.

It is not what you do that will make you happy, but how you feel about what you do. I know that I could be sitting in a room by myself with nothing to do and still feel happy. I am able to entertain myself no matter where I am. You should be able to bring joy to yourself no matter what you are doing. Happiness is an attitude.

Smiling And Laughing.

The first thing you can do to be happy is smile. That's right just adjust your lips and put a cheerful smile on your face. Smiling can be so cheerful for you and others. If you don't smile often you must practice smiling. Smile more often to be happier. To practice being cheerful spend about twenty minutes a day smiling and laughing. When practicing smiling put a heavy smile on your face. Tense your face to smile for long periods of time, so you are used to smiling. Practice smiling for bad situation and for difficult situations. Here are smiling exercises for you. Smile as you reply to each statement.

- A person tells you they don't like you. *Smile cheerfully as you say,* "Why don't you like me."
- A person wants to fight with you.

Smile cheerfully as you say, "I am not going to fight."

- You were told you didn't get the raise. *Smile cheerfully as you say,* "I deserve more money. Why didn't I get the raise?"
- You must get up twice at 2AM in the morning. *Smile cheerfully as you say,* "It's too early to wake up in the morning."
- You fall as you are walking. *Smile cheerfully as you say,* "I should watch my step."
- You wake up with a sore back. *Smile cheerfully as you say,* "My back is sore. It is time to go to the chiropractor."
- You are pushed by an employee at your work. *Smile cheerfully as you say,* "Why did you push me."
- You are punched lightly. *Smile cheerfully as you say,* "Don't hit me."

Laughing To Make You Happy

To be happy you must laugh a lot. Laughter in your life will make your life happier. I have some important exercises that I want you to do. These exercises will make you happier. You do want to be happier, don't you? Of course you do. You must practice laughing with a loud bellowing laugh that shakes a room. Practice this type of loud laughter with difficult and unpleasant situations. Practice this type of loud laughing twenty minutes a day, while repeating the below statements as you laugh. Do this exercise until you are used to laughing. If you keep practicing this loud laugher and smiling you will become a better cheerful person and you will be liked by many people. To practice laughter in difficult situations, I have picked a statement or an act. As you "say" or "do the act" on his list, then burst out and laugh loudly for one full minute, for the first step. For the second step, you would listen to the statement, then laugh loudly as you reply to the statement or act. Do both exercises so you are used to laughing in hard and difficult situations.. These examples are just exercises. For the real situation, you don't have to laugh as hard. Do this exercise for twenty minutes a day

- You are told, "You are not getting the raise." *Your reply as you laugh, loudly* "Well, why not. Can you tell me why I am not getting the raise."
- You are told, Your friend stole your money." *Your reply as you laugh loudly,* "How much money did my friend steal?"
- You are told, "Your bank lost your money." *Your reply as you laugh loudly,* "How much money did my bank lose me? Who told you?"
- You are told, Your wife is leaving you. *Your reply as you laugh loudly,* "Did my wife tell you she was leaving me."
- It just happened. You just fell off a chair. (actually do this) *Your reply as you laugh loudly,* "Oops, I just fell. Accidents can happen."
- It just happened. You just stained your favorite shirt (stain a piece of cloth). *Your reply as you laugh loudly,* "My shirt is ruined. I have to get this out with stain remover.
- It just happened. You are slapped in the head by another person (do this to yourself). *Your reply as you laugh loudly,* "Why did you hit me on my head? I don't deserve that."
- It just happened. A car cut you off on the road (act out yourself driving) *Your reply as you laugh loudly,* "You should watch your driving or there will be an accident."

If you practice this smiling and laughing technique, other people will like you more and give you more. When practicing laughter, practice with a loud hearty bellowing laughter. Practice loud for all of your irritating and difficult situations. Do these exercises so you can be happier. You do want to be happier, don't you? Of course you do.

How Can You Be Happier Today?

You can be happier today. How? It's simple. Think of pleasant things and do fun things and smile or laugh. Think of things that will make you happy or that have made you happy in the past and smile or laugh. Do fun things and smile or laugh. Previously we spoke about how it is possible for a well-adjusted person to be doing nothing at all and still be happy. Fill your mind with good memories, memories of joyful moments and bring them to life in your mind as you smile or laugh.

I remember that when I was 10 years old I went on an outing with my Cub Scout troop. It was a glorious February day, and a blanket of freshly fallen snow surrounded the log cabin that they had rented for us. Try and imagine 40 young kids in one large cabin. I was only there for a about a week, but when I think back it seems like I was there all winter. I was a annoying kid; the kind that irritated people just because he wanted attention. The scout leaders felt that I should be taught a lesson. One day, as I was menacing the inhabitants of the cabin, they grabbed me, tied me to a chair and wouldn't tell me what they were going to do next. Well, I found out! *I was to get the peanut butter surprise!* Every scout waited patiently in line for a chance at the peanut butter jar. Each, in turn, scooped out a finger full and smeared the goo onto my face. By the time the last little scout had taken his turn, I looked more like "The peanut butter Blob" than like a ten year old camper.

I laughed through this peanut butter ordeal. As you can tell I have a good sense of humor. I always have and I always will. When I think of this incident, I laugh. I encourage you to do the same; think of the good times, the funny times or any pleasant time that you have had. You will truly see a change if you do this simple thing.

A man once told me that he would be happy once he made a million dollars. He told me that a million dollars would solve all of his problems. He believed the money would bring him happiness the moment it was in his hands. Was this man right? Maybe, but if he wasn't happy before, there is a chance he won't be happy after he gets his million dollars. If you are waiting for certain events to make you happy, there is a chance you will be disappointed. Happiness lies in the present, not in the future. Make the best of your life now and have fun and be happy.

A long time ago, a good friend of mine Aaron, was having difficulties with his mother and he told me something very interesting. As we were driving down College Boulevard in San Diego, he said, "Dave, my mother had me because she thought I would bring her happiness." She didn't realize the truth that happiness comes from within. Another person can't make you happy; it has to come from yourself."

How right he was. Aaron's unhappy mother had him expecting that a new baby would bring her happiness. She believed he would somehow provide the things she lacked. She raised him alone. She was a bitter woman and she transferred that bitterness to her son. It's no surprise, then, that he grew up in her image. He never could bring his mother the happiness she sought because she was unhappy inside, and never took the steps necessary to change her condition. You have to make yourself happy, no one can do it for you.

A terribly depressed man I know told me once that he would be happy if only he could marry a past lover; his "lost love", he called her. Happiness, I tried to explain, only sometimes lies in the future. You have to try and make every moment happy by having fun and don't expect someone else to furnish happiness.

It is said that you can tell how happy a person is by watching how often they smile. People that smile a lot are usually happy people. When I meet a business associate this is one thing I look for; I seldom do much business with people who don't smile. In my experience they are not as trustworthy or dependable as those who smile often. Take note of the people in your life and the quality of your relationship with them, and try and relate that to how much they smile. *Do you smile a lot?* If you don't, try and get into the habit of smiling. Smile often. As I told you earlier, you will find that the physical act of cheerfully smiling will make you happier.

What Is Happiness?

You will be happy when you are doing what you enjoy and you are getting the most out of all the wonderful things that life has to offer. Have you ever wondered what happy people have in common? A survey was given to a number of people who considered themselves to be generally happy about their lives. They were asked, *"What do you feel when you are happy? What do you do to be happy?* They all answered in different ways. They all felt differently when they were happy, and they each had their own activities that made them happy. There is no one thing that will make everyone happy. Do what you enjoy and bring joy to yourself. Have fun in your life and be happy.

Another interesting thing about this study

that I want to share with you is what happy people think about happiness. According to the survey, most happy people don't even think about being happy because they are busy doing something. These people never contemplate the meaning of happiness because they are busy doing something that makes them happy. They are enjoying life and all it has to offer. Are *you* enjoying life and all it has to offer? You should be.

If You Only Had Six Months

What would you do if you only had six months to live? Would it be dramatically different from what you are doing right now? People that are happy wouldn't change a thing. They are doing the things right now that give them the most satisfaction. I've asked this question to many people and one of the answers I get is, "I would quit my job." Those people don't like their work very much. I know I wouldn't quit my job even if I was to die in six months. I enjoy my job. The same should be true for you. Ask yourself, "What would you do if you had only six months to live?" If you would make any changes, make them now. You should enjoy to the fullest, the fun things that life has to offer. Why take second best? Your life is special, so don't settle for less than the very best. Some people wait until they are about to die to enjoy the best life has to offer; don't be one of them. Enjoy your life now and do fun things. Put these fun things on your list of things to do.

Fun Things For You To Do

- Go to a movie theater and watch a big screen movie.
- Watch a newly released movie on your big screen television.
- Bowl at a popular bowling alley.
- Ice skate in a rink.
- Roller skate outside with others.
- Ride a bicycle down a bicycle trail.
- Go swimming in a large pool.
- Invite others and have a barbeque in your yard.
- Have a picnic in a popular park.
- Go to an amusement park and go on all of the rides.
- Go to a football, baseball or basketball sports event
- Go to a theater and watch a theater play.
- Play basketball, baseball or football in a park.
- Go out and get an ice cream sundae, frozen yogurt, or a milk shake.
- Go camping with tents or a rented recreational vehicle.
- Eat in a fine restaurant with family.

Sigmund Freud On Happiness

The goal towards which the pleasure principle impels us - of becoming happy - is not attainable: yet we may not - nay, cannot - give up the efforts to come nearer to realization of it by some means or other. The pleasure principal Sigmund Freud refers to is the tendency of people to seek pleasure and avoid pain, and strive to fulfill our most basic and primitive urges, including hunger, thirst, anger, and sex.

Mrs. Rudkin: Becoming Successful At Something You Enjoy

Let me tell you about a woman who became successful by doing things that she enjoyed. One of Mrs. Rudkin's children needed a special food. Now, Mrs. Rudkin was a good cook, so the doctor suggested that she bake some old-fashioned whole-wheat bread. The doctor told her that this type of bread contained all the nutrition that her child needed. She loved to cook, so she taught herself how to make this special wheat bread.

Mrs. Rudkin said, "I got down an old cookbook and looked up the recipe for homemade bread. The ingredients it called for came as a bit of a shock, especially the stone-ground flour. But I decided, for the sake of my son, to stick to the recipe. I got the whole wheat from the local feed store and ground it myself in a coffee mill. Soon my whole family was enjoying the bread that I

106

baked to help my one ill son."

The bread she made tasted very good. She finally found a miller who would grind her whole wheat; and soon, she was making bread for her friends as well as for her family. Eventually, she began to wonder how well her bread would sell in the marketplace. She knew her bread was of good quality and she believed that it would sell well. She was determined to make money by cooking. She left some of her bread with her grocer. About three days later, other grocers contacted Mrs. Rudkin, wanting her bread. The news spread and grocers all over the state of New York wanted to carry her product. People were even writing in to buy the bread by mail. Her bread came out in the late 1930's. Even though she sold her product for twice the price of commercial bread, people were willing to buy it because of its quality.

Mrs. Rudkin took something that she liked to do and turned it into a booming business. By 1940, she sold 55,000 loaves a week. She called her newly formed company Pepperidge Farms. Today, Pepperidge Farms sells baked goods and other products all over the United States. The thing that Mrs. Rudkin liked to do created an empire for her.

When Will You Be Happy?

This story illustrates that you will only be happy when you are pursuing your goals. If you don't have a goal to pursue, your powerful mind will have nothing to work for. Choosing not to give your mind goals to work towards is like driving in circles around a block. You use a car but you just don't go anywhere. Do you want to go places? Give your mind fuel, set your goals and let your powerful mind help you catch your dreams. The process, as well as the results, will bring you happiness.

This is the most important thing that anyone can tell you about happiness. The reason that so many of us are unhappy is because we have no purpose. Having purpose, pursuing a goal, can make great things happen for you. Take some time out right now and decide what you want to do with your life. As soon as you do this, you will start to see happiness.

The key to happiness is having a purpose in life and having something to work for. Know exactly what you want and then go after it. This will give your life purpose and make you happy.

In previous chapters I have included a goal setting master plan. Follow this goal setting plan and watch your level of happiness and success increase.

Unhappy People

What do unhappy people think about? Some people believe happiness lies in a different city or in a different country. Some of these people get very disappointed when they find out that their new environment is just as disappointing as the old. The truth is, if you are not happy where you are right now, you won't be happy 'where you are going. Feeling happy about what you are doing will make you happy.

What about material acquisitions? I mentioned the man who believed he would be happy when he made a million dollars. He should be happy with himself first. All the money in world won't bring some people happiness. Material things can make you happy. If you are unhappy inside, you may remain an unhappy person. It is your attitude that will make you happy. Create a happy attitude and become happier.

Why Do We Feel Pain?

Why do we all feel pain? It is our body's way of telling us that something is wrong, so feeling pain is necessary for our survival. Without it, we would fall to pieces. If a person experienced no pain when he had an stomach ulcer, how would he know that treatment was needed? Imagine the condition of an ulcerous stomach that never got treatment?

Our mind sends out signals to tell us whether our success-oriented mechanism is on track and doing its job. When our mind sends us pain, we must change what we are doing. Conversely, headaches and other stress-related pain occur for a good reason. The pain warns you that you are on a bad course. If you are experiencing any stress-related pain, the first step in taking care of the problem is to examine yourself very carefully. Is there anything about yourself that you don't like? Are you happy with yourself? Is there anything about yourself that you would like to change? Make those changes and make your life happy. Remember, you can only change others to a certain degree, but you can change yourself.

Making Mistakes

A potential cause of pain stems from the mistakes that we make. We all make mistakes. If we learn from the mistakes that we make, then we will be more successful. I have made more than I can count, but I believe that making mistakes has actually turned out to be a good teacher. People that don't make mistakes, or don't learn from their mistakes, don't accomplish as much. The only way you will ever learn is by trying. If you don't try, you won't learn. Your success will be determined by how well you handle your mistakes. The golden rule is that you should try to limit your mistakes and never, never make the same mistake twice. That's right, you heard me correctly. *If you make the same mistake twice, you are not learning.* Learn from your mistakes, they are the greatest teachers you will have. Make an effort to understand why you made the mistake and try to correct that error. If you learn from your mistakes you will not make the same mistake twice. Successful people learn from their mistakes.

Are You Happy When You Are Secure?

This discussion returns us to an important point. Are you happy when you are secure or when you are insecure? Insecure is when you are working on achieving your goals and secure is having completed your goals. Try to guess before you read on. Alright, I will tell you. For the most part, it is the journey to the mountain top and not being on the mountain top, which creates happiness. Doesn't that seem strange?

Aren't the best things in life, the things that you have to struggle to get? If you get them too easily, you just don't appreciate them, will you? I know people who make a lot of money but who are miserable, but there are others that make a lot of money and are happy. I would be lying if I told you that making money alone will make you happy. Don't you want to be more successful and happier? You are more successful if you are happy. Making more money will only be worthwhile to you if it makes you happier.

I want to return to discussing the value of being *bored.* When you have reached your goal, you will be secure. Security then, leads to boredom. It is the effort itself or the effort toward the attainment of a goal - that creates happiness. When you finally get what you want, you become bored because the challenge is gone. The troubles and the joys that you experience while trying to reach your goals are what bring you joy and satisfaction. They are what will make you happy. When you have completed your goal, start another goal. You must start another goal, this way you will not be bored. Before looking over the list of activities to lessen boredom, set your goals as outlined in previous chapters. Don't forget to set your goals and become happier.

List Of Things To Lessen Boredom

1) Go to the library and research topics.
2) Read a business or self-improvement book.
3) Listen to a business or self-improvement audio tape.
4) Watch a business or self-improvement movie.
5) Join a business or a self-improvement support group.
6) Take an adult school class.
7) Meet some old or new friends and spend time with them.
8) Make phone calls or house visits to friends and relatives.
9) Write letters to friends and relatives.

I have talked to many self-made millionaires. They tell me that they enjoyed the struggle it took to get to where they are. It was the journey to be successful that made them happy. That is why those who inherit money are not as satisfied or as happy as those who work for their money.

Your Key to Success

I am sure that you already know that people are your key to success. People who express their feelings well, are usually always successful. If you want to succeed, you have to market yourself. I can tell you that almost every successful person is able to communicate their ideas and their feelings well to others. Let me give you an idea of what some of the most successful people in America did before they were successful. Frank C. Mars, of Mars Candy, was a salesman for 18 years before he made his first cent on a candy bar. King C. Gillette spent 24 years as a successful salesman before he made money with his newly invented razor. These examples illustrate one point: Being a good communicator is an asset, an asset that you need in order to succeed. Remember, you don't have to be the salesman type, but you should be able to convey your true honest feelings to others.

To communicate well, you must be honest, open, caring, persistent, cheerful and expressive. This is how you create a winning personality and it is the way to become successful. Think about what I have said. Study it carefully and evaluate it. You have an opportunity to be the best you can be. Use the knowledge I've provided and make it work for you. Take this opportunity to better yourself; it is your first step toward riches.

Continue Laughing

The most important part of the chapter are the cheerful smiling and laughing exercises. I want you to get used to laughing and smiling. The more you laugh and smile the more successful you will be. When you practice smiling make sure you form a hard cheerful smile for many minutes a day. When you practice laughing, make sure that you let out a very loud bellowing laugh that shakes the

SUMMARY

- Happiness doesn't depend on what you have. It depends on how you feel about what you have.
- It is your attitude that will make you happy.
- Be cheerful and smile more often.
- If you keep practicing this loud laugher and smiling you will become a better cheerful person and you will be liked by many people.
- Start to feel happier by doing fun things and by thinking about pleasant things.
- You are happy when you are doing something that makes you happy.
- You are happy when you perusing a goal and bored when you have completed your goals. When you are bored, set new goals and start new activities to be happy, like taking classes and reading books.
- Unhappy people blame their unhappiness on their environment.
- It alright to make mistakes, but don't make the same mistake twice.
- Developing a better level of communication will lead you to success.

whole room. Here are more laughing exercises for you. These laughing exercises are to practice laughing in difficult situations. To practice the loud laughter, read that statement on the list then burst out and laugh loudly for about one full minute. Remember it has to be a loud bellowing laughter. Do this exercise for twenty minutes a day

- You are told, "You are fired." *Your reply as you laugh loudly*, "You can't fire me. I am a good employee."
- You are told, An employee just hit your car." *Your reply as you laugh loudly*, "Who hit it. I hope he has insurance?"
- It just happened. You are pushed as you are walking (push yourself). *Your reply as you laugh loudly*, "Don't push me."
- It just happened. A bird flew into your head (act out the bird diving) *Your reply as you laugh loudly*, "A bird flew into my head."

Become Happier

Some of the techniques I have shown you are new. You may never have seen them before. The reason for this is that I want to keep you up to date with the latest research in getting along with other people. You can be sure that these techniques are used by the world's greatest minds. It took some of these people 20 years to understand the concepts I am discussing with you. Successful people who see what I have done are amazed. How amazed? Amazed at how the knowledge learned through many years of experience can be learned overnight. They are amazed because they know how well these secrets of success work. I know you will be amazed when you see the riches that these qualities will bring you. Study them well and become successful.

Chapter Fifteen

The Wealth And Love Relationships

In this chapter I will show you how to develop good relationships and grand beauty as well. There is a secret that works at developing all kinds of relationships and when you are in this state you are better adjusted and better looking. When I say better looking, I mean that people in the state of non-attachment are pretty or handsome people. In other words, the best looking people you will see in a crowd are non-attached. Yes, I kid you not. What is non-attached? This chapter will reveal non-attachment to you. The secret is a very simple concept that you can master. Some of the greatest minds in the world guard this wealth and beauty secret dearly.

To achieve perfect harmony in all relationships, you must have an understanding of non-attachment. Non-attachment is one of the greatest fundamental secrets of success and love and it is where beauty lies. It is an attitude that allows meaningful relationships to flourish, and increased prosperity, more success and physical beauty. When I say *relationship*, I am speaking of any relationship. A relationship with other people, a relationship with yourself, and a relationship with objects such as money, toys, cars etc... Being successful depends on forming successful relationships. Once you are able to master the concept of non-attachment, you will be able to master the three types of successful relationships.

Once you master the concept of non-attachment you could have many things that you always wanted. Let me go over the three different types of successful relationships. They are:

1) Love yourself and be happy with everything you do.
2) Maintain caring and loving relationships with everyone in your world.
3) Develop prosperity and wealth, in your life.

If you are lacking in any of the three areas just mentioned, then this chapter will really help you. Non-attachment will change your life. I have all of these things now, and they started coming to me only as I began mastering the concept of non-attachment. It is simple to master, and its results could be truly amazing.

Your Status In A Relationship

Each person or thing you are associated with, involves a different kind of relationship. The key is to remain non-attached in all your relationships; thus the concept of *non-attachment*. When you are in the state of non-attachment, other people will say that you look better. In the state of non-attachment you could be pretty, beautiful, handsome or even cute. You may be in an attached relationship with one of your friends and in a non-attached relationship with another. The moment you become non-attached with an individual or thing you can develop perfect harmony in that relationship and you will look better. Believe me as you look in the mirror, you can notice a difference. Not only will your looks improve but the relationship will become more exciting and exhilarating.

Look at my interpretation of how the human mind works in the next diagram. The area of the human mind that we will be talking about is between action and thinking; it is the area in which our mental processes reside. An attached person thinks before he acts. A detached person acts before he thinks. A non-attached person acts in coordination with thinking and acting. They can think and act at almost the same time. You will see what I mean as I explain each state.

The Mind

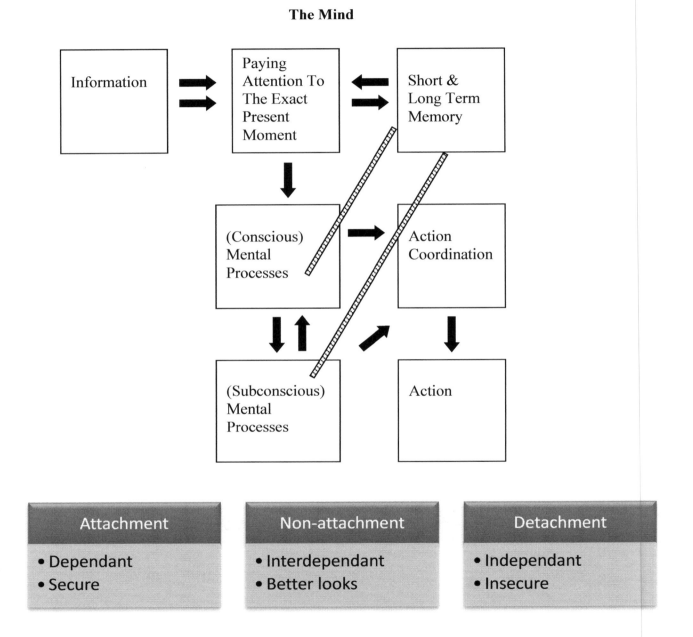

Before I go over the different states of attachment, let's see what state you are in. This quiz will tell you which state you are in regarding a relationship you may have with another like a spouse or family members or friends. Pick an individual with whom you have a relationship and try to determine which state you are in. Try writing in different individuals with whom you have different relationships. See how each relationship fares. Answer the following questions and see how they pertain to your various relationships.

Relationship Attachment Quiz

1)   Are you secure in the relationship?

7   6   5   4   3   2   1
Yes   No

2)   Could you let go of the relationship?

7   6   5   4   3   2   1
No   Yes

3)   Do you get everything you want out of that relationship?

7   6   5   4   3   2   1
Yes   No

4)   Do you have the freedom to go where every you want?

7   6   5   4   3   2   1
Yes   No

5)   Can you say whatever you want?

7   6   5   4   3   2   1
Yes   No

Relationship Attachment Score

Here is what the scores mean. If you scored between 5- 10, you are very detached to the relationship. If you scored 11- 17, you are semi-detached to the relationship. If you scored between 18-22, you are non-attached. If you scored 23-30, you are semi-attached. If you scored 30-35, you are very attached.

Here are the answers, according to which state you are in, for all five questions. 1-2 is detached. 3-5 is non-attached. 6-7 is attached.

Your Relationship With Money

Let's find out which state of attachment you are in regards to money. This quiz should reveal to you what kind of relationship you have with money. This test is not designed to discover your present wealth, but it should tell you, your relationship with your wealth. What matters is how you feel about the wealth that you have. You could be poor and happy, and you could be rich and unhappy. This test will tell you how happy you are in your relationship with wealth.

Money Attachment Quiz

1)   Do you have all the money you need?

7   6   5   4   3   2   1
Yes   No

2)   Could you easily give away some of your money?

7 6 5 4 3 2 1
Yes   No

3)   Can you confidently tell others how much money you have?

7 6 5 4 3 2 1
Yes   No

4)   Do you always get all the money you need?

7 6 5 4 3 2 1
Yes   No

5)   Can you spend whatever you want?

7 6 5 4 3 2 1
No   Yes

Money Attachment Score

Here is what the scores mean. If you scored between 5- 10, you are very detached in your relationship with money. If you scored 11-17, you are semi-detached in your relationship. If you scored between 18-22, you are non-attached. 18-22 is the best score. If you scored 23-29, you are semi-attached. If you scored 30-35, you are very attached.

Here are the answers, according to which state you are in, for all five questions. 1-2 is detached. 3-5 is non-attached. 6-7 is attached.

Beautiful, Handsome, Good Looking or Pretty

When is a person's appearance beautiful, handsome, pretty or good looking? It is when they are in the middle state. Which state is that? It is the non-attached state. That means when you become non-attached, you will actually start to look better. Within one hour you could be better looking. I kid you not. As you are looking in a mirror, you may notice the difference. Nature has a tendency to apply good looks to those in the non-attached state.

Attached People?

Attached people are people that cling to other people and are influenced by others like children are to their parents. You can be sure that every one of us has been in the attached state more than once. I know that I have. It is really better to be attached than it is to be detached. Attached people are usually good with other people. They are loving and caring and are trusted more. They are good at anything that has to do with other people. However, if they want to be good at most professions, they will have to lean more toward the non-attached state, which is a state of interdependent in regard to relationships.

Detached People

Detached people tend to be independent in their lives and seem insensitive. They tend to be alone a lot. They are loners. They have fewer friends then an attached person and are not good conversationalists. They find many people annoying and talkative. Most of what other people think or believe go right by them, since they are detached from other people.

Non-Attachment

How does a non-attached person differ from both the detached and the attached person? It is the midpoint. At this point, they reach the perfect ability to adapt to all relationships. It has been proven that true love takes place in the state of non-attachment. If you put yourself in this state, you will find more happiness. Beauty also takes place in the state of non-attachment. If you are in this state you can look pretty, beautiful or handsome.

Let me draw a little chart to show you where the different states of attachment lie. Remember, you can switch from one state to another all in the same day. Your level of attachment depends on what is affecting you. In other words, you may be attached to one person and detached to another. The best relationship you can have with any person or thing will occur when you are non-attached. It is possible to act either attached or detached in a situation as long as you are being yourself.

What Is Non-Attachment?

I have told you what you can gain by being non-attached, but what? You may be asking, what is non-attachment? It is the state of a relationship in which you are the happiest and the best looking. This can be a relationship with a car, a person, an attitude, yourself or with anything.

Non-attached people are both good listeners and good talkers. They appreciate the relationships they have because they understand what their lives would be like without them. They are good communicators because they are willing to walk away from those who don't listen, but they also listen to those who talk. They don't compromise themselves. They are loving and caring, and yet can be assertive and aggressive, depending on the situation. Their feelings guide them, so their actions are spontaneous. They are better looking and fall into the class of pretty, beautiful and handsome. They are always in a state of interdependence. They are always themselves because they know themselves.

A Non-Attached Person

How would a non-attached individuals react to losing money? They accept the fact that they may lose their money any day. They want to keep and appreciate their money, but they realize and accept the fact, that they may be without their money one day. Because they feel that they might lose their money, they are constantly looking for ways to preserve their wealth. They may double their money just by looking for ways to save it. If they lose their money, they would be hurt, but their loss would prompt them to understand why their loss occurred. They would then reclaim what they had lost. This is the attitude that the most successful millionaires have. Only in this state can you completely appreciate what you have.

Going From An Attached State To A Non-Attached State

I am going to show you how to achieve non-attachment in a relationship with another person. This person could be your boss, your friend, your employee, your wife, or your lover, etc... You should maintain this type of an attitude with any relationship that you have.

To achieve non-attachment, you must be able to contemplate walking out of the relationship wither it is a job or an investment. You may have already created alternative plans. The truth is that you want the relationship, but you are willing to leave it. You would leave when your feelings dictate that you should do so. You want the relationship and its benefits but you don't want to continue doing something that goes against your beliefs or feelings; so you prepare to leave. The possibility of leaving the relationship is always present in your mind. You should actually visualize what you would do without the relationship. To summarize; you want the relationship, but you will leave it if you have to put up with something that rubs against your grain.

I don't want you to get this state confused with what a detached person feels. A detached person always makes plans to leave the relationship. A detached person doesn't want the relationship as much

Going From A Detached State To A Non-Attached State

Next, I will tell you how a detached person goes to the non-attached state. The benefits of the non-attached state are success, love, beauty, prosperity and money. How does this person become non-attached? A detached person must force themselves to be in a relationship, by spending a lot more time with one special person and other people. They must keep seeing the same one special person and the same people again and again, even if they dislike other people. It takes a bit of getting used to, but the rewards of having relationships are worthwhile.

Non-Attachment On The Job

Let me illustrate the states of attached, non-attached and detached with your job situation. Employees who constantly do whatever their bosses tell them to do, are attached employees. These employees are slower and may have some difficulties. They just put up with a lot of problems on the job, and, in time, resent their jobs.

Detached employees don't care that much. They feel that a problem is always the other person's fault. To most people, they seem insensitive and self-centered. They constantly talk back to management, blaming most problems on management but never on themselves.

Non-attached employees, in contrast do care but with reservations. They really enjoy their jobs and do their best and do want to keep their jobs. However, if management gives them a hard time and they feel that they have been wrongly stepped on, they may try to find other work. They know that they have nothing to lose by voicing their opinions. They are sincere, honest and open about their feelings, but, if management continues to step on them, they will complain.

Remember this important point about happiness: Happiness is not related to what you have, it is related to how you feel about what you have. Non-attachment will bring you wealth, happiness and beauty because of the new attitude of appreciation you will develop toward other people. The state of non-attachment will give you personal freedom which, in turn, creates good honest communication. Communication helps to determine the success of a relationship. You must gain your personal freedom in order to achieve good communication in a relationship. There are two states that will give you personal freedom: detachment and non-attachment. The personal freedom we gain from detachment does you no good because, in this state, your attitude is self-centered. Your attitude in non-attachment is more positive.

We can achieve good communications with other people and better looks, only when we have a non-attached attitude. When I talk about good communication, I mean in-depth communication through which all true feelings are brought out. Your true feelings can only come out in the state of non-attachment.

SUMMARY

- Attached people cling to other people and are influenced by others.
- Detached people are independent people that have tendencies to be alone.
- An attached person may get bored and a detached person may get lonely.
- Non-attachment is an attitude that will create better and more meaningful relationships and good looks like being pretty, beautiful or handsome.
- You can have a different "attached" attitude for each relationship you have, like a person, your job or an investment.
- You will be happiest and best looking in the state of non-attachment.
- A non-attached person is spontaneous, considerate, confident, assertive and caring. They are good talkers and listeners.
- Going from attached to non-attached state involves contemplating leaving the relationship.
- Going from detached to a non-attached state involves contemplating staying with the relationship.
- Being non-attached allows a person to a person to develop better looks, a good attitude and allows a person to express their personal freedom.
- Giving people what they want, will not guarantee they will like you.

Giving People What They Want

Giving people what they want will not always guarantee that they like you. It may make them lose respect for you, or take you for granted, but overall they will like you. People don't always ask for what they really want. You must be yourself, and give others what you feel you should give them, that is from your heart. The old saying, *Give people what they want and they will like you,* is sometimes wrong. How must you treat people?

116

Let your feelings be your guide. When you feel like being nice to someone, you should be nice. When you feel like being rude, you should be rude. Your display of emotions will depend on how in touch you are with your feelings. That is why it is important to be in touch with your feelings.

A Sigmund Freud Quote.

Human beings are funny. They long to be with the person they love but refuse to admit openly. Some are afraid to show even the slightest sign of affection because of fear. Fear that their feelings may not be recognized, or even worst, returned. But one thing about human beings puzzles me the most is their conscious effort to be connected with the object of their affection even if it kills them slowly within. By Sigmund Freud

Chapter Sixteen

Creating The Wealth Attitude

This chapter will show you how to use the wealth attitude of *"Novanetics"*. I will go over why some people are successful and how others could be more successful. It is not a matter of intelligence as much as it is of controlling a difficult part of your mind. Once you have mastered controlling this part of your mind your success can be yours. The most successful people in the world know that this wealth attitude is the key to achieving great wealth. The world's greatest lovers will tell you the same thing.

I can tell you from my experience that gaining command over this part of my mind was the key to my success and prosperity. Once I conquered it, I did better with my life. Let's discuss the part of you that everyone sees, the part of you that makes you feel confident or timid. It is responsible for the way you feel about yourself. It is an important part of your mind. It determines your success and prosperity and it is at the heart of the wealth attitude.

Creating The Perfect Ego

The most dramatic part of my life was when I lost everything I had. It was truly a turning point in my life. Many years ago, I was over $12,000 in debt and the world around me started to fall apart. At that point, my self-esteem was gone. I disliked myself for being a failure. One day I sat in my room and lamented, because I knew I was to blame. I accepted the fact that I had created my own failure. My family fell apart, my wealth was gone, and so too, my health began to fail. I started to become ill. One day as I lay in bed, I realized that my love and my money were gone, and I knew there was only one thing left -myself. That, too, I sensed was slipping away. I knew that if I let myself slip away, there would be nothing left. It was then that I decided to turn my failure into success. I wanted to be the best I could be.

I became a humble person. My smaller ego made me a realistic person. I spent six months working on my life while I was in college, and I turned my life around. I bought the best self-improvement and business books I could find and I studied hard. I talked to some remarkably intelligent people with great minds and I talked to them and learned as much as I could. I wrote out my specific goals. I dreamed and visualized myself owning a large company and being successful. I repeated my goals to myself every day, while I attended college and ran a book company. I wrote the book *"How To Use Your Hidden Potential To Get Rich."* My company grew and grew and within a few years I published many books and two national magazines. My company was large and employed over a hundred people. I owned two nice cars and even bought a large home.

What happened to turn my life around? What made me much happier and much more successful? The answer is that my ego was shattered when I suffered failure. Every successful person knows that with the right methods, from failure comes a learning period and then a greater success. I believe that if I had suffered more, and worked harder, I could have been even more successful.

Before my failures, I thought more of myself

than I should have. I had a big ego. I had a false sense of reality and my failure was a direct result of this. I was doomed to fail. All my failure did was set the record straight and empty my mind of any exaggerated ideas I had about my success. My mind became a clean slate and I began to restructure my thinking processes. I absorbed new ideas and thoughts, which before my failure would never have penetrated my closed mind. You know the saying; you can't teach an old dog new tricks. Well I was an old dog and I couldn't be taught. When I lost everything, I became a new dog and learning was possible.

Empty Your Mind

Some of you may not have to fail to learn. The key to discovering success is to empty your mind of all your false assurances. Understand that you can pull the pieces and start again. Reward yourself when you accomplish something and don't assume that you know anything well until you have actually found that to be a fact. Try and view yourself honestly. Don't inflate your ego.

Since that time that I lost my money, I have earned countless millions of dollars for other people and myself. I was featured on "Life Styles Of The Rich And Famous" and other magazines and television shows. So many years have passed by and during that time, I have had many years of business experience. It was this experience that made me what I am today. I am an expert when it comes to making money easily for other people and I did help so many people. I had to learn the hard way and when it comes to setting someone up in their own business, few know as much as me. Mastering the art of "Novanetics" was one of the reasons I was so successful and wealthy. "*Novanetics*" includes many technique and concepts that the rich and wealthy guard closely.

Balancing Your Ego

A healthy ego, isn't that what you want? When your ego is correctly balanced, you will be able to win people over and be a happier person. Your accomplishments and defeats will have meaning if you are honest with yourself. Truth is the key to having a perfect ego. Be honest with yourself and others and you will know more truth. If you can verbalize to supportive others everything that you are thinking, you are being truly honest

with yourself, you will become more successful.

Let me tell you a story about a woman I met:

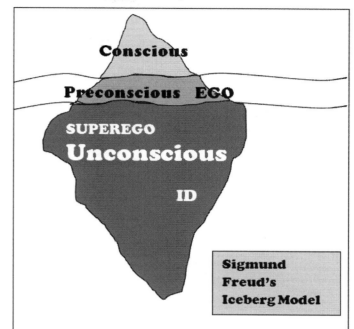

I had a conversation with a woman who was telling me about her numerous accomplishments, and the great places she was headed. She was trying to impress me. I wanted to feel superior to her so I continued to discuss all of my great accomplishments. It wasn't long before the conversation began to turn ugly. Hard feelings were being created and it was obvious that we were going nowhere, fast. I knew something had to be done, but I didn't know what.

I started to talk about things that made me look humble. I began to reveal some of my weaknesses to this woman. I felt as if I had vulnerabilities; I just told her the truth. I talked about my shortcomings and my accomplishments - like the fact that I had lost money but I had also earned a lot of money. I told her, " I learned twice as much because, I made twice as many mistakes." As I talked, she began to change. We began talking on a more personal level. She started telling me more about herself, and we began to get along really well. Let go of your ego, you will be surprised by the results.

Sigmund Freud's Model Of The Ego

The mind is like an iceberg,. One-seventh of the human mind floats above the water and is the conscious mind. The pre-conscious and the Unconscious mind is below the water line.

Freud proposed that the human psyche could be divided into three parts: Id, ego and super-ego. Freud discussed this model in the 1920 essay Beyond the Pleasure Principle, and fully elaborated upon it in The Ego and the Id (1923).

Do You Have A Weak Opinion Of Yourself?

Very few people have an ego that is exactly balanced to their personality. Most people think more of themselves, or less of themselves. Having a lesser opinion of yourself is more advantageous than having an over-inflated ego. With supportive people, it is very easy to go from a weak ego to a healthy one.

Every successful person has had many accomplishments and some failures. You should, at all times when you are with supportive people, portray yourself as honestly as you can, regardless of what your personality is like, or what other people think of you. You should not be afraid to express your honest feelings; even if you don't think highly of yourself, you should express those feelings openly to supportive people. Don't hide them. One way to conquer a weak ego is by expressing your feelings to others and explain your desire to improve.

When other people are annoyed by your feelings, you will start to change. Expressing your feelings truthfully to a supportive people, is the key to conquering a weak ego. A good friend of mine, Lloyd, once told me, "Dave, there is a purpose to everything we go through." At first I didn't understand, but later his words made sense. He meant that if you don't go through a certain experience, you can't learn from it. Express yourself truthfully and honestly. Don't pretend to be someone else, be yourself at all times. Be very honest, verbalize your thoughts and act out your true feelings to supportive people around you.

This is the only way to be you.

What Attitude Will Create A Good Ego?

Creating a positive healthy ego is a matter of rewarding yourself for all of your accomplishments. There are many things that you do well that you probably don't even notice. Reward everything that you do. This will help you create a positive self-image. Enjoy life and all of its rewards; every moment should be filled with excitement. As we have discussed in previous chapters, develop goals and due dates to complete those goals. Pick some things that you want to do, and do them. This will improve your life. Whether it is to be happy or to help those who are needy, that may be able to help you some day, set some goals in your life.

One of the things you should also do is to develop more friends. Pick supportive people who care about other people. This will be good for you. Develop a positive opinion of yourself by realizing that you are important and that you are needed by others. If you have but a few relationships, develop more relationships. All humans are gregarious. In other words, we need each other in order to survive. Small babies die if they don't get love and attention from their parents. Adults are stronger but they will die inside if they don't get love and attention. You need other people in your life and they need you in their lives. Talk to your friends, relatives, people at work and talk to all of the people you meet. Get to know them. You will find most to be quite responsive. Remember that everyone needs to feel special and important. You have this need and so does everyone else. Go out of your way to make other people feel special and important and you will develop more loving relationships than you ever thought possible.

Methods of Developing Better Relations With Friends & Relatives

1) Make telephone calls to friends and relatives on a regular basis.
2) Write letters and emails to friends and relatives on a regular basis.
3) Visit the homes of friends and relatives.
4) Have barbeques, picnics or other outings with friends and relatives.
5) Celebrate holidays like Christmas, Thanksgiving, New Years and Easter with friends and relatives on a regular basis.
6) When getting an invitation to a party, make a commitment to attend the party, since it is a special event for many people.
7) Upon hearing of a party and you want to attend the party, contact the organizers of the party or

those attending to get an invitation.

8) Join a business or self-improvement support group and build friendships.
9) Join an activity group like a bowling group, a happy hour group and attend their functions to build friendships.
10) Attend an adult school classes and build friendships.
11) Faithfully attend class reunions or other reunions.
12) On a regular basis attend religious services based on your faith.
13) Meet some old or new friends and relatives in a restaurant or other venue and spend time with them.
14) Join social networking sites like Facebook.

Strengths & Weaknesses

A well-adjusted ego comes from the understanding that you have a lot of strengths, but that you also have weaknesses. This attitude has two purposes. It allows you to appreciate the good qualities in yourself, and that in turn gives you confidence. It also allows you to look at the weaknesses in yourself and understand them, which is the first step toward converting those weaknesses into strengths. Every person has an Achilles heel, and the sooner you acknowledge your special problem, the sooner you can correct it. It is important to discover your strengths and weaknesses, and bring them out into the open and to convert them into something positive.

Coming To America

Let me tell you about a man who accepted his weaknesses and acknowledged his strengths. He came to this country with a wife and four children when he was 23 years old. Imagine the hardship involved in finding yourself in a foreign land with the added burden of having to support a family of six. He knew it would be rough, but he decided that he was willing to take the chance on starting a whole new life. One of his weaknesses was he didn't know English well. He knew he needed more education, and he knew deep down he had the potential for success. He knew that he could learn quickly. He took night classes to learn English. He worked as an apprentice electrician during the day and worked another job at night. He always had at least two jobs.

This man had a dream. He left his native land to create a new life for his children and for himself. He was willing to work day and night until he achieved his life-long dream of success, which to him, meant escaping the nine to five

jungle. To fulfill his dream, he knew he had to harness his strengths and his skills. He knew he had a strong aptitude for learning and for creating ideas. It was these strengths that made him a success. He decided that he wanted to be independently wealthy. His goal at the time was to have his own electrical company within a few years. By the age of 26, he had started his own electrical company. By the age of 34 he founded a construction company that put up shopping plazas. By the time he was in his 40's he had accumulated about $3,000,000 in real estate holdings. This man is my father.

Complete The Winning Attitude

Reward yourself for each accomplishment. When I say accomplishment, I mean any accomplishment. An accomplishment could be drawing a picture or writing a poem. Wait until you accomplish something before you reward yourself. Some people reward themselves even when nothing has been accomplished. This boosts the ego without reason. It creates a false self-opinion. People like this will tell you that they can do things very well, while in reality, it is very likely that they have not done many of those things. Reward yourself when you have made accomplishments, instead of dreaming that you have done more than they actually have accomplished. This is the opposite of a weak ego.

You want a well-balanced ego and I say again, that the only way that you can do this is by acknowledging and rewarding your strengths and accomplishments. Only in this way will you have an honest opinion of yourself. Recognize your strengths and weaknesses this way other people understand the person that you are. Here is a quote by Marilyn Monroe, "I'm selfish, impatient and a little insecure. I make mistakes, I am out of control and at times hard to handle. But if you can't handle me at my worst, then you sure as hell don't deserve me at my best."

Spontaneous Communications

As you appreciate and reward your good qualities and recognize your weaknesses, the information gets stored in your subconscious mind. Once it is stored, you don't have to think about it. As you speak information is spontaneously brought up. It is an amazing process that happens as you just express your thoughts by talking. Your level of communication speeds up and becomes more intelligent. You will sound better and more people will listen to you. Communicating with others creates a feeling of confidence, because your accomplishments will speak for themselves. You know the saying, "If you have money, you don't have to talk about it." That's because information on money is kept in your mind and as you speak, you infer that you have money.

Being Close-minded

A person that is close-minded limits their mind, because they think they already know. If you "already know" then new information can't enter your mind. When you empty your mind of all current grandiose thoughts of yourself, new thoughts can enter your mind. If the old thoughts remain, your new thoughts can't enter. Your subconscious remembers every little thing about you. When your mind is empty of egotistic thoughts, brand new ideas can enter your mind and be imprinted. Your mind will be able then, to store and relate information to others more accurately.

See Yourself As You Are

Today, I am able to get along well with everyone I meet. How do I do it? I am completely honest about myself when I express myself. If a person won't accept me the way I am, then we may not get along. I want other people to accept me as I am, but if they don't, it becomes clear to me that we just aren't compatible. I can understand this early, by communicating openly and honestly.

Do you understand this attitude? I want another person to genuinely know me, then that person can choose to accept me the way I am. If they won't, I will just work out my differences. This is a non-attached attitude, and it is the attitude that you need to succeed. When you accept yourself as who you are, you develop a strong sense of honesty. When you accept yourself, you become more confident. The rich and wealthy are confident. Are you? If you aren't, you can be.

Being perfectly honest with supportive people will do wonders for the relationships in your life, while a lack of truth usually means the relationship isn't as honest. If you want supportive people to know who you are, you can accomplish this; by being truthful. Being honest, it is one of the best ways to influence people.

Defensive and Negative People

Have you ever met someone who is very defensive or negative toward you? I am sure you have. I have always wondered why people are like that. I was surprised when I found out the truth. You may have created these negative feelings inside of them. Their feelings about you may have created their defensive behavior. What you say or do to others will create certain defensive or negative feelings towards you. What do I mean by that? Their reaction to your words or actions is negative to them, which means they did not like what you said or did, because it was bad for them. Did you ever arrogantly talk a lot to another person? Talking a lot may make you feel superior while it makes others feel defensive and negative; because they are were offended by what you said. No one wants to feel defensive. Everyone wants to feel good. When what you said or did was not good for them then their defensive value structure will make them resent you.

Jim Was Defensive

Jim was a shipping clerk in a company with 50 employees. He told me he couldn't understand why so many people in the company resented him. He felt that he was kind and thoughtful of other people and he did his job well, but people just didn't like him. As we talked, I discovered what his problem was. He described a confrontation with a certain co-worker, Tom.

Jim said he and Tom discussed the company in general. Jim began to tell Tom how well he got along with people in the company. "I can't understand it," Jim said, "I just told Tom that I knew the president and the vice president on a personal basis, and that they could do favors for me." I asked Jim to describe his relationship with the president. His relationship with the president wasn't as strong as he had claimed. Jim seemed to have exaggerated most of what he told his co-worker, Tom.

Remember, conversations are a two-way street. The other person will respond according to what you say. There is a simple attitude that will take you places if you adhere to it. Once you achieve this attitude, you will not believe how much success you will have with other people. The secret of this technique is in letting go of your ego and be more humble. Having a big ego and talking a lot makes certain other people defensive and negative.

Boasting About Yourself

There were times when I wasn't making money in my business. I didn't tell other people that I wasn't making money. I told them that I was making more money than they were making. In order to compensate for my own insecurities, I made myself look better than I was. It is true that success breeds success and it is also true that failure breeds failure. That means that when you are successful you attract successful people which make you more successful. When you are a failure, you will attract other failures which will make you less successful. I learned the hard way that you must be honest with yourself and with supportive people, so you can get back up. You don't gain or keep many supportive friends by bragging or by being dishonest.

Learn From Others

I am sure that you have felt some type of resentment for another person whom you felt was too vocal. I have, but this type of resentment can help you learn. It seemed to me that the person was bragging about how much better he was than me. This conversation makes me feel so inferior. I feel this type of a feeling some of the time. It could be my mind telling me that it is time to do something different. As soon as I feel it, I know that I have to evaluate and maybe change something in my life. I had an experience that was the turning point of my business career. My

competitor was two years younger than me and was making more money than me and accomplishing more in the book selling industry than I was. This infuriated me. I was jealous and upset; it really bothered me. It irritated me so much that I decided to do something about it. I made some changes in my life. The first thing I did was to accept the fact that he was smarter than me. The second thing I did was to accept the fact that this person could teach me a thing or two. So, I got to know him, and I learned. I learned, and I increased the sales of my company. At first I was upset that he was competing with me. Later, I realized that he was responsible for a great turning point in my career. Thanks to him, I am doing a better. Learn from people who you feel are better than you, and you, too, can be the best you can be.

Expectations

There was a time in my life when I felt that it was safe to have no expectations. As a result, instead of taking control of my life, I was controlled by everything around me. A good friend of mine, Sherry, told me that high expectations are healthy. But I thought that high expectations could lead to disappointments. 'That is true," she said, "but having high expectations will always lead to success." You must take risks in order to succeed." She taught me a very valuable lesson.

Attached people have high expectations of people and things around them, with no expectation of disappointment. There is nothing wrong with having high expectations, but they can lead to disappointment. An attached person fails to consider this. A non-attached person expects the most, but prepares for the worst. A detached person doesn't expect anything. Not understanding the concept of expectations could lead to failure. That's right, it could lead to failure. I have failed in the past because I didn't prepare for the worst. I was so positive, I only expected the best. That is only good if the best always comes around. It doesn't always. Not only that, if you prepare for the worst, you can avoid the worst.

Milton S. Hershey used this concept to his benefit. On Hershey's fourth venture, he made money. He founded The Lancaster Caramel Company in 1887. This company just made caramels. He expected the best from himself and

123

at that point, he began to live out these high expectations. This company grew to cover a city block and employ 2,000 workers. Hershey wanted to prepare for the worst. He wanted an assurance that his company would do well in the future. So, in 1893, he bought some chocolate-making machinery from Germany. He experimented making candy bars in his spare time. Working with chocolate didn't make him a cent at the time. He just wanted to prepare himself for something new, just in case he had a setback.

In 1901, Hershey sold the Lancaster Caramel Co. for one million dollars to a group of his competitors; but he kept his chocolate-making machinery. Later, he decided to sell chocolate bars. He did very well, so well, in fact, that he was able to build a city from the money he made on chocolates. By 1908, his chocolate company was worth $60 million. Hershey prepared for the worst and eventually his empire became 60 times greater.

They Will Live Up To Your Expectations

Other people will live up to your expectations; but before they give you what you desire, they have to know what you desire. There is a simple method. It is so simple that I always wonder why people don't use this technique. How do you get people to do what you want them to do? Just tell them what you want from them. You will be surprised at what they do for you. If you don't relay that information to them, they won't know what they can do for you. That's right. People will live up to your expectations. People want to be liked, admired and rewarded so they will try to please you.

SUMMARY

- Failure can be a great teacher. Failure could create a learning period and later a greater success.
- Expressing your feelings to supportive people, is the key to conquering a weak ego.
- Creating a healthy ego is accomplished by rewarding all of your accomplishments and admitting to your weaknesses.
- Accept your ego the way it is and be honest and truthful about yourself to supportive people
- See yourself as having a lot of strengths, but understand you also have weaknesses.
- Being close-minded limits your mind.
- Empty your mind of egotistical thoughts, so you can fill your mind with new ideas.
- Have high expectations, but prepare for the worst.
- People will live up to your high expectations.

If you want to be admired, liked and rewarded for who you are, follow these steps.

I. Evaluate your strengths and good qualities. Develop more confidence in yourself by building up your strengths.
II. Recognize your weaknesses and vulnerabilities and develop a game plan for conquering them. One way to conquer your weaknesses is to express them to supportive people and ask for feedback.
III. Empty your mind of any conceit or false ideas you have about yourself and reward yourself for accomplishments only when you earn the rewards.
IV. Express yourself truthfully and honestly to the people around you. Express your weaknesses as well as your strengths to other people.
V. Plant the thought in your mind that you can do anything. Create a backup plan if your plans don't materialize.

Chapter Seventeen

The Treasure Chest Of Feelings

Being in touch with your feelings and emotions will allow you to be in touch with everything around you. A mark of a very successful and prosperous person is the ability to express their deepest feelings. The smartest people are in touch with their feelings. The ability to think very quickly starts with being in touch with your feelings. Expressing your deep feelings is not easy but it can be accomplished with practice. Once you are able to express your deep feelings, you are able to think quicker and think better and you will become more successful than other people. The purpose of this chapter is to show you how you can express your deepest feelings and present yourself in a way that will make you attractive to others.

I included the discussion on the state of non-attachment for a good reason. One of the benefits of non-attachment is that it lets you expose your true feelings to yourself and to others. You have to be perfectly honest in order to express your true feelings. The attitude of non-attachment allows you to do this. Acting out your feelings could be unpleasant if you are in a detached state, but if you want to be successful, it must be done. Make sure that you listen to any feedback you may receive after you have acted out your feelings. The feedback that you get when you expose your feelings will help you to be the best that you can be and maybe the smartest cookie on the block.

Expressing Your Feelings

When I tell you to express your deepest thoughts, do it so it can be understood by others.

The key to expressing your feelings is to tell others what you are thinking. Whether it is about them or about yourself, or even about business affairs, you should express what you are honestly thinking. It is as if you were thinking out loud. I know many of you are uncomfortable expressing your most intimate thoughts, but don't worry, other people will understand you.

If the thoughts that you are expressing are true, does it matter? Your actions reveal what you're thinking anyway. When you express your true feelings, all you are doing is explaining the way that you feel and why. If you hate someone, tell them that you hate them and why you do. If you love someone, tell them that you love them, and tell them why. If you want to describe products or services, give others the complete features and benefits. Many people will have great admiration and respect for you if you can relate what you are thinking to others honestly. Do this and you will become better and better at communicating and selling. When you express your true feelings, you will start to think faster and you will become smarter.

Be Honest With People

It is difficult for us to see ourselves objectively. You could be hurting or helping someone while being unaware that you had any effect on them at all. If you tell people what you think, you will be letting them know your impression of them or the details of a product or service they may purchase. Others can now see themselves or your products or services as you see them. People appreciate this. Some people will tell you what you want to hear. Do you respect a person that agrees with you and is a yes person? People like that are a dime a dozen. Don't you respect a person who tells you what is really on his mind, no matter what it is? I know that I do. If you can be honest with people, you will build relationships that you never thought possible. The more that people will understand about you or your business, the more they will know you.

Express Your Thoughts

If you want to know others, you must know yourself. If you verbalize all of your thoughts and true feelings, you will be able to know yourself and your product and services. Just expressing your feelings allows you to subconsciously think-out a situation. Have you ever been in the middle of explaining a problem to someone when suddenly, out of nowhere, the answer just comes to you. I am sure that this has happened to you. Could you imagine what would happen if you were able to express your thoughts and feelings all day long? Your ability to act out your thoughts and feelings all day long will bring you amazing insight into everything that happens in your life. Others will also be able to understand you better and they will also buy your products and services. The most successful and wealthiest people can express all of their thoughts to other people.

If you are bold enough to embark on the road to express your true feelings to those around you, you can be one of the privileged few? You can start by expressing all of your thoughts and feelings honestly, all of the time about yourself and your products and services. Expressing your thoughts and feelings helps you to get in touch with your true self, and enables you to develop an interesting and strong personality. When you express your thoughts and feelings you will start to think faster and quicker and you can become the smartest cookie on the block.

Expressing Your Harsh Emotions

There are some cases where you try to express your feelings and all you get are harsh emotions, so you get angry and you cry or yell. Why is that? Maybe your subconscious lets out your feelings in an extreme mode. Why does that happen? Maybe something is very wrong? Just talk it out with supportive relatives and friends. Explore the facts and act. Intuition or hunches are light feelings. Your actual feelings are moderate. But emotional outbursts are a high level of feelings, being let out. The feelings burst out because you didn't express yourself to others. Pay attention to your feelings and your emotions and express your feelings to supportive people. Let me tell you about Judy.

Judy Expressed Herself

Judy became very resentful of her job. She felt that her boss didn't understand her. She couldn't stand the situation any longer, and so she began looking for other work. She told me, "When I first started working for Mr. Settle, everything was OK. As time went by, I began to notice his insensitivity towards me. I did everything he asked me to do. I just couldn't understand why he wouldn't do anything for me, not even the little things." "Like what?" I asked her. "You know, he would go out and get lunch for himself and, can you believe, not even think to ask me if I wanted anything." I then asked Judy if she had ever told her boss about the things that were bothering her. She told me that she had never mentioned a thing. A few weeks later, Judy came to me and said that she had decided to express her feelings to her boss. "Things are better than ever with my boss," she told me with a grin on her face, "I just don't know why I didn't speak to him sooner."

The only way you will attract a person who is compatible with you is by being open and honest and sincere. When you possess these qualities, you will be able to tell others what type of person you are. They, in turn, will determine if they are attracted to you. Openness and honesty is a must in any type of personal encounter. Openness and honesty with supportive people will also make you think faster and quicker. You know you are a good communicator when you can verbalize everything that you feel. Talk to other people about your feelings. No matter what the situation is, you will come out ahead.

Understanding My Feelings

It was one of those wet Fridays. I dragged my feet into the office wondering what I had on my agenda. I was to go over my new advertising schedule. Just as I was reviewing my plans for the next six months, I got a phone call. The background hiss indicated to me that the call was long distance. A tough voice cut loudly across the wires. It was an old friend Mark. He asked me how I was. "Fine," I told him. He then said, "Dave, I want to come out to California. I need to relax." "I have three weeks off and I think it would be nice to see you." "What do you say, Dave?"

Mark caught me at a very bad time. I had a lot of work to do and very little time to entertain anyone. I had other things to do. What was I going to tell him? Because I believe it is best to be honest, so I told him exactly what was on my mind. I told him very seriously, "Mark, it would be nice to see you." "It's just that I'm really busy right now." "I have a lot of things I have to do and I wouldn't be able to spend as much time with you." "Three weeks is a long time." "You could stay with me but I just won't be able to spend that much time with you."

Mark was very insulted. He told me, "Dave, I don't get that much time off." "I wouldn't object if you wanted to come to New York." "Friendships are a give and take." "Don't be selfish, think of me." I was very insulted and told him that there was no point in continuing our conversation. He said, "Fine," and hung up. I thought about this conversation. Was I wrong? Was it wrong to do what I wanted instead of what Mark wanted? Who was right? What do you think?

Who's Right To The Rabbi

I am going to tell you a story that will show you who was right. A wise rabbi was called in to council a Jewish couple. The man and woman argued often and were having difficulties staying together. They wanted the rabbi to hear them out. The woman entered the rabbi's study and told him and his aide, her side of the story. The rabbi listened to everything she said and when she finished, he told her, "You're right."

The woman left the Rabbi's study and the man entered room. The Rabbi then heard the man's side and, after he finished, he told him, "You're right." The rabbi's aide was very puzzled, so he asked the rabbi, "How can both of them possibly be right?" The rabbi turned to him and said, "You're right." What is the moral of the story? You can't invalidate another person's feelings.

If you feel something, you are right. If someone tells you that you are wrong, you will get upset. Who was right, Mark or I? We were both right. He was right for acting out his feelings and I was right for acting out mine. If you act out your feelings, you are going to do things that make you feel good. The only way I am going to "know" is by acting out my feelings. If I have been selfish, many people will tell me that I am selfish. What does all this mean? Acting out your feelings means doing what you feel. Doing what you feel involves doing exactly what you want, regardless of what others say. You did hear me correctly. We are all subconsciously influenced by what others say.

Let's say that you are at an elegant cocktail party and you feel strongly about hitting a person. What should you do? If you acted on your feelings you should hit the person. If you hit this man, you would be thrown out of the party and wind up feeling humiliated. If you hit this man and then were thrown out, do you think that you would hit a second man at a future cocktail party? You probably wouldn't. The idea wouldn't enter your mind the second time around because you imprinted what happened in your subconscious mind. By acting out your feelings, and experiencing the negative consequences of your actions, you gave instructions to your mind as to which response is proper or not proper.

You Will Be Attracted To Certain Types Of People

Past experiences of other people are locked in your subconscious mind. Your mind understands the people you know. What does this mean in regards to other people you don't know? Well subconscious mind will recognize similarities in different people. Suppose that you see a person who is attractive to you, and you have the urge to approach them? Let's say you were able to arrange a date. It may work out, but the chances are that you would be more likely to be involved with a person, because your past experience was positive with that type of a person. That person could have been like your relatives, like your father or mother or brother or sister or close friend and your subconscious mind knew that type of a person, so you were attracted to them or fought with them.   What does acting out your feelings and getting to know different people do?   This information is imprinted deep inside your subconscious mind.   It modifies your behavior, creating the personality that is most advantageous to you and it senses similarities between different people.

Coping With Other People's Emotions

Our emotions are always changing. Everything around us is in a constant state of flux. One day you may be very happy and the next day, you may be glum.   It is human nature to be emotional.   No feeling is permanent.   We are all in a state of change.   We change from day to day. Look at yourself.   Are you always in the same mood?   A clear sign of maturity is the ability to adapt our emotions to the various situations and moods in which we find ourselves.   What about other people?   People change on a daily basis and we can't judge them on what we feel on a certain day.   Something a person told you yesterday may not hold true today.   It is important to deal with the situation as it is right now.   If you express your feelings of the moment, you will always make the right decision and expressing your feelings will make you a smarter and faster thinker.

Spontaneity

Being spontaneous just means acting from your feelings at any given moment.   Are you spontaneous?   A survey showed that people find spontaneous people fun and that they enjoy being with this type of person more than any other.   Isn't it true?   Don't you enjoy people who live for the moment and do what their feelings dictate? People that have to think before they act are not as fun.   They are too self-conscious and tend to act the way that they think other people want them to act.

If you think before you act, you can't be spontaneous.   To be spontaneous, you must act without thinking about it.   Express your lively feelings.   I mean your deep feelings.   Express your every feeling, as soon as you feel it and you will be smarter and you will also think faster. Expressing your feelings, in turn, will help you to enjoy life a lot more and help you sell products and services.   As soon as you have the urge to do something, do something lively.   Don't hesitate.

You will be able to enjoy yourself a lot more. Becoming spontaneous will make you fun to be with and other people will like you more or it could make some people scorn you.   Live for the moment and go with your feelings.

You Are Quick When You Act Out Feelings

Acting out your feelings is like using a muscle in your body.   When you need to move your hand on a steering wheel while you are driving, you just move your hand.   You wouldn't think about this, you would just move it.   Quick people would move their hand quickly and slow people would move their hand slowly.   A person who acts out their thoughts and feelings quickly to supportive people, is a smarter person.   Do the right thing with your honest feelings.   As soon as you feel a feeling, you must either talk or act out a reply to supportive people.

Honesty

Honesty is a virtue.   I strongly believe in it. No matter what you do or who you associate with, you will be judged on your honesty.   Honest people earn trust; their own trust and the trust of others.   The more honest you are, the more you will be loved and admired by others.   The reward for honesty is that people will hold you in higher regard, and you will, in turn, think more highly of yourself.

As an example, think of a salesman who is trying to sell a product or service.   For this example we will use a product.   Would you trust a salesman who gave you all of the honest details of the product?   I mean not some details, but all of the honest details.   I know I would trust this salesman.   If I wanted to buy that same product again, I would go back to that salesman that explained the honest details of the product and buy again.   I would.   How about you?   What would you do?

When I talk about honesty, I am talking about a deep honesty, an honesty that allows you to verbalize your every feeling; an honesty that helps other people understand you and your product and helps you to understand yourself and your product. It is an honesty by which you are true to yourself. People with this level of honesty enjoy life to the utmost because they feel a deep sense of joy in themselves.   To develop a truly deep honesty you

128

must act out your feelings. No matter what anyone says or thinks of your actions or words, you must express your feelings with a deep honesty to supportive people. Develop this type of honesty in yourself and you will reap its rewards and become much more successful.

Reward Other People

Express your positive feelings. Tell someone that they look great and the compliment will go a long way. The secret to getting people to like you is to praise them. People enjoy giving, but only if their giving is appreciated. This is a very important point. If you don't show appreciation for what you receive, you may not receive anything again. Give rewards for those that give to you unless you don't want their gifts. Everybody needs rewards, approval and recognition for what they've done. If someone helps you in any way, tell that person how much you appreciate their actions. If a woman you know looks good, tell her! There are situations where a person takes advantage of you when you reward them or are kind to them. If that is the case you should tell them how you feel about their arrogant behavior. In this example you would say, "You did a good job and I like you, but I am not about to give you any money today." Or you could say, "I really want you explaining the details to me, but I can't pay you what you want."

You should not, however, show gratitude or appreciation if you don't mean it. Show other people appreciation or gratitude only when you truly feel it. Express this honest gratitude and appreciation to others and you will see the joy in their eyes; remember, everyone wants to feel special and important. Praising others will really make people like you.

Here are some examples of how you can best state your appreciation of others: *I really appreciate the way you..,... Thank you very much for....., You are very good at ....., You were very nice to ....., You look pretty today. You look great tonight, etc.* It would be unwise to overdo your appreciation, just be honest. An overdose of appreciation appears insincere, but if it is true, say it.

One type of appreciation that all people enjoy is praise. People look to others for approval. You should give praise, however, only when it is deserved. If you praise people when they don't deserve it, or if you praise people too much, you will lose your credibility and it might boost an ego. Being insincere might cost you something. If you are insincere your praise will seem phony, like you don't really mean it. Don't exaggerate your praise. Make the praise as warm and sincere as you can. I urge you to be honest when giving any type of appreciation. Praise only when you feel that the act or the person deserves it.

Smiling & Laughing To Cope With Negative Feelings

Smiling is great for you, and smiling will make people like you more. It will add a positive flavor to your attitude and allow you to make difficult and bad situations more positive. Smiling and laughter will also make the people you know happier and more joyful. It is a good idea to practice smiling, this way you will be a happier person. If you don't smile you must spend more time smiling. It is a good idea to practice being cheerful about twenty minutes a day or less. Put a heavy smile on your face when practicing smiling. Smile for long periods tensing your face. This will help you get used to smiling. You should smile for bad and difficult situations.

Laughter

Add laughing to your 20 minutes a day of being cheerful. You must do this. Practice loud bellowing laughter, that type of laughter that makes the whole room shake. This laughter will help you get through bad and difficult situations. Keep practicing loud and hearty laughter as well as smiling, so that you become a cheerful and better person. This will help you be liked by many people. Now say or act out the subject on the following list. You should then burst out and laugh loudly for one full minute. To get you used to laugh in bad or difficult situations keeping doing this laughing exercise. Remember for each statement practice your loud bellowing laughter.

- You are not getting the promotion.
- A family member stole your money.
- Your bank account is missing.
- Your husband/wife is leaving you.
- You just fell off a chair. (actually do this)
- You just tore your favorite shirt (tear a piece of cloth)

People will like you more if you are cheerful and positive. Practice this laughing and smiling technique so that people will like you more. It is important to remember that when practicing this laughter, you must do a loud hearty bellowing laughter. For all of your irritating and difficult situations practice a loud bellowing laughter and heavy smiling.

Yelling And Anger

To become a likable person it is better to laugh and smile often. There are times where a serious, disciplined personality is a better alternative and in those times you must be loud and harsh. In important times or times of emergencies, it is not possible to be a pleasant and happy person. If you are loud and you use harshness in your voice tone people will act. You must yell and sound mean in some situations. It will amaze you how quickly people will do what you want when you yell with a harshness in your voice. Commanding the situation may require anger in your words.

Express Your Negative Feelings

Every one of us has gotten upset more than once, which causes stress and anger. What is necessary is a method to lessen this stress and channel that energy in a positive way. Depression and frustration are signals from your body. Your mind is telling you to learn from those bad experiences in your life. Take your bad feelings and direct them along the right channels. If frustration and depression are not vented, your condition will get worse. You may even explode, thus harming yourself.

Express your negative feelings to supportive people in your life and work out your problems. Do this on a regular basis and you can improve so much of your life. First, let me point out that

SUMMARY

- A silent aggressor is a person who holds in their aggression.
- If you honestly express your feelings, you will vent tension and you will feel better.
- Expressing the honest details of the product or service you are selling will get you the more sales and commissions.
- By expressing your feelings honestly, supportive people will understand you more and you will begin to feel better about yourself.
- Do what you feel, regardless of what others say, but after you act, pay attention to the feedback.
- We are constantly changing. It is natural to be emotional. Deal with a situation as it occurs, right now.
- Being spontaneous allows you to enjoy all of the moments of your life.
- Having a deep sense of honesty in sales of products and services or to supportive people will gain you respect and admiration from others.
- Show others appreciation and praise and they will appreciate you.
- Laughter and smiling will add a positive flavor to your communications and help you will difficult situations.
- Practice loud bellowing laughter and lengthy heavy smiling to help express negative feelings.
- To command an important or an emergency situation you must yell with anger in your voice.
- Express you negative feelings privately or with supportive people.

having negative feelings is one of the best opportunities that you have for learning. By resolving your negative feelings you will become a better person and a more adjusted person. Your life could improve, if a negative experience becomes a positive experience. Learn from your defeats. Take your failures and turn them into successes. Make depression and frustration work for you.

Depression And Anger

The power of *"Novanetics"* is within all of us, all you have to do is take it. *"Novanetics"* uses an easy method of taking negative situations and making them positive. You can turn around your failures by expressing your negative feelings, then expressing your positive solutions.

1) If your thoughts is: "My financial situation is terrible" then you would say, "I would feel better about my finances if I got a second job."
2) If your thought is: "We have to do something about this debt." Then you would say, "We could solve our money problems if we move to a smaller house."
3) If your thought is: "I don't want her coming here." Then you would say, "You can just tell her to call before she comes over."
4) If your thought is: "We should be with the family." Then you would say, "We have had such good times with them so we have to spend more time with the family."

I know it sounds simple but it really works. Tell yourself how upset you are or how depressed you feel and I know that you will feel a lot better, after you talk about your positive solutions, this will make you more successful.

Depression and anger can be very useful in completing our goals. Learn to express all of your feeling - both good and bad. We must be able to use aggression and frustration in a positive and constructive way.

If someone dies who is close to you, or if a valuable relationship comes to an end. Express your anger and pain to supportive people around you and explain your positive solutions. If you don't express everything that is on your mind it may scar you. Get if off your chest. Verbally express, from the bottom of your heart. Do this and you will see a better *you* emerge. Expressing your deep feelings will make every aspect of your life better.

Express Your Negative Feelings To Other People

Not only should you express your negative thoughts to yourself you must tell other people in your life how you feel about them. If you hate relatives or friends you must tell them how you feel constructively and why you feel that way. This will benefit both of you, after you resolve the situation.

If you want to be successful and prosperous you must get out from under that *rock* and tell people how you feel about them. Express your hate, envy, and jealousy constructively to other people when you have these feelings, this way both of you can benefit. Your goal is to express or act out every thought that you may have, whenever you may have it. If you can do this, you will think faster and become smarter and you will also become more successful. Let me tell you a story about a man who expressed his negative feelings to another person.

Stan was one of the guys I used to work with. He was a very agreeable guy. One day his boss, Joe, told him that he wanted him to arrange 2,000 envelopes in zip-code sequence for a bulk mailing. It was a big job. Stan agreed to do it. Stan came over to me and said he thought Joe was being unfair to him. Stan was always complaining about something, and it was always behind Joe's back. Every now and then he would burst out and have a fit. I asked Stan why he never told Joe how he felt. He told me, "He shouldn't have to." Finally, one day, Stan mustered enough guts to tell Joe how he felt. Joe was stunned; Stan had never spoken up before. Stan and Joe worked it out and now both of them get along better than ever.

Expressing Aggressive Feelings

There are times when all of us are so stressed that we find it hard to control ourselves. At these times, all that matters is expressing those angry feelings. Do this privately or with supportive people, but do express your aggressive feelings, so you understand yourself. Many people can only express their angry feelings at such explosive times. At times like this, they should count to five before speaking. When those people hit a high level of stress, their feelings erupt and shower all those around them with hostility, which is not good. A person who holds his in their feelings until they explode, is a person who does not express their feelings well. This is a very unhealthy condition, but the release of those emotions must take place one way or another.

The better way, of course, is in a positive way and in a gradual release. Talk to the supportive people you know on a regular basis. You should try and make sure that you and your loved ones express your feelings on a regular basis. If everyone were to express their feelings regularly, there would be less crime, and a lot more love in this world. Don't hold your feelings in, express them honestly and openly. This in turn will help you think quicker and become a smarter person. Good luck with your feelings.

Chapter Eighteen

The Secret Of Making You Rich With Novanetics

This chapter contains engineering methods of using the power of the mind that are unknown to many people. Only the very successful and privileged few understand the capability to the mind to understand and utilize intricate amounts of detailed information. The all-powerful mind can outperform an expensive computer when it comes to engineering logic. Learn about these exciting concepts and put the power of *"Novanetics"* to work for you. Let me tell you more.

A business associate ten years my senior asked me this question. "How is it that you know more than me when I have more experience than you?" "Experience is meaningless if you are not aware of the experience," I told him. What did I mean by that? We all experience things in life on a continual basis. Do we all learn from our experiences? Do we ever make the same mistake twice? Do we forget details and as a result of not paying attention or getting something wrong? These questions relate to being aware of what you are experiencing at every moment of every day. It has to do with seeing things as they are and understanding what you are seeing and doing. We can always pay attention to what we like or love. If you enjoy an activity you will pay attention to it and understand the details. People with a good sense of curiosity pay attention to the details of an activity. When we understand the details of what we are seeing and doing, then we can become more successful and more prosperous.

Enjoy The World Around You

Enjoy the world and the experiences and details it has to offer. This ability to experience the world will bring you joy. I know a woman who was very bored and depressed much of the time. I spoke to her, and she told me that she is now a happy woman. "What changes did you make?" I asked her. "You know, I don't do anything any different than anyone else," she said. "What do you do differently?" I asked curiously. "I am now very much aware of the things around me. I notice and appreciate everything now," she replied. "First I started out by becoming completely involved with the way I walk. I know it sounds silly but it really helped me. I became completely aware of the way my soft shoes touched the hard pavement; and of the way the muscles in my legs stretched and contracted with each step. I made it a point to notice every single detail about my walking. I did this by concentrating on my walking only. There are thousands of things that I notice now that I didn't notice before.

"I am aware now every time a cool breeze brushes against my face. I can smell the fragrance of green leaves. I notice the different shades of every color, and I view each scene as if it were a separate picture. The creamy color of the sky and the bright green color of the leaves; it can leave you breathless. You know, I can't get enough of it." "How were you viewing the world?" I asked her, puzzled. "I was asleep," she said. "I really didn't notice all the things I notice now. I would have taken that same walk in the park but I would have had something else on my mind, so I wouldn't have noticed or enjoyed any of the beauty around me. The things I didn't have were more important to me than all the wonderful things I can enjoy. The biggest change in me is that I can appreciate the things around me. So many people take for granted the beauty of the world." I told Susan that I really envied her for enjoying life so much; and I really meant it. Susan added, "This experience taught me a lot. Today I am enjoying the world around me a great deal more than I ever had."

An Opinion

There is an old Japanese saying that goes, "If you have an opinion, you don't know the truth." What does this mean? It means that an opinion, in this case, is a set thought and with a set thought, you are close minded. A set thought could distort the truth, when the situation has changed. The world around you is constantly changing, so you should change your opinion. New ideas can't enter your mind if you have a set opinion. You can't expect to hold on to an opinion or idea when everything around you is constantly changing.

I once had an encounter with a business associate, Sam, who had a preconceived opinion of me. Before our meeting, Sam bumped into a person who knew me. This person told him I was cold and close minded. Sam then created an opinion of me in his mind. When I met with Sam, he couldn't see my warmth because he had a pre-conceived notion of me. He had a set opinion.

Sam's set opinion of me blocked out my true character. Unless he is able to allow himself to really see me, he may never know who I really am. This is how having a set opinion can block out the truth. What should Sam have done? When Sam met me he should have had a different attitude; he should have cleared his mind of any expectations regarding my personality. In other words, he should have emptied his mind, and taken the time to get to know me. He should have learned for himself what kind of a person I am. To get to know me, Sam should have come to our meeting with an open mind and prepared himself to listen. Being a good listener will always pay off.

We all have opinions about ourselves. If these opinions are bad, we develop a negative self-image. You should recognize that any opinion you have of yourself or another may change. You are constantly changing; so any feelings you have should change just as frequently.

How To Enjoy Life

When you last saw a sunset, how did it look? Wasn't it a beautiful sight? But, if you were to see the sunset every night, you wouldn't appreciate it as much, would you? There is a way to keep appreciating the beauty of a sunset, no matter how many times you see it. It goes back to the fundamental concept of awareness. Watch and empty your mind of all its thoughts before you look at the sunset and concentrate on the event. If you use this technique, you will notice you will be looking at the sunset as if you are seeing it for the first time again. If you want to learn the truth about what you see and appreciate the beauty of the things around you must empty your mind and concentrate on the event. It involves seeing things through virgin eyes; with no prior ideas or images. Adopt this attitude and you will see the truth. To get the most out of any interaction you should use this technique.

Paying Attention To John

Let me tell you what used to happen to me. Years ago, I was having a conversation with a neighbor of mine, John. He was a real talker. I guess back then I didn't have much of an attention span. John told me about his new boat. He started talking about his boat and I started thinking about the boat I wanted to get. I didn't hear two words John was saying because while he was talking, I was thinking. I should have paid attention to what John was saying. I should have concentrated on what was happening instead of falling into my own dream world. Instead, I didn't hear much of what he had to say and I merely said *yes* every now and then as he spoke. The next day John came over to my place in his shorts and asked, "I thought you agreed. Are you ready?" "Ready for what?" I asked, surprised. 'To see the boat I was telling you about yesterday." "Oh yeah, it slipped my mind, John," I said. "I'll be right out." I was lucky I had nothing else planned that day. John could talk people into things they didn't want to do. I must have agreed to go boating with him while I was in my trance. In this situation, I didn't pay attention to all of the details. This incident really started me thinking. I didn't want to find myself in this kind of a situation again.

What Did I Realize?

I should have been paying full attention to what John was saying. If I didn't want to listen to what he had to say, I should have told him so. During the conversation, I was analyzing what John was telling me. Because I was analyzing what he was saying, I didn't *hear* what he was telling me. I should have concentrated or tuned in to what was going on at that moment. I should have been a better listener. I can't think and listen at the same time. No one can. Now, when someone talks to me, I listen. When I am alone, I think.

I Analyzed The Situation

Believe me, there is nothing wrong with analyzing. The ability to analyze a problem is a gift. If we couldn't analyze, how could we solve problems? But there is only one time to analyze a situation. If you analyze a situation while it occurs, you will not know all of the details of the situation; my experience with John illustrates this point. If this happens, the whole purpose of analysis is defeated. When should you analyze? After you have listened to the details.

After The Situation

Really seeing what is happening or concentrating is the only way you can get the most out of the details of the situation. You can really see the situation once you have some distance from it. When you have seen the details of the situation as it was, you then can judge it. While the details of the situation is occurring you can't analyze it. You must concentrate on the situation while it occurs and while you are concentrating pay close attention to details. After you have understood the situation, you can analyze.

How Do You Pay Attention To The Details?

If you really like what you are doing, you will pay attention to the details. Like anything in life it is a love for work, a love for a hobby or a love for a discipline, which makes a person see the details of it. I may watch a television movie, but if I don't

like the theme or the movie, I will not pay attention to the details. If I am watching a television movie and I like the movie and the theme, I will pay attention to the details of the movie. If you like or love what you are doing then you will pay attention to the details. Learn to love or do what you love to be better at paying attention to details.

Activities That Help You Pay Attention To Details

1) Engage in telephone conversations.
2) Engage in in-person conversations.
3) Playing video games.
4) On line games and group activities.
5) Entering a competitive contest.
6) Quizzes' and tests.
7) Social Media.
8) Real time texting.
9) Timed games.
10) Instructional videos.
11) Subscribing to magazines like Popular Mechanics

WHAT HAPPENS IN YOUR MIND?

Your mind is capable of doing only one thing at a time. It can either pay attention to the exact present moment or it can be thinking (mental processes). When you are in thought, then, your mind can't absorb any external detailed information that may be present. At any one given moment you can either pay attention to that exact moment, or you can analyze the situation. You can't do both. You must do one or the other. Concentrate or observe to what happens at each exact moment and pay attention to details; then analyze later.

The three steps to Paying Attention

1) **Enjoy The Present**
2) **One Thing At A Time**
3) **Clear Your Mind**

Enjoy The Present

Tune into the present moment. Any opinion or thought you may have will pre-occupy your subconscious mind. If this happens, you will confuse your mind and jumble the messages it receives. There is one simple rule that, if followed, will ensure 100 percent comprehension: CONCENTRATE AND DO ONE THING AT A TIME AND PAY ATTENTION TO THE DETAILS.

One Thing At A Time

You will have to make a choice; you can either "listen to concentrate to an experience or event", or "you can listen and concentrate on your own thoughts." You will not be able to do both at once. Make a definite choice between the two and you will see that you are able to get more out of all the experiences in your life. The key to doing one thing at a time is the ability to concentrate. I want you to practice doing one thing at a time. Try to fully master this talent. I have a simple exercise for you that will help you to concentrate.

I want you to sit in a chair perfectly relaxed. Let every muscle in your body relax. Now I want you to concentrate on your breathing. Count each breath and pay close attention to the way you breathe. Become aware of each and every breath you take. I want you to become completely aware of every sensation and feeling you have while you breathe. While you are concentrating on your breathing, I want you to make the suggestion of you developing better concentration. Keep saying this suggestion to yourself so it is imprinted in your mind. Don't think of anything other than the way you breathe and your suggestions. Concentrate and don't let anything interfere with your breathing and those thoughts. Try this for ten to fifteen minutes.

Hard, isn't it? I was told to do this years ago. When I first tried this, I couldn't block out the many other thoughts that continually entered my mind. Eventually I mastered this technique. After you have mastered this exercise, you will notice that you are more aware of everything around you. You will also be able to concentrate better. The most important thing of all is that you will have more control over your mind.

Empty Your Mind

If you empty your mind and watch as you flow with an activity instead of thinking about that activity, you will do better but don't forget to study and to constantly practice for the activity. The key to enjoying the things around you is emptying your mind, then doing the act while you concentrate.

SUMMARY

- Enjoy the world and get better at what you do by paying attention to details and being more aware of the things around you.
- We can always pay attention to what we like or love. If you enjoy an activity you will pay attention to it and understand the details. People with a good sense of curiosity pay attention to the details of an activity.
- If you have an opinion, you may not know the truth. An opinion could be a temporary point of view.
- Watch and empty your mind of all pre-conceived thoughts so you can pay attention.
- You can't think and pay attention to something at the same time. First practice an activity and then just do it while you are concentrating on details.
- Enjoy the present moment as it occurs without analyzing it. Thinking or analyzing should only occur after the event.
- Study and practice an activity for days and weeks before you do them. Practice makes perfect.
- Concentrate on only one thing at a time.
- Information on doing complicated programs is locked in your subconscious mind because of rigorous practice.

Your mind must be cleared of everything. When it is clear, you will be able to learn. Empty your mind and fill your pockets. A great skier doesn't think about skiing when he skis. The skier does practice skiing again and again for months and years and when the skier skis, they just know it. How is it possible for someone to ski expertly? What could be that skier's guiding force?

The State Of Being

It is a state of being. Let me explain. Have you ever skied, or participated in some type of athletic activity that demands precision? Have you ever tried performing a difficult move while thinking about that move? What happens? I am sure you know; you usually wind up on your rear. The same thing will happen no matter what activity you are involved in. Do you want to fall? Of course not. There is a method to doing something well. You know the saying, *"Practice makes perfect."*

PRACTICE AND STUDY THE ACTIVITY AGAIN AND AGAIN

After you practice and practice and practice, your mind writes a program that lets you effortlessly do a routine or activity. Study and practice and practice and practice different aptitudes and then you will be able to do them effortlessly. The world's best athletes know that in order to compete successfully, they can't think about the competition while they're competing. They constantly practice a routine and then during the competition they just do the routine (without thinking about it). In order to be successful, you must be living in the moment. If you have ever taken up the martial arts, you know that this is a fundamental. If you want to be good at some activity, you must be, in the moment and not be heavily thinking about it. Practice extensively and study the activity before you do it. Then concentrate while you are doing it. Have you ever been overly careful about something you didn't practice? I am sure you have. Regular extensive practice will ensure you will improve your abilities.

Activities You Can Study and Practice

1) Practice activities in different chapters in this book.
2) Practice and do an athletic routine.
3) Practice and do a telephone conversation.
4) Practice and say a speech out loud.
5) Practice and write a letter.
6) Practice and sing a song.
7) Practice a school study exercise.

His Subconscious Mind

All the information on skiing is locked up in his subconscious mind, because the skier practiced and studied skiing, this created a program. While the skier is skiing, the subconscious mind is an "automatic pilot." Its powerful ability leads the skier down the hill. If the skier begins to think consciously about skiing, the skier will be interrupting the automatic guidance system that the skier created in their mind, and then the skier might fall.

The List To Boost Your Performance

1) Love or care about the activity you participate in, so you will know the details.
2) Empty your mind of all pre-conceived thoughts so you can pay attention.
3) Don't think and analyze at the same time, so you can pay attention.
4) Practice and study every activity you need. Do this for days or weeks. You will get the most out of any activity if you let your subconscious mind run on automatic. It is a very powerful tool.
5) Concentrate on what is happening and try to be part of the situation. Don't think about the situation until it is over or your subconscious mind will not be able to function properly. Leave your activities to the power of your mind.

Chapter Nineteen

Using Persistence To Gain Success

In order to be successful you must have a big desire to have many of the good things that life has to offer. If you really desire these things, you will develop a good sense of persistence. Your burning desire to become successful will determine how successful you will be. Persistence will guarantee you will become successful. Without strong persistence, you have little chance of a big success. That's right, little chance. Why would anyone want to drastically lower their chances for success? I don't know. Yet only one out of ten people are persistent. You are going to be one of those ten. You must have the qualities of being persistent to be successful. You hired me for a mission; and that mission is to make you successful and prosperous. I will not let you down. If success is what you want, that is what you will get. By the time you finish reading this chapter, you can be more persistent.

What creates persistence? A burning desire for something. I know that at one time or another, you must have had a burning desire for something. Did you get what you wanted? It's not enough just to have a burning desire, you have to put that burning desire into action. There is a simple method to put achieve your goals. In seven words, it is: HAVE A BURNING DESIRE TO BE SUCCESSFUL. Now, isn't that simple? Always act on your desires. Let me tell you how one man's persistence has paid off.

Goodyear's Persistence Paid Off

At age 21 and in the year 1821, Charles Goodyear worked in his father's hardware store in Philadelphia. Goodyear was intrigued by the manufacture of early rubber products. In those years, rubber products were primitive. Back then, these products were near useless because anything made of rubber got hard and brittle in the winter and hot and gummy in the summer. Goodyear was determined to make rubber a usable product. He devoted all his time to the creation of rubber that could withstand heat and cold. He had a burning desire to accomplish this task. He was determined to succeed.

The government awarded Goodyear a contract to make rubber mailbags. The government later gave up on the project because in the heat of the summer, the mail bags melted right on the backs of the mail carriers. All of the rubber manufacturers of the time had to deal with the same problem; rubber couldn't withstand extreme temperatures.

Even though Goodyear had no background in chemistry, he was determined to improve rubber. He would randomly mix substances together just to see what would happen. Time and again, he thought he had found the secret of durable rubber, only to be disappointed. But Goodyear was persistent. He was determined to continue until he accomplished what he had set out to do.

Goodyear Sacrificed Everything

Goodyear had such a desire to improve rubber that he sacrificed everything and was put in prison many times for not paying his debts. There were times when his family suffered extreme poverty. Goodyear was determined to improve rubber, however, and refused to give up until he did. Goodyear sought the secrets of improved rubber for 18 years. For 18 years, people thought he was crazy, but he didn't care. He had a goal and he was determined to achieve it.

Goodyear had a wife and five children. After 18 years, his wife lost patience with her husband. She begged him to stop working on his rubber. But Charles Goodyear persisted. Eventually, when his wife could no longer stand his quest, she forbade him from ever working on rubber again. He agreed. But Goodyear was determined to achieve his goal, so he worked on the rubber in secret.

Goodyear Worked In Secret

According to the story, this is how Goodyear found the secret for improving rubber: One cold day Goodyear was kneading a pile of rubber and sulfur together over his stove when he heard his wife returning home. He didn't know what to do, so he threw his pile of rubber and sulfur in the stove. Later, he took his mixture out. His rubber had changed. It had vulcanized. It was then that he realized that adding sulfur to rubber and then heating the mix, would cure it. Improved rubber was created.

One man's persistence paid off. A burning desire to create durable rubber not only insured Goodyear's place in history, but created an empire. Goodyear knew he was going to improve rubber. Nothing was going to stop him: not poverty, not prison and not sickness. He was determined to succeed and he did, for the whole world.

Positive Assertive Attitude

Being a persistent, goal-oriented individual will help you fulfill your goals. You should have a positive, assertive, forward-moving attitude. When you encounter problems, work on solving them, and keep moving forward. Solve your problems but keep moving ahead. Don't stop until you have completed your goals.

Win People Over

Everyone admires a persistent person. Persistent people know what they want and go after it. Why does persistence make people feel important and special? Persistent people go after

what they want without regard to rejection. They can do this because they are driven by their instincts. They act in accordance with their own burning desires to get rich, regardless of what others think. They look within themselves and let their feelings dictate their actions.

No Matter What Others Think

Set your goals to a good level of prosperity and wealth, then use persistence to achieve your goals. Whether your goals are getting more education in school, studying online courses, investing in income property, reading books, joining clubs or getting certain jobs. Go forward to achieve your goals. Work hard to achieve your goals and "No matter what others think" continue to achieve your goals. This is an important concept to remember. If you follow your success oriented attitude, and you will understand that your actions will be dictated by your feelings, after you set your goals. Even if someone is threatening to deny you an opportunity, follow your feelings, that you want to succeed, and don't cave in to that person's demands. Only when the situation disintegrates to the point of hopelessness, should you give up; but you should only give up when your feelings of being prosperous, dictate that you should. Believe me, if you follow these steps, that won't happen very often.

If you want something, go after it. If it is not for you, you won't get it. Never give up, your goals of being successful. The only time you should give up is if your feelings, based on your future wealth, tell you to stop. People who don't take risks never make it. Do you want to make it? Think about it. Your ability to persevere will make you prosper. Be persistent and prosper.

The Inventor Of The Telephone

Alexander Graham Bell was born in 1847 into a family of speech instructors in Scotland. He wanted to succeed. At the age of 12, Bell was persistent with his inventive abilities, and spent time building a simple dehusking machine that was used in a mill for several years. Bell wanted to do well in his life and was determined to have a good education so he taught and studied in college at a young age, but in 1870 he left Scotland for Canada. Bell wanted to earn a living and help deaf people so in 1872, Bell who was persistent with his goals, became a teacher at a Boston University, where he taught deaf mutes to speak. This was not enough for Bell who had a strong desire to be successful, which led his to his experiments to build the first telephone. Bell worked and networked with other people in his attempt to invent the first telephone. Many years of hard work followed.

The Persistent Bell Got Patents

Bell kept experimenting day and night and in 1875 Bell heard vocal sounds as he worked on a device that transmitted plucked reed sounds over the telegraphic wires. The persistent Bell, kept working on his telephone invention to perfect it. Alexander Bell's hard work had paid off for him and in 1876, only three days after he was awarded a patent for transmitting vocal sounds telegraphically, Alexander Bell made a great leap for mankind. In his Boston laboratory where he worked with his assistant Thomas Watson, Bell spoke the first telephone words "Mr. Watson, Come here, I want to see you" into the transmitter. His assistant Watson, who heard the hissy words in the next room, walked to Bell and told him that he heard his words. At that moment the telephone was born. The jubilant Bell was excited. After many years of persistent dedication, he was able to get the first telephone to work. Alexander Graham Bell went on to prosper with fame and fortune. After Bell invented the telephone, he became one of the founders of huge American company, American Telegraph and Telephone, which is AT&T. You have heard of AT&T.

HOW TO INFLUENCE OTHER PEOPLE BY USING PERSISTANCE

If you are persistent, you will eventually get what you want because people find it easier to give in to you than to continue to resist. If you keep asking for something that is within reason, you will get it. The following are steps you must take in order to use persistence effectively with other people.. Here are the five steps to influence people with persistence.

1) **Use A Direct Statement**
2) **Repeat Your Request**
3) **Don't Lose Your Temper**
4) **Get The Other Person To Make A Commitment**
5) **Fulfilling The Commitment**

Use A Direct Statement

In some cases, just using a direct statement will get you what you want. All that is involved in a direct statement is telling a person what you want. Here are some examples: *I want to ..., Tell me..., Show me.... Give me......* If this doesn't get you what you want, go on to the next step. Be polite when making a direct statement. Words such as *please* should be used when making a request of another person.

Repeat Your Request

Repeat your request over and over to the other person until you get what you want, or at least until you get a reasonable compromise. Don't let the other person distract you with excuses or accusations. Keep repeating your request no matter what the other person says. The other person will try to distract you. Don't let that

happen.

Don't Lose Your Temper

You must be calm and collected at all times during your persistent request. The other person may try to get you off track - don't let anything change your request. Key in on what you want. Always be calm and pleasant, and remain persistent in asking for what you want. If you continue to ask for something you will eventually get it. Persistence pays off.

Get The Other Person To Make A Commitment

The other person may give you a vague answer to try and satisfy you, such as, *We'll see, Soon, Later,* or *Maybe.* When you get a vague answer, push for a firm commitment and an exact date. It is very important to define the terms of the agreement and the exact date. Be specific as to the cost, date, and anything else that pertains to the agreement. The terms of the agreement should be repeated to the other person to ensure that there are no misunderstandings. After you repeat the terms of the agreement to the other person, have the other person repeat them back to you.

Fulfilling The Commitment

Make sure that the person(s) who made the commitment to you does what they agreed to do. If they are not living up to the agreement, be persistent and remind him of their obligations. Remind them as many times as it takes so they must hold up their end of the agreement. If that person(s) demonstrates that they are unreliable, make sure never to enter into an agreement with them again.

Time and time again I have seen a pattern with people who break agreements. The behavior is repeated again and again. This type of person just can't be trusted. Always fulfill your end of an agreement. Don't ever go back on your word or you will develop a reputation as someone who can't be trusted. Those who deal with me know that for a fair deal my word is as good as any contract. When I give my word, I fulfill the terms of the agreement.

HOW TO MASTER THE ART OF COMPROMISE

In many cases, all you will be able to achieve by being persistent is a compromise. Compromises are good because they put you a step closer to your goal. If, for some reason, you can't accept a compromise, then don't accept it. Offer whatever you can, and nothing more. This, of course, may result in an unfavorable settlement. The following are several steps that show you how to compromise while getting the most possible out of a bargain.

1) **Tell The Person Exactly What You Want.**
2) **Be Strong And Persistent.**
3) **Don't Agree If You Are Not Sure.**
4) **Offer 35% Less.**

Tell The Person Exactly What You Want

Make sure you know exactly what you want.

When you do know what you want, tell the person exactly, and in terms they can understand. For example: *I need more..., I want two...I must have $300...* etc... It is also important that you give the other person a chance to benefit from the agreement. For example: "I need more money so I can do a quality job for you with the best possible workmanship."

Be Strong And Persistent

You must get around the other person's excuses and rationalizations. You must be persistent until you feel that you have hit the other person's bottom line. You may find that the other person is trying to manipulate you, but if you are strong and persistent, you will make that impossible. Keep making your request to the other person until you feel that, the other person will go down no further. If your request is fair, the other person will give in to you. Keep hammering away.

Don't Agree If You Are Unsure

If you are unsure of what you want, don't agree to anything. If you unsure of the facts, don't agree to anything. You must completely know the situation before you compromise. If you need more time, tell the other person that you need more time. If you need more money, tell the other person that you need more money. Make sure you can live with the agreement before you make it. Don't commit until you personally know that you can fulfill the terms of the agreement.

If you have made an agreement and you know that you will lose money if you complete the agreement, then go back and re-negotiate. Don't continue with an agreement that will make you lose money. Tell the other party that you will lose money and you can't fulfill your terms of the agreement because you will lose money. You may be in court if you do this, but that is better than going broke.

Offer 35% Less

To get the best out of a compromise, you should offer the other party around 35% less than the discounted price, you are willing to pay. This will give you a bargaining chip when negotiating. If the other party wants $10,000 for equipment and you are only willing to pay $6,000, offer them $4,000, which is about 35 percent less. They will then start negotiating up and you can negotiate down. Don't pay more than you feel your offer is worth.

THE KEY TO NEGOTIATING

The secret key to mastering the art of negotiation is silence. Ask questions rather than talk. *They say that the first person to speak loses.* The first person that names their price or condition will lose. Most good salesman know this, and that is why they will try to get you to name your price. The standard rule to follow is, if you know little about the situation, say nothing. If you know what you are willing to pay, make a price or condition that is far lower than you are willing to pay. Anytime you can get the other person to talk, then be silent. Let the other person do the talking and you take all the benefits.

If you are unsure of what you want, don't agree to anything. You must think the situation over entirely before you make a compromise. If you need more time, you should take more time. Make sure that you can live with the agreement before you make it. Don't ever strike an agreement that you don't feel right about.

Work With Your Feelings

It is critical that you use this technique in relation to your true feelings. If you feel that a compromise doesn't fit your needs, don't agree to one. Don't compromise yourself. If you don't feel right about it, then walk away. Walking away is a commonly used technique in negotiation. Walking away often helps persuade the other party to give in, to compromise. This is a good indicator that they were going to bluff you. I highly recommend sticking to an agreement that you feel good about. If you are satisfied with walking away with nothing, walk away with nothing. If you walk away, you may come out ahead. I want to tell of an instance when walking away enabled me to get a better deal.

How I Negotiated A Car Deal

I walked into the car dealership and looked for a good-looking Mercedes Benz sports car. I found a car I liked. I told the salesman, "I don't

SUMMARY

● Having a burning desire to achieve a goal creates persistence.
● Being persistent means being a positive, aggressive, goal-oriented person who is constantly moving forward.
● No matter what others think, always move forward.
● You can use persistence to win people over to your way of thinking.
● If you keep asking for something persistently you will get it.
● A compromise can be one positive outcome of persistence.
● Don't agree with the agreement, if you are unsure of the facts.
● The secret key to mastering the art of negotiation is silence.
● If you don't get what you want, walk away. You could get the better side of the deal by doing this.

want to discuss the price. First, I want to find a car that suits my needs, then we can talk price. I also expect a good deal." The first words out of this salesman's mouth were the classic closing line. He asked me how *serious* I was. His best sales pitches followed. The salesman asked, "If I can get you the deal you want, will you take the car home today." I told him yes. I could see his face light up.

The Mercedes Benz sports car on that lot looked good to me. The paint sparkled. The whole interior was a nice brown leather. The car looked so striking and sporty. I went to the salesman and told him quickly, "I don't like to waste time. Let's get right to the point. Let's go into your office and draw up the papers." This, I know, got the salesman excited.

We were writing up the papers and, true to form, the salesman asked top price for the car. I told him to lower the price or he would lose a customer. We had been negotiating for about an hour and the salesman had come down only $2,000. He was asking $54,500 for the car and all the extras. I told him that I wanted the car for $51,500. He brought his manager into the discussion and I was informed that I could forget it, because at that price, the dealership would be losing money. I said I would think about it. These guys didn't say much to that statement. They told me that if I thought about it too long, the car would be gone.

I started to walk out of the dealership. The salesman said the car was mine for $53,000. I said *No* and kept walking. Just before I got in my car, he reluctantly agreed to my price. He later told me I got the car at a steal and asked me not to mention the deal to others.

Could I have bought the car for less money? What do I know? But one important lesson to be learned is that I had nothing to lose by negotiating. I felt the car was worth $51,500 and walked out. I took no risk. I could have always walked back into the dealership and bought the car for the $54,500 price. I had nothing to lose by walking away because I could have always reconsidered. Try this technique; it can help you to get the best deal possible.

Chapter Twenty

Others Will Make You Wealthy

Success and prosperity seldom happen without the help and support of other people. All people are gregarious, in other words we all need other people. You need the ability to get along and work with other people in order to succeed. One of the fundamentals of *"Novanetics"* is getting along with other people. I emphasize *other people* in this book. There is a good reason for this. Other people can help you to succeed. Your own knowledge can be multiplied many times if you work with other people.

I want to help you to work with others. Remember, ten minds can work better than one. If you strive for something alone, you are taking the long route. Take the short route and work with other people. Anybody with wealth and success will tell you that it was other people who made the difference. You can benefit greatly from other people, and to get the most out of other people, you should follow certain guidelines.

Know What You Want

It is really important that you know what you want from a relationship with another person. Think about this for a minute. Do you know what you want? If you do, then write down what you feel you would like from a relationship with another person. I will help you out. I will write down qualities I want from a relationship with another person. This may give you an idea of what characteristics you want from people in your life, which could be similar to your own characteristics. Write down what you want from other people in your life.

What I Want In Other People	What You Want In Other People
Honesty	
Confidence	
Loyalty	
Cheerfulness	

Spontaneity	
Wise & Informative	
Hard-working	
Responsible	
Creativeness	
Expressiveness	
Informative	
Openness	
Supportive	
Friendliness	
Adventurous	
Politeness	
Positive Attitude	
Funny	
Motivating	
Passionate	

Misc	
Misc	

After reading the list you may think that I am interesting, but I did write additional qualities I thought deserved to be on the list. Do you compromise yourself by having friends who you don't feel good with? You should have friends that you like. You can choose your friends. Pick friends who will support and care for you. I am sure that that is what you want.

Look over your list. Are you happy with it? Take a look at yourself and ask this question: Does your list describe you? If it doesn't, take a second look at yourself. Are you lacking some qualities that you would like to see in others? You can develop these qualities in yourself. If you would like to see yourself with these qualities, add them to your goal list. Work on them and they will be your own qualities.

The People Around You

There is an old saying that goes, "You are what your friends are." There is a lot of truth to this. Ambition in your friends will fire ambition in you. Failure in your friends will cause failure in you. Your friends can be an asset or a liability. Your choice of friends will also determine the route you take in your life. Choose successful friends who are good. Do you want to travel on the path to success? If that is your decision, associate with people who follow that same path as you.

There are some people who will ridicule you if they know your goals. They are jealous of those who have more or who aspire to do more than they do. Your success would make them feel inferior, so they condemn such effort and may try and block you before you even start. Make an attempt to be with people around you are supportive of your goals.

If you tell a man who rents an apartment that you want to buy a $500,000 home, he may laugh and ridicule you. If you tell a man who owns a $500,000 home that you want to buy a $500,000

home, he will believe you and may give you advice. He knows it can be done because he has done it. A small man will try to de-motivate you, a big man will support you. You want to associate with people who believe in you. If they believe in you, you will believe in yourself. If you associate yourself with negative simple people that is the way you will be. Choose your friends carefully. Choose successful friends with admirable qualities.

Why Re-Invent The Wheel?

When I first started my business, I was stubborn. I wanted to do it all by myself. I spent half of many days trying to figure out how to get my business started. I could have asked my neighbor, John, what the steps were that he used to set up his business. He could have told me in five minutes. Eventually, I asked myself, "Why not take advantage of other people's knowledge and save myself the time and expense involved in making unnecessary mistakes? Why not make it easy on myself," I thought. Why should you try and re-invent the wheel? If the wheel has already been invented, find out how to make it from someone who knows. Get advice from your family and friends. Why would you want to figure it out from scratch by yourself? Getting support and advice is one advantage to belonging to a support group.

Apple Computer Was Formed By Two People

Other people can make you wealthy. Steve Jobs one of the first of two Apple Computer partners was born in San Francisco. He attended Reed College in 1972, dropped out and got a job. In 1974 Jobs traveled though India to seek enlightenment while studying Zen Buddhism. In 1974 he returned to San Francisco and looked up his old high school friend. Stephen Wozniak who worked for Hewlett-Packard suggested that him and Jobs start a company. Wosniak was designing his own computer and circuit board. Hewlett Packard later turned down Wozniaks design in 1976. Steve Jobs sold his Volkswagen minibus and Stephan Wosniak sold his programmable calculator, they took the money and built a logic board in Job's family's garage which they called the Apple I. To sell Wozniak's Apple I computer they both co-founded Apple Computer in 1976. A year later they both gained celebrity status and success with the improved model Apple II. Wosniak designed the Apple II computer with a keyboard and a specially designed plastic case.

Today, Apple Computer which has a dedication to quality has become one of the largest companies in the world so Steve Jobs and Stephen Wozniak's dedicated work had paid off as the team that founded Apple Computer. Having partners and working with other talented people can make you very successful.

YOUR SUPPORT GROUP

I urge you to create a support group of success-oriented people. Setting up a support group will have a great impact on your success. You need people around you who will support and help you. Every support group that I have ever become familiar with has been of great benefit to all those who participated in it. Belonging to a support group, whose members all have the same goals and desires, will help you to become more successful. The members will not only support you and your ideas, but they will probably be able to offer you help and advice. Your fellow members can help you learn.

Form Your Support Group

This point should be stressed. You will not be as successful as you could be, without the help of other people. Positive people will help, support and assist you. You need people. I understand this necessity that is why I emphasize getting along with other people all through this book. I urge you to create your own support group, a group that can and help create success for you. Large corporations have these groups because they know that they lead to success. Now that you may have decided to form your group, let me go over its specifics. You *have* decided to create a group,

haven't you?

The group should consist of four to six people. Having too many people will take away the small, personal appeal of such a group. It is helpful if each member has different or varied interests. I know of such a group in which the members of several different professions would get together once a week for breakfast. This type of group is great if you are self-employed. If you are self-employed, I urge you to create a group like this. Let me tell you about this particular group. It consisted of a photographer, a printer, an insurance salesman, an advertising man and a stockbroker.

Each of these members was in a different field, so they didn't compete with each other. It was a support group that worked. The members gave each other referrals and discussed their business problems. Each of them was able to increase their business and break through their obstacles. It was a great arrangement. Do you think that you could create a breakfast arrangement with people in different fields?

Get about four to six people together once a week. In this meeting, you will discuss your goals and anything else that you feel is of interest to the group. You will learn a lot, and will also be able to share your knowledge with those who need it. It is an opportunity to grow with other ambitious, positive people. It is an opportunity to become successful through the help of others. If you are having trouble forming a group or would like to know which people in your area would like to form a group, please contact me. I would be happy to help you.

GUIDELINES FOR YOUR SUPPORT GROUP

1) Have four to six people in your support group.
2) Make sure everyone in the group is supportive and positive. Negative people will inhibit your efforts.
3) Set a firm meeting time once or twice a week. A breakfast meeting would be fine.
4) Make one person the president, leader or coordinator of the group.
5) If you are self-employed, the group will be more helpful if its members are in different professions.

I have already discussed the guidelines for those in your group. You will be working closely with them, and they will have a great influence on you, so decide carefully who you will invite to be in your group. Make sure that they are people you like and admire. I have some guidelines that will help you get the most out of your friends and your group members.

Here are the six guidelines for your support group.

1) Associate With People Better Than You
2) Show Appreciation Of Others
3) Help Others As Much As You Can
4) Model Yourself After Those You Admire
5) Reward Others For Helping You

Associate With People Better Than You

Associate with people better than you. Look at people as a resource and let them help you. If a person knows more than you, don't be scared, you can learn from them. If this person is successful, that is all the more reason to seek their advice. You could be better than a person in one field while they could know more than you in another field. You could both learn from each other. Find out what makes this person successful and develop those qualities in yourself. Remember, success breeds success.

Show Appreciation Of Others

One way to have other people help you is to acknowledge their wisdom. Learn from others, they can help you to achieve your goals. Make sure that you acknowledge what others have done for you. Tell them that you appreciate them, and recognize that they are helping you. Do this, and they will continue to help you.

Help Others As Much As You Can

There is a saying that many people believe, "If you do good things then, they will come back to you." In other words, if you do good things for others, then others will do good things for you. This is especially true of your support group but this is good in many other situations. If you help

SUMMARY

- Other people can lead you to success.
- Know exactly what qualities you want in other people by writing down the qualities you admire.
- The people you know can help you to succeed or they can help you to fail. Choose positive, successful people to be with. .
- Take advantage of other people's knowledge by knowing them, and save yourself time and expenses.
- Create a support group of about four to six people.
- In this support group associate with people better than you, acknowledge help from others and show them appreciation.
- In a support group, help others as much as you can and, and reward people that help you.
- Model yourself after those you admire.
- Pets alleviate loneliness and boredom and also provide health related benefits like exercise.

people in your group, they should return the favor help you.

Model Yourself After Those You Admire

Think about who you admire and try to analyze what it is about them that makes you feel that way. Model yourself after those that you admire. To be successful, you must learn from successful people. Model yourself in the image of someone who you admire. If you do this, you can quicken your quest for success.

Reward Others For Helping You

When someone does something for you, remember that person and acknowledge them. Always reward people who help you. This reward may be as simple as a *thank you,* or may even involve some kind of material gift like a card, flowers or a pen. Whatever reward is, it will serve as an acknowledgment from you; and it will show your appreciation of others. If you want to encourage people to help you, you must reward them. I have shown you qualities that will help you with your group and friends. Remember this: "To have a friend, you must be a friend." There is a lot of truth in those words. Be good to other people and they will help you up the ladder of success.

HOUSE PETS AND HOUSE PLANTS

Having a pet is a great idea. Studies show that every household has at least one pet. Pets are great companions that warm your whole house and are a pleasure when coming to your home every day. Pets alleviate loneliness and boredom and also provide health related benefits like exercise.

Dogs And Cats

By far dogs and cats are the most popular pets that have become man's best friend. These animals have added so much to many people's lives by being people's companions. Many say that the relationship between people and their cats and dogs have lowered stress, decrease depression, increase physical fitness and just bring joy to their owners.

Birds

Birds are great pets to have. Many overlook their noisy behavior and their butting nature, just for the enjoyment of having a chirping companion in their home. Bird pets are always kept in cages that have to be cleaned on the regular basis. Consider also buying a bird feeder and bird bath in your yard. Bird feeders are inexpensive and many stores sell the bird seed that is filled in the bird feeder.

Guinea Pigs & Hamsters

Kept in a cage with plenty of food, guinea pigs, hamsters are energetic and amusing pets that require little maintenance. They are small and like to keep active and can bring many hours of delightful watching.

Fish In An Aquarium

Fish in a aquarium were popular pets in years gone by. Having fish in aquarium is not only a rewarding and exciting type of pet, but they give much pleasure to their owners who can watch the fish swim in the clear water. Don't forget an air pump that bubbles oxygen in the water. Feed your fish on a regular basis and you are set. Seriously consider owning tropical fish in your own aquarium.

Ant Farms

Ant farms have given their owners much pleasure over the ages. Ants live outside in a warm climates and if you view a garden you can watch them gather and carry food in long lines. An ant farm lets you see what the ants are doing to support their active home. In an ant farm, two pieces of plastic sheets surround the soil so that you can view hundreds of ants working in their colony.

House Plants

You must consider growing plants inside your home. Studies have shown that people feel better and their health may improve with the growing of indoor plants. An indoor planter or even an indoor plant pot is fine for growing regular or tropical plants in your home. Of course, you can plant indoor plants in hanging baskets by the windows of your home. Don't overlook the beauty and wonder of having indoor plants in your home.

Chapter Twenty One

Listening To Riches

Listening skills are valuable and they can make you successful. It can become one of the most valuable tools that you have to gather information. If you can master the technique of listening to other people, you will be able to influence other people. Listening can break down communication barriers, and it is one of the techniques that can work for you. You will become successful, if you are a good listener.

HOW LISTENING & SPEAKING WILL MAKE YOU SUCCESSFUL

Listening has been valuable in every successful person's climb to the top. Developing an ability to listen has helped many people become successful. Napoleon Bonaparte was highly regarded for his expert listening ability. He paid very close attention to anything said to him. His ability to listen carefully to others helped move him up the ranks of the French Military, all the way to Emperor. I want to help you to become a better listener because I know that developing good listening techniques will help you to succeed. I have outlined the steps necessary for you to become a good listener. Look over the steps and study them. Influence others by listening.

Listen To The Best People

Listen to the better people in your life. They can help you get where you want to go. Their advice and experience is invaluable. Let them educate you. People are dying to tell other people what they know. It makes them feel important.

Don't hesitate to ask the better people in your life what they know. And when they tell you, listen to them. After you listen to them give them feedback. Make sure it is constructive criticism. Always try to ask for advice. Their advice will be valuable to you. If the advice you get is negative and critical, get a second and even a third opinion.

Eliminate All Distractions

Distractions will inhibit your ability to speak and listen well. It is important that you remove all distractions when listening to another person. You want to create a warm and comfortable atmosphere for the speaker. This way you can listen to a speaker.

What Questioning Will Do

Questions arouse the thinking processes of those who are asked questions. When you ask questions, you give others the chance to express their own ideas and feelings. The only way you will discover information about others is by asking questions. Asking questions helps people think. If you are able to help people think on their own, with non-objectionable questions, then they will respect and like you. Your help has enabled them to do something for themselves that they were unable to do before. By listening to others, you also fulfill their need to feel important. Through your concern, they will feel special.

Keep The Conversation Open

In order to listen, you must keep the conversation open. Some people won't tell you everything that is on their minds. You may have to keep questioning them just to keep the conversation going. If the person gets upset at your questioning, then ask, "Are these questions upsetting you." If the questions do upset them then you could talk about yourself or keep the conversation shallow. All of your questions should relate to *who, what, when, where, why* and *how*.

What Questions Do You Ask?

The questions you ask must have a specific purpose. If they don't, you will lose credibility. People must fully understand what you are trying to ask them. First give them a reason for the questions like; "I know you would like this car, I just need more information so I can help you with your choice." "I am trying to romantically know you and just want to know if it would work out between us." "I don't go to this place often, but you seem like the kind of person that would enjoy ...."

Don't confuse people by asking complicated or compound questions. Instead, try and break a complicated question up by asking one part at a time. Try to get others to tell you *why*. *"Why"* is one of the best questions to ask. The reason for asking people questions is to get definite answers. Your questions should prompt definite answers, and you should discourage others from guessing at the answers to your questions, unless the answers are upsetting. The therapeutic value of questioning is lost when people guess at answers.

Changing Subjects As You Speak

If you are going to change subjects during a conversation, tell your listener that you will be moving on to another topic. If you confuse your listener, they may not listen. It is easier for a person not to listen at all than to try to follow a confusing conversation. Don't make it difficult for your listener.

How to Resolve an Argument by Listening

I have solved many arguments just by listening. It may be hard to believe, but it really works. It works when someone is trying to get

their point across; trying to convince you how right they are by yelling as loud as possible. Even if the argument is meaningless, listening will enable you to control the situation and wind you up on top.

The first thing you should do is to listen to what the person has to say without interrupting. This is where your listening skill will come in handy. You should say *yes, I understand,* or just nod your head occasionally every now and then to demonstrate that you are truly listening. It is important that you understand the other person's point of view. Even if you don't feel they are right, you must at least let them know that you understand their point of view.

When the other person has finished saying what they have to say, ask them, "*What can I do for you?*" This statement throws many people off because they don't expect it. Do what you can for the person at this point. If what the person asks for is unreasonable, explain your position and tell the person you can't do what they want, but you are willing to do something. You might say, "*Yes, I understand your situation, but I can't do that, but is there something else I could do.*" If you can give that person all they want, all the better. The point that you are trying to get across is that you are willing to listen and to try and help. You will find, after using this technique that most people give in to your point of view. That is because you listened to them, and they feel part of their problem is resolved.

How Listening Made Me A Friend

This happened years ago, but I will never forget how I handled an angry customer. It was a cold Monday morning and I was rushing to get caught up on my paper work. A man came in the front door and started yelling and screaming at my secretary claiming that my company had filched his money. I told him that this was not true. I politely asked this man to have a seat in my office. In a harsh voice, he told me he sent in $20 and had not received the book he ordered. For nearly ten minutes he accused me of all sorts of things. I just nodded my head every now and then and took notes on what he was saying. I listened very carefully.

I waited until he finished talking. I then asked him what I could do for him. He told me he wanted the book or a full refund. I told him there was no problem getting either because our policy is

100% customer satisfaction. I was upset that he didn't get his order. I agreed with what he had told me and I told him, "Orders are shipped out of this office within 48 hours. I would be angrier than you if I didn't get my order. I don't blame you one bit for being angry. I am also upset that you didn't receive your order."

We found his name in the computer but with it was a completely different address than the one he lived at. He was considering moving at the time and had used a relative's address. He told me that he had forgotten all about that, and that he would check with his relative to see if the book had arrived. I gave him a free copy and told him his relative could keep the book. He then told me I had been very kind and that he was glad that I had listened to him before I took any action. This man has been my friend ever since.

HOW TO MAKE OTHERS LISTEN TO YOU

It is important to listen to what other people have to say. It is also important for others to listen to what you have to say. This way both parties can communicate to each other and transact an understanding. This section will teach you how to create the most impact with what you say. Here are the six steps to make others listen to you.

1) **Get the Other Person's Attention.**
2) **Make Your Message Understood.**
3) **Make Your Message Benefit-Oriented.**
4) **Begin Discussions with Agreements.**
5) **Give Reasons for Your Requests.**
6) **Give Them The Choice in your favor.**

Get the Other Person's Attention

The first thing that you must do when trying to make a point is to get the other person's attention. Make sure that the other person is listening to you before you begin talking. If the other person is not listening to you, you are wasting your time. Your time is valuable, so if someone to whom you are trying to communicate won't listen to you, either get them to listen, or talk to them at another time. You will find that there are plenty of other people that will take the time to listen to you.

Qualify the conversation by making sure the other person wants to hear what you have to say. By qualifying, I mean you should ask the other person to determine if the person wants to hear what you have to say. To qualify ask, *"Would you be interested if I can ... ..., Can I take a moment of your time to ... ..., Can I have a word with you to explain....., Can I talk to you about... ..., I would like to introduce myself and I would like to speak about.......* If they say yes, begin to talk, if their attention span wanders, then stop talking. Boring someone will not get you anywhere. If you can't attract the other person's attention, either improve your talking skills or find someone else to talk to.

Make Your Message Understood

Make sure your message can be fully understood by the other person. Don't use language or terms that they will not understand. Try always to use familiar words. Here are some examples. Instead of "construe" use "understand." Instead of "gregarious" use "outgoing." Instead of "enervate" use "weaken."

After you have finished talking, try testing how much the other person has absorbed of your talk by asking a few questions. The questions you ask will tell you if that person understood what you've tried to explain. You can even ask the person to repeat what you said. It will be quite obvious by their answers, how much of the conversation they paid attention to.

Make Your Message Benefit-Oriented

The key to getting people to listen to you is the answer to the question, *"what is in it for me?"* If there is some perceived benefit, a person will listen to you. People want to hear what you will do for them, not what you want from them. Fill your message with benefits. The following example shows how this concept works. *"Listen to me and I can get you the cash you need." "I don't have the kind of money you want, but I can give this to you." "Here take my card, it will help you." "If you listen to me, I can show you how to be a better person."* These reasons are much more appealing than, "Listen to me because I am smarter than you."

What you say will have a dramatic influence on people if you can answer this question for them: "*What can I do for you?*" If you can answer it then you know how to word the conversation. Before you begin to talk to a person, find out what they want. If you understand what a person wants, you will have them listening to you with wide eyes.

You create alliances with people when you give them what they want. Show other people that you can do something for them.

Begin Discussions with Agreements

When you begin a conversation, open with something about which you have some mutual understanding and agreement. When a person argues about the price of a product, you should agree with them then give them a benefit. Here are two examples of this concept, *"Yes, I understand the book costs $30, but the valuable information in it is so good that it is well worth the $30. Yes, I know we have our disagreements, but we get along most of time, so this outing would be good for both of us."*

If you want someone to turn the lights off when not in use, you should not say, "Keep the lights off, you ###!.." You should say, *"We both want to conserve energy and save money, don't we?* Wait for that person's answer. This person is obviously going to say yes. After that person agrees, ask them if he thinks the lights could be turned off when they are not in use? Of course they are going to say yes. This works because the concept agreement is that person's own idea.

Give Reasons for Your Requests

When you tell someone to do something you should always have a good reason. Just because you want it done, or because it is a rule, are not good reasons. Give that person a reason to listen to you. If you ask someone to follow a policy or rule, tell him why you expect him to follow it. Make them see the benefit they will receive by following the rule. You must always justify a request. If you don't want people to smoke in your home, tell them why. Explain to them that; "You don't want them to smoke because you are allergic to the smoke and that the smoke stains your ceilings." Another example is; "I want you to study this business class, because they you will be more educated and you will earn more money." One last example is, "I want you to use a ladder, because you may fall off the chair and hurt yourself."

Give Others The Choice

People resent being told what to do. They would rather make the choice themselves. People prefer that you ask them, rather than tell them. This leads us to an interesting point. If you don't give people the chance to say *no,* then most of the time they won't say no. Ask them a question in which the answer is always YES.

Let me show you what I mean. Let's say that I want you to buy my book. Instead of asking you if you want to buy my book, I ask you whether you want the hard bound or soft cover edition, or whether you want to pay by check or money order. You see that with these questions I am not asking you if you want to buy the book. If I ask you that, you might say *no.* I am asking you these trivial questions that assumes you already want to buy the book. Let us try that again, "Will you be using a check or a money order? You would say a check. Then I would say, "Make out the check to my company." Here is another example if you want your wife to come to a seminar, you could ask her if she wants to go to a business seminar with you. Your wife may say no. The better question is do you want to go to the business seminar at 7PM or at 7:30PM. If she gives you a time then she has already said yes. Use these types of questions. You will notice that you become more influential with other people. You will also notice that you will get more of what you want.

HOW TO HANDLE ADVERSITY

The five steps in handling adversity.

1) **Prepare For Adversity.**
2) **Learn Adversity's Lesson.**
3) **Focus On Your Goal.**
4) **Be Willing To Pay The Price.**
5) **Act On Your Ideas Today.**

Prepare For Adversity

Always expect success, but prepare for adversity or harsh conditions. Unpleasant things happen to all of us, so don't feel singled out. Even the billionaires of our time have felt the sting of adversity. Your goal is to use adversity for your benefit. Prepare for the worst, but expect the best. For example if you think a venture may be risky, set some money aside, so that you can pay for necessities in case you lose your money. Another example is that if you feel that your computer equipment might break, then buy insurance or have a spare computer ready.

Learn Adversity's Lesson

Adversity is a great teacher. Learn its lesson to do better. You can learn from your mistakes. Mistakes are lessons that can help you excel in your life. Obstacles are challenges to overcome. For example if you fall on hard times while you are supporting your family, and you have lost your job, then train yourself for either a better job in the same field or another job that pays more money. If you work hard enough you will be in a better position than when you first experienced your hardship.

Focus On Your Goal

When adversity rears up, focus on your goals. A horse will not finish in first if it runs right and left and wanders away from that track, A horse needs blinders so he isn't distracted by people or objects. You need blinders so you don't stray from your goal. Nothing should be able to stop you from reaching your goal. Whether it is to get a higher paying job, get a small business, get a training certificate or a earn a college degree, commit to your goal and keep working on completing your goals. Be clear on your purpose and don't stop moving forward. You have no limits, and nothing will stop you in your path. If you want to gallop across the finish line, you must focus on your goals.

Be Willing To Pay The Price

You are going to have to pay a price for your success. Nothing comes easily or cheaply. Recognize that you will have to work hard and that you will face adversity. Both of those qualities are signs that you are on your way to success. Develop communication skills so you can work with other people. You will never make it alone. You must be able to listen to other people. Their knowledge and wisdom will be valuable to you. Listen to them and accept their help, and only reward them for what they do for you. If people get rewards they will help you again in the future.

Act On Your Ideas Today

Make it a point to plan and act out your ideas

SUMMARY

- Listening is a skill that can make you successful.
- Listen to the better people in your life, their accomplishments, education and job skills can help you become successful.
- Questioning prompts other people to think and allows you to direct the conversation.
- Eliminate distractions and keep the conversation open.
- You can resolve arguments just by listening.
- To make others listen to you, get their attention, make your message understood, and make your message benefit oriented.
- To make others listen to you, begin discussions with agreements and give reasons for your requests.
- Give people a choice in your favor and you will be able to Influence them.
- Act now and don't procrastinate.
- To handle adversity, Prepare for adversity, learn adversity's lesson, focus on your goals and be willing to pay the price for your success.

today, by setting your goals, then completing your goals. Do whatever you must do to get where you want, but act on your ideas today. Act now to be successful. Don't procrastinate. As soon as you know you have to do a certain task, do it now or put it on a schedule to do it at a set time, but don't procrastinate. The only way you achieve success is to act now. Don't waste time and don't procrastinate. Your completed tasks will determine your success. Set your goals then commit to following your goals.

Becoming More Influential

I have included these sections in this chapter because I feel it will help you become more influential when communicating with other people. Being more influential has helped many people become more successful. Helping good people will bring you more love and riches than you may ever see in your life. Follow the steps outlined in this chapter and you will be amazed at the results.

Chapter Twenty Two

Knowledge: The Key To Riches

You need knowledge to be successful and the more information you study, the greater your success will be. What type of success? You will earn more money. You may never get paid for what you know but you will get paid for what you do with what you know. You must know specialized knowledge to get paid. In this chapter, I will tell you how you can add tremendously to your level of success and prosperity by increasing your knowledge.

Let me tell you about people who used knowledge to become more successful and prosperous. I know a man who worked at a grocery check-out. He felt that he could do more with his life. He wasn't very proud of working in a supermarket. He finally decided to enter a different career. He wanted to be a realtor because he enjoyed people and was intrigued by real estate. He took some night classes in real estate at a local college and kept his day job at the grocery store. He finished the courses and took the real-estate exam. He passed.

He persuaded a real estate company to let him sell residential housing. He has made over $100,000 in commissions. This is quite an accomplishment, and he achieved it because he knew the value of knowledge.

Commit Yourself To Learning

Gaining knowledge from learning is so important. You must set aside time every single day for learning and gaining knowledge. This commitment will be so important in your life. Make a commitment now to increase your level of

knowledge. Do this after work or even in the early hours of the morning, but you should do it daily. Would you like to be smarter? I am sure you would. Spend about thirty minutes to two hours every day reading business or self-improvement books. Take an educational school classes or business seminars to increase your education. Go to the library for thirty minutes to two hours every day and keep up on business or self-improvement topics.

Using Knowledge To Succeed

One man I heard of, had devised an ultimate plan for creating wealth, but that for some reason, he couldn't seem to turn his vision into reality. He wanted to open a gift shop in a retail outlet. He had done his homework. He knew everything except how to run a store. This man lacked *specialized knowledge.* He decided that to make his venture a success, he needed specialized knowledge. He got information on gift stores and sought out the advice of a consultant. His problems were solved. He learned everything he needed to learn and his store became a success. You are not paid for what you know. You are paid for what you do with what you know. That is why there is a need for practical knowledge, specialized knowledge and financial knowledge, all of which will make you money.

The Software Of Your Mind

Your subconscious mind will do your decision making and computing for you. There is only one small thing that your mind needs. One small thing. It needs data or specialized knowledge to put in the "mind software." Knowledge is so important. Call it what you will, but your mind needs it. You see the mind is like a powerful computer and it's software needs information. Do you know what a computer can do without data? Nothing. What about a smart phone without data. Nothing. Do you know what your mind can accomplish with information? Quite a bit. Find specialized information that you will need, and then study this information so that it enters the software of your mind. Learn and understand everything there is to know about the topic of your choice. This knowledge will help you overcome failure and to achieve success.

Specialize In Knowledge

Knowing a lot about a few things will pay off a lot more than knowing something about everything. You must know something about what you want to succeed in. You must specialize in a particular area. If you want to sell cars, study cars and salesmanship. If you want to go into the income property business, with no money down, study the income property and specialize in this field. Choose a field in which you want to succeed and then learn everything and anything you can about it. When you have done this, your subconscious mind will use this information to help you achieve more business and social success that you desire. (As a favor to readers, I have included the "no money down" income property plan. Refer to the real estate "apartment addition" section of this book. I included these chapters to help you get started with your life.)

You must search for specialized knowledge. This type of learning will definitely get you ahead. If you enjoy acting, then study acting. If you want to be an artist, then study art. Learn everything you can about art and you may succeed in art. Take some night classes at your local college. If you are not able to do that, take a correspondence course. Learn by talking to people who know. Use this knowledge to help you to move up in your company or to create more loving relationships.

Chrysler Studied A Home To Become Successful

Walter Chrysler's father who was of German and Dutch ancestry was born in Canadian city of Chatham, Ontario in 1850. In 1858 his family migrated to the United States. Walter Chrysler was born in Kansas, in 1875. He knew the value of hard work and began his successful career as a machinist and railroad mechanic in Ellis. Chrysler a freemason, wanted to improve his financial situation and further his education with a specialized school degree. He didn't have the time, but knew that having a good education was very important. He took correspondence courses from International Correspondence Schools in Scranton, Pennsylvania, and studied hard, to earn himself a specialized degree. Chrysler was overjoyed when he graduated from his home correspondence program that earned him a valuable mechanical degree. Chrysler's hard work had paid off, and in 1911 Walter Chrysler started to work for Buick for a $6,000 a year salary. The educated Chrysler had set his goals to become rich and left Buick with a huge sum of money, making him one of the richest men in America. In 1925 Chrysler used his money to buy a controlling interest in Maxwell Motor Company. Later Chrysler merged it into his new 1925 Detroit, Michigan company called Chrysler Corporation. Chrysler also included the Plymouth and DeSoto automobiles, and in 1929 Chrysler purchased the Dodge Brothers company which he called Dodge. He had made it to the top and in 1928 Chrysler financed the construction of the Chrysler building, and finished construction in 1930. The successful Walter Chrysler had finally fulfilled all of his dreams and in 1928 was named Time Magazine's man of the year.

Organization Of Knowledge

You need knowledge to be successful, but it has to be organized. If you have access to that knowledge, you can put it to good use. You should know where to get the information or knowledge that you need. It could be the library, an online source, a magazine, a book store or even your own information library. If you know people with specialized skills then their phone number is all you need to access specialized skills and knowledge on a particular topic. When you talk to people that have experience in your field, get their name and phone number and keep this contact information in a file.

I know a man who makes a million dollars a

year in mail order sales. When he started he knew very little about advertising and nothing about the mail-order business. How was he able to put together such wealth? He hired an advertising agency to do his advertising and a mail-order specialist to manage his company. He didn't have to know how to run his company. All he needed to know was where to find someone who could do the work. In this case, the knowledge he needed was how to hire the proper people. He needed to know who would do a good job and who wouldn't. Developing knowledge about how to choose the right people and delegate the work properly, helped him build a business and create a fortune.

Many people hire companies that they need to make their venture successful. It can be expensive, but you can too. While there are many advantages to this approach of hiring companies, there are also a few disadvantages. It will save you time, but it will cost you more money and you won't have as much control over what you are doing, but you will get a better quality job.

There is another method of hiring a company or hiring trained people. You can join a support group that has many talented people; these contacts can help you further your business ventures. Ask them for references from people they know that can do the work at a much lesser price. Make sure that if you join such a group, you have some knowledge to offer. One such group I know of includes an insurance salesman, a printer, a lawyer, a product marketer, an advertising specialist and a dentist. All of these people work together to help each other. Their support group is for their mutual benefit. The minds of six people can solve many problems. You should do the same.

Where To Obtain Business Knowledge

You don't have to know all the information that you will need to be successful. You do have to know, where to find that information. I have provided a list of sources of information.

- Buy specialized business books or other types of books.

- Go to the public library and borrow books & videos.
- Call a relative or friend that knows something about your business needs.
- Call a specialized business consultant.
- Join a specialized business support group.
- Join a national or local organization in your field.
- Subscribe to a magazine in your field.
- Check with internet listings for information.
- Buy information and expertise from a business consultant.
- Purchase a franchise.

Doolin Specialized In Chips

In 1932, 29-year-old Charles Doolin was unable to keep his ice cream store running profitably. It was during the depression years, and his competitors were lowering their prices in order to survive. Doolin was making less and less profit. He expected his store to do well but he also prepared for the worst. He started looking for another business to start. Doolin wanted to concentrate his efforts in the retail snack field. He thought of marketing the Mexican tortilla, but was discouraged by others, who told him that the product had a short shelf life and became stale easily. Despite those warnings, Doolin decided to specialize in the tortilla. He studied the tortilla and learned everything he could about it.

He found out that in order to prevent theft, ice cream shop owners used glass jars to display their potato chips because they knew a rattling lid would get their attention. Doolin, however, felt that putting chips in glass jars was impractical. One day, when Doolin was in an ice cream shop, he noticed tortilla chips in a stale-free package. His subconscious mind clicked. The ideal product was found. He set his mind to work and discovered what he had been seeking.

Doolin discovered that the maker of the corn chips was a Mexican who only wanted to make enough money to return to his homeland. Doolin gave the man $100 for his recipe and corn-chip-making machinery. Doolin had only $75 and had to borrow the remaining $25. With the help of his mother, Doolin raised the rest of the money and began manufacturing and selling his chips. They were, and continue to be, a success. A large part of Doolin's success was due to his ability to find the information which he needed. If any of you are wondering what he called these chips, I'll tell you. He called these chips FRITOS corn chips. Have you ever eaten his chips? Of course you have.

Knowledge and You

Doolin's story illustrates what can be accomplished by sheer determination. He was determined to learn all that he could and to succeed. The information he had gathered clicked in his subconscious and the result was his incredible success. You can enjoy the same success as Doolin. Study, learn, and buy specialized knowledge in the particular field in which you are interested.

How Your Ego Can Stop Learning

We are always learning. No matter how much you know, there is still more to learn. The ability to admit that you don't know something about a topic will enable you to learn about it. Your acceptance of your weaknesses will give you the ability to learn. But if you believe that you know everything, then there will be nothing that you think you need to learn.

Jesus is known to have had this attitude toward learning. Someone told Jesus that he was good and he replied, "Why callest thou me good?" He was not even willing to admit he was good. Once you consider yourself good, you are unwilling to try to be better; once you think you know everything, you are unwilling to learn more. What is the bottom line? It is that you should understand and learn from every experience and contact. You will never be able to learn if you have the opinion that you know it all already. When entering new situations, you should pretend that you know nothing. Try this; you will be surprised at the results.

SUMMARY...

- Commit yourself to learning more knowledge.
- You don't have to know all the information, but you need more, you must know where to find the information.
- Know all sources of information and knowledge, like people, books, courses, videos etc.
- Your mind needs knowledge to solve problems.
- Specialize in a certain field of knowledge in order to succeed.
- When you don't know certain information, you are open to new ideas and knowledge.
- You may make mistakes by thinking that you know something that you don't know.
- It is difficult to learn under pressure.
- Practice ahead and you get through difficult situations with ease.
- Study, read and learn to be successful.

My plumber happens to be one of the nation's authorities on plumbing. He has 40 years of experience and owns a large plumbing operation. I am sure that this man could redo the plumbing for part of the Empire State Building. Yet, if you were to ask him if he could repair a simple leak for you, do you know what he would tell you? He would tell you what he always tells me. He says, "I'm not sure; let me have a look at it." This man makes very few assumptions about his knowledge.

I once asked him why he never will say that he knows something. He told me, "I used to think I knew it all. That was when my problems began. There was a time when I would approach every job as though I knew what was wrong and how to fix it before I even laid my eyes on the problem. When I was wrong, it really cost me. Now, I approach every job thinking that I know nothing. If a new problem comes up, I am able to handle it properly because my mind is open to anything new." His ability to admit to his imperfection helps this man do well at something at which he is already an expert.

Learning Under Pressure

Experiments on laboratory rats suggest that learning under pressure is very difficult. Rats subjected to stress don't learn as well as rats who are not subjected to stress. Humans react to pressure and stress the same way. Where does that leave you? You should try to absorb knowledge when you are relaxed. When you are relaxed, your mind is able to learn.

Why is it hard to learn under stress? It is because stress is an obstacle. Have you ever frozen-up in a stressful situation? I know that I have. A friend of mine once told me about an experience he had had. He belonged to a bowling club. One day, he was to go to the front of the room to tell members of his bowling group how he felt about them. He wasn't used to public-speaking and was extremely nervous. He told me he tried to talk, but just couldn't say anything. He tried and tried, but no words came out. The more he tried, the worse it got. Finally, he had to leave the room embarrassed.

The Solution To Freezing Up

I am going to show you how to get through any situation, stress-free. In order to conquer stress you must first understand it. Your mind is responsible for all of your thinking and acting. You cannot do something while you are thinking about it. You either can think about it or you can do it, but you can't do both. Your mind gets confused when you try to do both. If you ever freeze, don't think, just act.

You must act spontaneously, instantly and without thinking. Your mind can handle it. Give full control to your subconscious and you will not freeze up. I am sure that you have reacted spontaneously to a situation before. Have you ever avoided a car accident by the speed of your reflexes alone? Have you ever made a split second decision in an emergency situation? I'm sure you have. Your mind works in an automatic mode. When you start to think, you obstruct its proper functioning. How are you able to overcome a stressful period? You can by practicing the situation when you are relaxed. Go through the motions over and over again until you know exactly what to do.

A Bowler Who Overcame Stress

A man once called to tell me how he was able to master the art of bowling. He told me, "I used to get real nervous and jittery on the alley. I was always worried that I wouldn't bowl well and that the guys would make fun of me. I wanted to be competitive and bowl as well as they did, at around 200. I think I just tried too hard." "A few months ago, I solved my problem. I stood in front of the mirror and pretended that I was bowling. I imagined that I was bowling tremendously and showing up all the guys. I could see myself throwing strike after strike, just like a pro. Every day I practiced with my ball in front of the mirror. I also dreamt about being a great bowler." "It really worked. I can bowl great now. I'm no longer nervous or jittery. Now, when I am on the alley, I make my buddies look bad. They're always asking me what my secret is. I tell those guys the same thing every time they ask. I tell them, it's all in the wrist."

Five Things You Need To Be Successful

First, You must believe in yourself.
Second, You must have a burning desire to succeed.
Third, You must set your goals.
Fourth, You must use your imagination to make your goals real.
Fifth, You must prepare the things necessary to achieve your goals. You must gain all the knowledge that you can and contact other supportive people that will help you. Preparation is the key to making your plans work. With knowledge, you can make all of your plans in life come true.

Chapter Twenty Three

Managing Your Time For Wealth

Managing your time is an important element of organizing your life. I am going to show you how to do more things, in less time. Your productivity will have no bounds. To use time management you must have certain goals and objectives in mind. Time management will make your goals and objectives realistic. In order to complete the goals you have already chosen, you must organize and manage your time. Not only will you have more leisure time but your wasted time will be replaced by productivity.

Henry Ford Wanted To Speed Up Production

Ford wanted to eliminate wasted time and produce a good quality automobile at a much lower cost so that many more people would buy a Ford car. He wanted to speed up the production of automobiles. Automobiles were just too expensive to manufacture and he had to find a way to manufacture them cheaper. Henry Ford studied and worked on the problem of making a car for less money. It was said that Henry Ford got the original idea for the assembly line from the Chicago slaughter house where carcasses were butchered and moved along a conveyer, like an assembly belt so that machines and workers specialized in different jobs. Fords attention was caught on the act of one worker doing the exact same job quickly again and again. He was impressed with the time saved. Ford was excited and wanted to use this method of manufacturing to make quality cars cheaper. The cost of manufacturing a 1908 Model T was $825. Ford knew he could lower the cost of manufacturing a car with the use of a time saving assembly line. In 1913, the assembly line that was developed for the Ford Model T had begun operations. By using conveyer belts on the assembly line, the production time for manufacturing a Ford Model T was reduced from multiple hours to 93 minutes, which was much faster than a regularly manufactured car. In 1914 Ford car sales went past 250,000. By 1916 Ford car sales for the basic touring car, had topped 472,000 and the cost of a car fell to $360.

The purpose of time management is to save time and thus to make more money. By reducing time wasters and doing regular work more quickly, you can make more money. If you manage your time properly you will be able to work faster and more efficiently. Henry Ford knew this and he set about to create a method of lowering the cost of a manufactured car so he could sell more cars and make more money. He wanted to make a bigger profit. By 1913, Henry Ford was selling so many cars and making so much money that he decided to pay automobile workers an astonishing new high wages. In 1914 Ford set the new wage rate at over twice of what regular auto workers earned at the time. He paid a staggering $5 a day wage.

The Five Time Management Principals.

1) **Evaluate Your Time Schedule**
2) **Make Your Enjoyable Activities Productive**
3) **Evaluating Your Activities**
4) **Handling Productive, But Unenjoyable Activities**

5) Task Time Chart

Evaluate Your Time Schedule

It is important for you to know when you are the most productive and when you are the least productive. Ford did this with automobile production. He analyzed the time and effort it took to manufacture his Ford car, before he came to a solution. His solution was the assembly line manufacturing method. When you recognize how your time is spent, you will know when you are the most productive and when you are the least productive. When you recognize how your time is spent, you can improve your time schedule. For the next week write down everything you do. Make a complete record of how you use your time and when you use it. When you review this schedule you will be able to pinpoint your wasted time and procrastination, as well as your productive time.

Task Time Chart

You must have a good understanding of your tasks, chores and activities. Ford kept track all of the expenses involved in the manufacturing of the Model T. With this statistical data, he was able to analyze time and cost savings of the assembly line and improvements in the assembly line. Keep a complete record of the time and expenses spent on each of your daily activities. This list will help you later on when you compile a complete schedule of all of your daily activities. A time chart of your activities will tell you how much time and money to allow for each chore in your diary. Keep a diary of your activities and work. It is also essential that you know which activity is wasteful and which activity is productive. To determine this, evaluate your activities. You must determine the purpose and objective of each. On the page that you have listed all of your activities, write down what your reason and objective is for carrying your activities out.

Evaluating Your Activities

After you have fully evaluated your activities, I want you to rate them on a scale of 1 to 10. Give the activities that you like most and the activities that most helped you to reach your objectives the higher score. The activities that

you, least enjoyed and that you felt contributed the least amount to your goals, get a lower score. You are the judge of what is productive and what is wasteful in your schedule. You may have found certain activities you didn't enjoy were contributing to your goals. You may have also found that certain activities were enjoyable but wasteful. The next few paragraphs will help you with those problems.

Make Your Enjoyable Activities Productive

Do the things you enjoy and love. **First**, if you love your work, you will get ahead in life. People tend to do much better when they do the things they love or like. If you like a certain field or a certain work, then work in that field. Do the things that you love or like, this way your life will improve. As Confucius said, "Choose a job you love, and you will never have to work a day in your life." Make sure that your enjoyable activities are productive. Your activities must be productive or you are just wasting your time with them. Don't keep doing time wasting activities that you like. If you find that activities you liked were unproductive, think again. If you enjoyed those activities, they must have been productive in some way. **Second**, the activity may be productive but you see it as unproductive. This circumstance is a question of relativity. Some people feel that being with another person is enjoyable but not productive. If you enjoy being with another person then you are productive because you are getting happiness from that activity. Look at your activity closely and make sure that it is productive. **Third**, you may be involving yourself in an activity that you think you enjoy, but that you don't really. Sleeping 12 hours a day may be enjoyable to some but it is unproductive. You will only need the amount of sleep that you expect yourself to need. You may only need seven hours of sleep. Studies show that less than 8 hours of sleep is fine. You may only need seven hours of sleep. Try to improve your activities so they are truly enjoyable or you won't want to work. Productive activities that you enjoy are the best choice for you.

Handling Productive, But Unenjoyable Activities

If you find that productive activities are not enjoyable, consider this: **Step One**, the activity isn't really productive; in this case you should evaluate the activity to make sure it is productive. Once you have evaluated the activity and you recognize that it isn't productive, you may stop enjoying it. If you still feel it is productive, but un-enjoyable (boring or difficult). Give out rewards like more money, for doing un-enjoyable work. Go to Step Two. **Example:** To some, going to school is unenjoyable but productive, and let's not forget that school is necessary. The rewards of educating yourself will only be felt later in your life. **Set Two:** Get paid to go to school or if you don't get paid. Visualize the future rewards of education so that you are able to enjoy schooling. See yourself in a rewarding position, so you can see what the effects of this activity will be later on. This way you can continue unenjoyable and productive activities. Pay yourself to go to school. You should also keep practicing the work so you know it well. If you keep practicing and working in a certain field, in time you will learn to like it more.

GET RID OF TIME WASTERS

A list of seven time wasters.

1)   **Television**
2)   **Phone Calls**
3)   **Visitors**
4)   **Shopping**
5)   **The Perfectionist**
6)   **Get Others To Work For You**

Television

If people would spend more time developing themselves than their knowledge of television programs, we would probably have a great many more successful people. Watch TV if the show is something you will benefit you. Some people say drama or comedy shows help their lives. These types of shows help them with their work or family. A television show in your field is always good. If you are in the business field then try to watch documentary or educational television shows that help your field. A television show that will help you in some way is good. Don't sit down in front of the set and watch just because you think the program is interesting.

Sleep

I just have to touch on one of our greatest time wasters. I have seen people sleep 12 hours and feel good about it because they feel they needed that much sleep. I was one of those people that slept more than 8 hours a day. I changed my habits when I met a woman who told me she sleeps five hours a night. I felt that was impossible, considering the relaxed state I saw her in. My conclusion at this point was that some people needed more sleep than others. I was then surprised to hear that she did sleep 10 hours a day. She was tired of wasting her time sleeping. She decided to sleep five hours a night and feel good about it. That is exactly what she is doing now. I am sleeping seven hours a night now and feel great. If you believe that you only need seven hours of sleep, then try it. The amount of sleep you need is determined by you and an alarm clock. Use your smart phone alarm or buy a good alarm clock and sleep less. Create your own sleep schedule instead of the "eight-hours-a-night fallacy."

Phone Calls

Telephone calls are so important and you absolutely must call family and friends on a regular basis. Every person should have at least two phone calls a day to family and friends. This way you will constantly keep in touch with family and friends. Telephone calls can also waste a lot of your time and make you to lose your train of thought when you are in the middle of a project. You must get people that call you, to tell you the bare facts and forget the town gossip. Here are ways to end wasteful conversations. Limit your calls to 10 minutes. Use a watch to time them. Tell the caller, "*I have only a few minutes, so what can I do for you?*" This statement will get them right to the point. When you are talking to someone, don't ask questions or elaborate. A good way to screen your calls is to use an answering machine. If you want to talk to the caller, pick up the phone; if you don't, let the machine handle the calls. When making telephone calls, make a list of what you want to talk about. This will save you time.

Visitors

Visiting friends and family is so important. By no means should you compromise on your visits to family and friends. Visitors, like telephone calls, can waste time. You must limit the amount of time each visitor takes up. Here are a few things you can do to conserve time. **First:** Plan to spend only a certain amount of time with your visitor. Set a time limit of, let's say 20 minutes. **Second:** Always tell your visitor why you could not spend more time than your time limit with them. Just say that, you are very busy with some project or that you were just going out. **Third:** You must tell people that you enjoy their company and that they make your life better because they are in your life. To do this, tell your visitors how nice it is to hear from them and that it is great seeing them. **Fourth:** You must put a value on your time. People who visit you without telling you ahead of time are not respecting you. Don't feel bad telling them that you are busy. **Fifth:** Try to get the visitor to tell you what is on their mind, but be empathetic to their needs and wants. **Sixth:** If the unwanted guest still won't leave, tell them, "It was nice seeing you, let me walk you outside." **Seventh:** If you are right in the middle of doing a chore and the visitor will not leave, ask them if they want to help you with your work. Most people say "no." They also won't come over uninvited very often.

Shopping

Organizing your shopping can save you a lot of money and time. **First:** Before you go shopping, make a list of exactly what you want to buy. Write that list in a book, and take that book shopping with you. **Second:** Buy in quantity so you don't have to keep going back to the market. If you know you are going to use it, why not buy more now? This will save you time and money. **Third:** Mark on a calendar all special occasions for the next year. Indicate on the calendar what you want to buy the people on your list. Buy all your gifts in quantity, including the cards. This way you don't have to run around looking for gifts and cards. I personally keep a case of wine in my home. If I am invited to a friend's house for dinner or a party, I take one of the bottles. This is always a nice gesture showing you appreciate them. **Fourth:** It is a waste of time and gasoline when you have to drive to different parts of the city to complete errands. Take care of your errands when you are in the area. I always get some supplies on the way home from work. -- I don't wait until I need them.

The Perfectionist

Being a perfectionist is a big waste of money. Wanting everything to be perfect is a big time waster. Getting the job done is sufficient unless the job calls for exact specifications. If you need exact specifications, then you must be a perfectionist. Almost all jobs don't call for perfection. Quality work is one of your objectives, but getting 90 percent of the quality in half the time is a better bet. You must look at a job and calculate how you can get the greatest return on time and energy. Don't work at a job until it's perfect, unless it is necessary to get the job perfect.

Get Others To Work For You

Trying to do work you are not good at is a time waster. Why would anyone work for two and a half hours at specialized job when an affordable professional can do the same work for less than thirty minutes? Not only will you save time but a professional is less likely to make a mistake. If you make a mistake you may have to pay out for damages. An example of that could be fixing the plumbing. If you make a mistake with the plumbing, you may have a flood in your home. Always try to do the most cost effective work.

The same is true for having employees. Contract out or hire people to work for you so you save money and you are more productive. Delegate jobs and duties when you have to. Everyone has weaknesses and strong points. People should do what they are good at. You will never be able to do with efficiency everything you want. Countries trade so that they can sell us what they are good at producing and we sell them what we are good at producing. Countries have tried in the past to produce everything themselves. It is possible but it has cost them a lot of time and money. Humans are the same way. If you want to increase your productivity, you must delegate duties.

TIME MANAGEMENT BASICS

Do The Activities That You Enjoy

You have now determined which activities are productive and which are wasteful.

Remember, it is important that you fully enjoy all of your productive activities. If you don't enjoy productive activities, you will not be productive. You must learn to enjoy productive activities. You must imagine yourself years from now as being very successful because you are participating in productive activities. You should be able to taste the success that productivity brings. After you determine what activities you must fit into your schedule, you have begun the first step to a "*better you*." You must do the work that will make you "*grow rich*."

Write Everything Down

In order to plan effectively for the future, you must write down your plans. Planning is almost impossible if you don't write down what you want to do. One of the best ways to document your plans is with a calendar. Getting a calendar or diary that has enough room to write down your daily activities will save you a great deal of time. It is also useful to get a calendar with a daily "things-to-do" section. Write down your schedules and plans in your calendar or diary.

Plan Your Entire Day

After you purchase your diary, use it to plan your whole day. From the time you get up until the time you sleep, your day should be planned out. Schedule in your work and leisure activities in your diary. Plan more productive activities into your schedule and remove wasteful ones. When planning your day, consider your energy cycles. Some people work better at night, while some work better in the morning. If you do your best work at night, do your most important tasks at night. As a general rule, people with low blood pressure work better at night while people with high blood pressure work better in the morning. Plan your day around your own capabilities and energy level. The way you plan your schedule is up to you, but make sure you strictly stay with your schedule and that you don't compromise.

Combine Activities

Why just stick to one activity when you can save time by combining two? Housework and listening to music can be combined to save time. You can learn a new language while you exercise.

SUMMARY

- Evaluate your time schedule.
- Make your enjoyable and unenjoyable activities more productive.
- Create a task time chart.
- Get rid of time wasters. Manage time used for television, phone calls, visitors and shopping.
- If you are a perfectionist you will waste time.
- Get others to work for you to save time and become more successful.
- Do the activities you enjoy.
- Don't procrastinate by delaying what you can do now.
- Plan your entire day, combine activities and use scraps of time.
- Write everything down in a calendar or diary and create deadlines for all activities.

You can watch a video while you run on a treadmill. The choice is up to you, but make the best use of your time by combining non-conflicting activities.

Even Scraps Of Time Can Be Productive

Every minute of your day should be converted into productive time. Even small amounts of time can be used. Create a list of things you can do if you have a spare 10 to 15 minutes. The time you spend waiting in a dentist's office could be used to read magazines. The time waiting in line could be used to make phone calls. The time you are held up in traffic can be used to do something. Even your lunch or break time can be useful to you. Take out that magazine you want to read, make phone calls or do small chores for ten to fifteen minutes. You can even tour a park or catch up on chores with extra spare time.

Create Deadlines For All Activities

Deadlines should be placed in your schedule

165

for all of your activities. A set time will help you to stop wasting time with your daily activities. Make sure that you are doing your chores, activities and tasks within the specified time. Just to conserve time, see if you can do the same activities more quickly. Use a stopwatch and time your activities. You may be able to wash your car in 30 minutes instead of one hour. You may be able to mow the lawn in twenty minutes instead of one hour. Long-range goals should also have deadlines placed on them.

Don't Procrastinate

If you know you have to do something, then do it now. Don't wait until the last minute to start your projects and tasks. Start on your objectives and tasks as soon as you know what they are. Don't procrastinate. If you don't feel you are ready to start, start anyways. If you think your work will be incomplete, don't put it off and do what you can today. You will feel good about yourself later if you don't procrastinate. Always try to keep an open schedule by doing the things and activities TODAY that you plan to do tomorrow.

CONCLUSION

The secret of making money lies in successful goal-setting, decision-making, problem-solving, time management and the ability to handle adversity. Mastering these simple skills can get you ahead in life. Study these skills and use them so that you can benefit from using your subconscious mind or what I call, *"your hidden potential to get rich"* Many people that have had financial problems have used the methods in "Novanetics" to become rich. You can too.

Chapter Twenty Four

How To Win People Over

To earn the wealth that you want, you will need to win people over. You will need success qualities to win people over. All people want to be rewarded, liked and loved. What does it take to win a person over to your point of view? I am going to give you a list of things that attract people to others, and a list of things people find unpleasant. Use these qualities wisely, in order to win people over with the power of your subconscious mind. .

THESE PERSONALITY TRAITS WIN PEOPLE OVER

Give Praise

Everybody enjoys being praised. People will like and admire you if you praise them. People look for approval of themselves from others. You should only praise people when they deserve praise. If you praise people when they don't deserve it, or if you praise people too much, you will lose your credibility and they may take advantage of you. Some people get overly confident and become arrogant when you give them too much. Don't exaggerate your praise. Just make honest statements. Make the praise as warm and sincere as you can. Praise people when they deserve it and they in turn will help you become successful.

Always Show Appreciation

Everybody wants approval and recognition for what they have accomplished. If someone helps you in any way, tell them how much you appreciate what they have done. Tasks that a person performs for you may not be repeated if you don't show appreciation. Many tasks are duties that should be done well, so why show appreciation when a person does what they are supposed to do. It may motivate them to do more and even do better.

Some people don't like giving appreciation to people who get arrogant. When you show too much appreciation you might get people asking for raises and promotions. Don't overdo your show of gratitude or you may seem insincere. Be genuine. Here are some examples of how you can best state your appreciation of others:

"I really appreciate the way you worked."
"Thank you very much for helping me out."
"You are very good at writing reports."
"I want to tell you how much it means to me that you worked on my wall.";
"You were very nice to buy this card," etc.

Care About People

Care about people and be empathetic about their needs. Empathetic means to understand their feelings. Care about people and people will care about you. People are concerned about themselves, and it is important for them to feel that others also care about them. People feel important when others care about them. Helping people get through daily trials in their life and sharing in their victories that they have won, makes people feel that you care about them. If you want people to care about you, you must care about them.

Be Confident

Confidence is an excellent quality to have. Most people admire and love confident people because they are good role models, and these people help others become successful. Confident people have good paying jobs, they get the right education and they have good families. Confident people step forward and do the right things in life that makes them successful and wealthy. Be confident with yourself. If you are not confident with yourself, people will not be confident in you. People admire and respect confident people. If you show others doubt, they will treat you with doubt. Be sure of yourself and play down your insecurities. Put your head up high and be confident.

SHOW PEOPLE THESE SUCCESS QUALITIES

Be Diplomatic

Everyone appreciates people who are polite and discreet and are able to tell the truth nicely. Be nice when you say something distasteful. Don't be angry and upset when you say negative things. Always be firm and direct, but you must say what is on your mind to get the desired action. Some people are just good at telling people the truth nicely. The best way to learn these qualities is from others. Study someone you would like to be like and learn how they conduct themselves. Always be firm and direct.

Share The Credit

When others have helped you accomplish something, share the credit with them, even if their contributions were not as great as yours. You will be surprised how generously people react towards you when you share credit with them. People will like you more when you do this because it is giving them something they earned. Giving another credit, is like giving a person a gift. Like with all gifts, if a person has earned a gift then you can give them a gift. If you give a gift to a person who hasn't earned it, they may take advantage of you and others.

Treat Small Things With Importance

Some problems may seem small to you, but they may mean a great deal to others. Don't ignore other people's problems, no matter how small. Certain small problems have a greater significance to them then you might imagine. Problems like giving rides, lifting objects, fixing things, helping move, seem small, but they are important to others. Help others solve their problems. Treating small problems with importance shows other people you care.

BEING SUCCESSFUL BY KNOWING THE TRUTH

Give People Your Undivided Attention

Everybody wants to feel important and special. To make a person feel important you must give them your undivided attention when communicating with them. Eliminate all distractions and be sure to have good eye contact. Good body language is also good. When you are communicating with another person, give them your complete, undivided attention. This also helps you understand their message.

Listen To The Other Person's Story

With a few good questions, in many cases, the other person will tell you everything you what to know. As the other person is telling you their side of the story, they will also realize what they have done. They will be able to uncover the true cause for their mistake. This is like psychological therapy. Once you and the other person understand the true cause, a remedy can be sought to settle your differences.

Use Empathy To Find Out The Truth

Try to find out as much as you can about the situation. If you are at fault, the other person may not know how to tell you. The only way you will be able to solve a problem is if you know exactly what has happened. Use empathy to discover the truth. Ask yourself questions, and see if you can answer them. Put yourself in the other person's position and visualize the situation from their point of view. Look at all of the facts carefully and

168

objectively. If you have a bad feeling then shy away if you have a good feeling then continue using empathy or your own feelings to get to the truth.

Get Advice From Other People

It is a good habit to ask others for advice. One you have talked over a problem or a situation that you have with another person consult with people you know. Explain the problem and the solution then ask the supportive people in your life what they think. Two or three heads are better than one. Get a second and third opinion and settle your differences with other people.

SUCCESS SECRETS AFTER MISTAKES ARE ADMITTED

Point Out A Person's Mistakes Indirectly

I sometimes like to blurt out accusations of wrongdoings, even in public. It does in many cases, pull apart relationships. Don't point a finger at anyone or openly blame anyone for making a mistake, especially around other people in a social setting. Use vague questions to get the other person to tell you what has happened and what they have done. This lessens any resentment they would feel if accusations were made incorrectly. Don't make remarks about personal abilities, intelligence, etc., even if the mistake was caused by the other person. The technique for constructive questioning is covered in a previous chapter.

Tell The Other Person What They Must Hear

Don't tell the other person what they want to hear, tell them what they must hear to improve their lives. Many people ruin their lives by doing the wrong things. You could easily make their lives better by telling them the truth or what they must hear. If you think they should be told something, tell them. You can tell people things like, "you love them", "admire them", "dislike their actions", "enjoy their company" and "they should change their attitude. Their behavior is despicable." When you tell someone what they must hear, tell it to them in a positive, constructive way so that they will benefit from your honesty.

Admit Your Mistakes

When you admit your own mistakes, people more readily accept you pointing out their errors. This makes it easier for people to admit to their mistakes. Telling others that you have made the same mistakes they have, and that you will help them by showing them how you solved similar situations. This makes them feel better about their own mistakes. Tell them, "I've made that same mistake many times, I know how it feels. I'll show you how I solved the same problem." "I have done this too, let me tell you what I did."

Make Them See The Problem Without Pointing The Finger

You don't have to point a finger at someone to get a problem solved, like saying, "You are the one who did it….. Or saying, "Tell me if Sid took the money … Or saying, "Why did you go to that house on 5th and Birch … ….. Have a conference with the person with whom you are experiencing problems. Tell them of your problem without mentioning any names or specifically saying who you are talking about. Just tell them the simple details of the problem without giving specific details, like names and addresses. This type of criticism is so indirect that, in many cases, it alone could solve the problem. It causes the other person to realize the problem and solve part of it or all of the problem, for you.

AVOID THESE HABITS THAT MAKE PEOPLE DISLIKE YOU

Don't Put People Down

Putting a person down can be very damaging to your relationship with that person. People feel degraded when called stupid, crazy, weird, dumb etc. Don't put people down, even if they are not present. If you do put them down, the word will get back to them, and you will look bad to others. You will have to try harder to get other people's respect and loyalty. You may lose the admiration of friends and family members when you do this. Always talk about people positively or in a constructive way. If you don't like someone and you know you will put them down, don't say anything about them to others, unless you think it is necessary. You will be amazed at the social advantage this gives you.

Don't Be Concerned With Your Interests Only

There is nothing wrong with caring about and looking out for yourself as long as you don't become entirely preoccupied with yourself. When you are preoccupied, you will seem arrogant to others. People resent selfishness in others. Try to make your concern for others more noticeable than your concern for yourself. Tell people that; You care about ……..and you are willing to ………for them, but you do want …., You understand their needs, and you give……..to them, but you need …... People will recognize and admire your generosity. Make sure others know you look out for them as well as yourself.

Don't Expect Others To Provide For You

The world is full of people in need and if you help them, many or some of them will return the favor and help you, some will not, but that's okay. If you have the time, try to do kind things for people you know, just to show you care, and it doesn't have to be money-oriented. It is the thought that counts and not the gift.

If you are unwilling to go out of your way for others, don't expect them to go out of their way for you. Doing things like, giving them things, , attend to their needs, driving them, shop for them, or doing other things for them are things you could expect them to do for you. Set the first example, by helping others on a regular basis, so they may help you in the future. If you help others, they will help you in return.

Don't "Show Up" Others

When you "show up" others, or degrade them, you do it at their expense. Showing up people in front of others takes away their self-respect. Degrading others makes them look bad and ruins their reputation. If you are better than others, they will know it. Putting other people down is unnecessary. Constructive criticism is better. You don't have to degrade or show up others to make yourself look better than them. Pick people that you admire in your life.

HOW TO MEET PEOPLE AND MAKE FRIENDS

People enjoy the company of others, and everyone wants to meet people with whom they can have close and lasting friendships. Here are some steps to follow if you want to become more successful at meeting people and making friends:

Waving, Shaking Hands & Saying Hello

Waving is a great way to break the ice. It is an excellent way to introduce yourself and a great way to say goodbye. Wave at people you meet and people you want to know. Make it a point to wave at people on a regular basis. Do this and other people will like you more. Don't forget to wave at people as much as you can. Wave, wave and wave.

What is the first thing you say when you answer the telephone. It is Hello. What is the first thing you could say to a person, when you first meet them? It is hi or hello. You can even say hi or hello to total strangers. When first meeting people say either hello or hi. It is a great way to start off a conversation. If you are at an event and you want to add a positive atmosphere, try saying hi and hello and even waving to liven people's spirits.

Try to always say something nice when you first meet a person. A good thing to start a conversation with any stranger is a comment on the time of day. When first meeting someone, and it is the morning. *Say, "Good morning."* If it is the afternoon, then *say, "Good afternoon."* If it is the evening then *say, "Good evening."* If it is the evening and time to go you would *say, "Good night."*

Try to ask a person you know (or sometimes meet) how they are doing. It is very polite to do this and it shows concern for other people. People like other people that care. Other people appreciate people that are concerned with their health and well-being. Here are many examples of statements you must use with people you know (or sometimes with people you meet). *"Hi, how are you doing?"* *"Hi, how have you been?"* *"I haven't seen you in some time, what have you been doing?"* Regarding Family: *How is your mother or father doing?"* *"How is your family doing?"* *"How has your family been?"* Regarding Health *"How is your health?"* *"How is the health of your family members?"* *"I hope your health is good."* Regarding Work. *"How is your job?"* *"How is work coming along?"* *"Are you still working at the same company?"*

If it is a holiday, or a special day then say good things to others. If it is Christmas, then say *"Merry Christmas"* to other people. If it was a Jewish holiday, you would say in Hebrew, *"Day Good"* If it is Easter, then say *"Happy Easter."* If it is a birthday, say *"Happy Birthday."* If it is an Anniversary, say *"Happy Anniversary"* Always tell people that are celebrating an occasion, the *right salutation.*

Shaking hands is a great way to introduce yourself to another person? Every business meeting starts with handshakes and every introduction could start with a handshake. A great way to start a meeting even with a stranger is with a handshake. Make it a habit to shake other people's hands or to rub knuckles when you first meet other people. Consider hugging. Hugging is good also.

Practice making other people feel more important by waving at them, by saying hello and hi and by asking how they are or asking about their health and saying good morning, good afternoon, and good evening and saying joyful statements about a holiday or special day. .

Introduce Yourself

When you first meet your prospect, say hello and shake their hand (or rub knuckles). This gesture is courteous and needed for all introductions. If you want to meet a person say hello, how are you, my name is _____, then shake their hand.

Let your prospect know who they are dealing with. Visualize them as a friendly, considerate and kind person. Give them information that will make them receptive to you. Make the information benefit-oriented for them. Try phrases like:

● I overheard what you were saying, and I was really fascinated by how much you know about……..
● You write very neatly, it shows you are accurate and artistic in your writing, I know …….
● Your smart pants and shirt go well together, you are a sharp dresser, I can …….
● I really like that dress on you, it brings out your pretty blue eyes, would you …...

Ask Leading Questions

Ask the person you are talking to a leading question. A leading question is one that provokes more of a response than a mere "yes " or "no." Here are some examples:

● Do you attend a lot of these charity balls?
● How do you know the host?
● Do you work at the same company, as …..?
● What do you do during the day?

The other person's responses to these leading questions will let you know if they are interested in you or not. If you try to sell yourself to the person immediately, you will get resistance. If you push too hard or don't ask your leading questions with true interest and sincerity, you will get negative answers, and the conversation may quickly come to an end. Try to make the person feel that you want their consent to expand on an idea that may be of interest to them. What you actually want is their consent to get to know them better. If the other person shows interest in you and begins to communicate with you, feel free to go a step further.

Open Yourself Up

Once the other person opens up to you, you can begin to open yourself up to them. You have their attention, and that person is interested in you. Once you feel comfortable in their presence, tell them what your strongest attributes are, the ones that will appeal to them most. Financial terms are always good. You could say, "I work 9 to 5, every day, except weekends and I earn a good salary and I own my own home in the eastern part of the city." If you get a positive response, you have successfully sold yourself to them. At this point, you can feel free to further develop your new friendship. If the person is unresponsive, it may be that you sound pompous and boastful to them or they are not interested. In this case, you should lower your volume a bit and sound as humble and sincere as possible.

Make The Final Close

Determine the purpose of the introduction and then make the final close to complete your goal. Sometimes you are at a function and you just want to socialize or quickly know a person. You see a person and you want to sell them a product or you want to get to know them quickly. In that case you can get right to the point and try to close the sale. There is a greater chance of rejection with a final close, but you can try it anyways. Here are some examples of a close.

- I don't usually bring up business at these functions. I can help your property. Here is my business card. Call me with any questions.
- I have been watching you. I think you are cute. Would you like to go out? This Friday at 6PM is fine.
- I would really like to go out with you and get to know you. Can I get your phone number so I can call you? I have a pen here.
- I am in the insurance business. I can call you with a quote that could be lower than your insurance. Can I get your business card, so I can call?

Make The Introduction

If you go to a function where there are many people. You could ask another person to introduce you to a person of your choice. The person you "ask for the introduction", doesn't even have to know the person you want to meet. You could start out, with, " I come to these functions on a regular basis. Could you help me with something? I want to get to know that person across the room." Could you go there and introduce me to that person. The person you send should say, "My friend who is …… would like to meet you ……would you…..

How To Handle Negative Feedback

Be prepared for some objections from the other person in the course of your conversation. Respond to each of their objections and try to agree with some part of them. Don't linger or argue over an objection, accept the other person's point of view without forcing your opinions upon them. Make sure that their objection is legitimate, not just an argumentative contest. First, agree that you can understand the other person's objection. Then ask the other person if there are any other reasons for objecting to your point of view. At

this point, the other person will tell you any underlying reasons for their objection. The "Yes, but..." technique works wonderfully with real objections. For example:

- Yes, I can see why you feel that way, but I feel that you should work later hours.
- Yes, I understand how you feel, but you will have a good time going out with me.
- Yes, I understand your dislike, but I want you to find another line of work.
- Yes, I understand your situation, but I still think we should meet at 6PM at the Corner Inn.

Winning The Battle

This part is the easiest part of your whole person selling approach. At this point, give the other person a choice. Don't give them a choice of whether to take you on or not, give them a choice of how to take you on.

- Instead of asking, "Could I have your phone number?" say, "Do you have a pen, or would you like to use my pen to write down your phone number?"
- Instead of asking, "Do you want to work together?, say 'You will work on the floor plan section and I will work on the income rental section."
- Instead of asking, "Do you want to go out with me?" say, "Would you rather go to a movie or out dancing?"
- Instead of asking, "Do you want to buy the bicycle?, say, "Will you be paying with cash or credit card for the bicycle."

Visualize The Future Results

This is the final step to your person selling approach. This method of visualizing the end results is more powerful than the previous exercise. If you want to do heavy selling use this method. At this point explain to the other person the future benefits of agreeing with you. Don't ask them what they want. Assume that they have made your choice and are enjoying the benefits of saying yes. Let me give you some examples.

- Instead of asking, "Could I have your phone number?" say, "You will enjoy spending time

172

with me. We will tour the lakefront and we could also eat a seafood lunch by the beach. You will have a great time. What time do you want me to pick you up?"

- Instead of asking, "Do you want to work together?, say "You will have a great time working with me. My expertise in rental income is very good and I know you will learn a lot from me. When you work on the floor plan section, I will help you. Do you want to start working at 8AM or 9AM.
- Instead of asking, "Do you want to go out with me?" say, "I love movies and I know you will too. You would really enjoy the *Metropolis Being"* movie. We could be in the theater at the afternoon matinee which starts at 4PM? I'll even buy us popcorn. I can pick you up at 3PM. Will you be ready by three?"
- Instead of asking, "Do you want to buy the bicycle?, say, "You will be able to speed down the walkway on your new bike. You can turn on a dime and the brakes will stop you quickly. You will be buzzing around the walkway on this bike, feeling great and losing weight. Believe me your health will improve. You wouldn't want to be without this bike. I can throw in the car rack for $35, so you can take the bike home today. It comes in blue or gray. Do you want the blue or gray bike?"

Reward The Commitment

After you have gotten the other person to make some kind of commitment, summarize the proposition and reward the other person for accepting. An example of that is: "Thanks for giving me your phone number. I'm really looking forward to seeing you Sunday evening." "Thank you again, for meeting me on Thursday, I do look forward to seeing you."

YOUR APPEARANCE AND CLOTHES

People will like you if you dress well. If you look good then you are a good person. This is how everyone feels. It is true that many can trust a snappy dresser, but they can't trust a slob. The best clothes to wear, is not to dress too casual or too formal for men and women, but dress right in the middle. Try to wear nice shoes to all occasions.

SUMMARY

- Give people praise and show appreciation, only if people deserve these rewards.
- Care about other people and they will care about you.
- Learn the truth of others by listening and using empathy.
- When mistakes are admitted by others, tell people what they must hear to improve their lives.
- Being arrogant and only being concerned with yourself will make others dislike you.
- Wave and say hello to everyone you encounter or meet. Shake hands and introduce yourself and ask about their life and ask about their health.
- When first meeting another person, ask questions to get to know the other person.
- Determine the purpose of the introduction and then make the final close. When making the final close explain your situation, then ask for action.
- Your appearance and dress is very important when first meeting others.
- If you look bad others will think you are bad. If you look good others will think you are good.
- Give others the best positive impression with your appearance and clothes and you will succeed.

Some people judge other people by their shoes. Always try to dress conservatively without flashy colors. Men should be well groomed, trim nose hairs and shave every single day. They should splash on cologne and wear a tie to formal functions. If you don't like ties wear a thin tie. Women should make sure they look very neat and nice. Some perfume and clean skin is always desirable. Hair should not be in the face. Makeup should be subtle.

Make sure your clothes are clean, without stains and are not torn. Poor people own torn, stained, dirty clothes that are badly out of style. If you wear these type of clothes, other people will think you are poor and treat you worse than the other people or guests. If you dress like a poor person, even the security will have to keep an eye on you. The way you look is very important to everyone. If your appearance is bad then others will feel you are bad. Always look good and you will do good.

Dress your best and you will do great. When an event is formal and it is an important event with important people, then you should look your best and dress formal. Good fashion is a matter of choice. Wear nice looking clothes and people will like you. Give the best impression and dress well and look neat. Good appearance is always a must.

Being A Target

Some people that are rich purposely wear old jeans and out of style clothes. I've seen many of them do this. Showing that you have money is always good, but showing off money, does have a way of ruining some relationships, due to bad deeds. Don't dress well or wave your cash around, in ghetto or poor neighborhoods, because you might be robbed. It could happen in other neighborhoods. All people think that good dressers with sharp clothes have money, which is good for the wealth crowd, but terrible for you in a poor ghetto neighborhood, because you may get robbed. You can become a target for your money if you showoff your clothes and money, so be careful.

Getting Along Better With Others

Getting along better with others is a matter of choice. Follow the principles outlined in this book and you will become a more influential person. Not only will other people admire and like you, but you admire and like yourself. Your choice to become a new person will be one of the best choices you'll ever make. Learn these simple principles so that you can influence people and win them over.

Chapter Twenty Five

Persuade People To Your Point Of View

Criticism is the expression of the disproval of others or things that is based on the perception of faults or mistakes. People that criticize are always blaming and looking for faults in others. Criticism is one way to persuade people to think and act a certain way. If you are expressive and honest you must criticize objectionable behavior in others, in order to solve problems. Like scolding, criticism can modify the behavior of other people. If people do things we don't like, we disapprove of their behavior by criticizing. The word "criticism" has a negative connotation in our society, but criticism is actually very useful. In this chapter we'll discuss criticism, which should be considered constructive persuasion, to solve problems. Follow the different methods when you wish to criticize constructively.

CRITICISM

Before you criticize someone, be absolutely sure that what the individual did was wrong. Know the person you are criticizing. Make sure you understand the person's character. If you know the person and their characteristics well, and you know they'll never change, you should still try to communicate to them. It is difficult to change habits of individual that are not capable of changing. Examples are stuttering, walking slow, not able to hear, etc. The reason for criticizing an individual is so you both benefit from the improved relationship. It is important that the person be bettered by your criticism. I have set several guidelines for you to follow when criticizing another person. If you follow these guidelines, you will find people following your suggestions.

Follow the following six steps to constructively criticize another person.

1) Understand the purpose of the criticism and write down the criticism in advance.
2) Make an appointment or time to speak to the other person, if you have difficulties communicating.
3) Tell them what the problem is and what both parties can do to solve the problem.
4) Don't accuse the person or degrade them when criticizing and try to add humor.
5) End your criticism with praise and thank them for listening.

CONSTRUCTIVE CRITICISM

Understand The Criticism And Write It Down

If you are having difficulties getting along with another person a problem may develop. The problem will get worse and worse over time. Go over the problem, you have with another person and evaluate what you want to tell them, to resolve the problem. Write down what you believe is the problem and what you believe will solve the problem. Write the problem, then the solutions in steps, so you understand what to say when you give constructive criticism. An example of the problem is: We yell at each other when we talk about my daughter. The solution is: We must both calmly listen to each other, then express our feelings about the situation.

Begin Criticism With Sincere Praise And Admiration

This is one method that some people use when criticizing. Everyone needs recognition of their strong points, as well as criticism of their faults. Begin your criticism by defining a person's strengths. Let them know how they please you and how much their actions mean to you. Then tell them that despite their strong points, there is one behavior you think they should change. After discussing their unfavorable behavior, end the conversation with more praise and admiration for their strengths.

Examples Of Praise With Criticism:

1)   He is a good boy, but he loses his temper so often.

2)   She is a pleasure to be with, but she takes things that aren't hers.

3)   He is such good hearted, but he tends to get angry.

4)   He is the finest person I know, but he tends to break the rules.

5)   She is a great person to be with, but she has a tendency to be loud and obnoxious.

Set A Time To Talk

You don't have to set a time to talk to another person. But it is a good method to resolve certain difficult problems. People use this method, if it is difficult to talk or if you are very busy and don't have time to talk, or if the criticism will be a lengthy talk that takes up a lot of time.

Tell a person in advance that you want to talk to them. Write down the time both of you agree on and the location. The appointment time you set should be a time that is convenient for both of you and it is a time that both of you are free. Remind that person to meet you at a desired location at the time you both agreed. Before the appointment, first understand what you are going to say and practice your criticism.

Add A Story Or Explanation For Difficult

Situations

If the situation is a tough situation that is difficult to talk about, then you may need to add a story or an explanation of the situation. If the problem is loud yelling, then you would give a story about another person that yells. If the problem is loud yelling, then you would give an explanation of the times both of you have yelled at each other. Giving an explanation will make it easier to relay your point of view. It is easier to communicate in difficult talks when you add a story or explanation. If you are criticizing a common problem that you both have talked about before then, get right to the point and clearly state the problem and the solution. If you don't know that solution, you could ask for a solution that will solve both of your problems.

Get Right To The Point

Overall, when criticizing someone, get right to the point and tell them specifically what their undesirable behavior is. This way you will both have an understanding of the situation. If you don't tell them exactly what they must work on, they may be able to correct their behavior. Telling them specifically what their undesirable behavior is, and making sure they understands why you are criticizing them, is the most important step in learning to criticize constructively. Later you can tell them, what both of you can do to solve the problem. If you don't have a solution to the problem, then ask for a solution and then discuss the solution. If you don't feel good about the solution, tell the other party that you disagree with their solution.

Add Humor To Your Criticism

There are times when you feel that you must criticize a fault that a person has. There is no way around you telling the other person that they are stupid for .... or incompetent for doing .... Some people put aside the criticism which is not good communication. You must talk about certain situations. In these cases it is better to use humor to tell the other person how foolish they are. If you must criticize a person's faults then follow two steps. First, laugh as you talk and you could change your voice tone as you laugh and talk, this is while you criticize the person's faults. Practice laughing as you criticize. Second, increase the description (in words) of the foolish act that you know. Don't say angrily, "You spilled that paint and ruined the floor." Do say (as you laugh), "You spilled my latex white paint, by kicking the paint can. The paint is all over the tile floor and the floor is ruined, ruined, ruined. It will cost you under a hundred (as you laugh)." If you laugh as you talk it is easier to criticize or talk to people in difficult situations.

Scolding Without Humor

There are times when you don't want to be as funny. You may want to criticize different people's characteristics or faults with a harshness so they understand the point. People more readily change when you scold them. You may be funny when you laugh at other people's faults, but many people will not take your criticism seriously. If your intention is to scold, then if you don't criticize people's behaviors with harshness, you can't expect them to consider seriously changing those behaviors.

End Your Criticism With Praise And Admiration

It is important for a person to know that you are criticizing them to help them. You mustn't make them feel that you are criticizing them because you want to hurt their feelings. End your criticism by restoring their self-esteem. When you've finished your criticism, thank them and tell them how much you appreciate their strong points.

Here is an example:

1) Don't yell at people, be calmer, after all you are the most liked person here.
2) Don't you dare go through that purse, leave it alone? You are always so good with other people's property.
3) You are yelling again, say it calmly to me, you look handsome when you do that.
4) Put back what isn't yours, you don't want them to accuse the best employee in the firm.
5) Don't ridicule him, it isn't good to do that to a man with a good heart.

TECHNIQUES TO USE WHILE

CRITICIZING

Criticize Only When Necessary And One Behavior At A Time

If you criticize a person too much, the purpose behind your criticism will be lost. The effectiveness of your criticism may be weakened when it is overused, and the other person may begin to resent you if you don't give them time to change. Only criticize when you feel it is necessary. If there are several undesirable behaviors you want the other person to change, criticize only one at a time.

Never Say "Never" Or "Always" When Criticizing

Words like "never" and "always" tend to put people on the defensive when they're used to describe their behaviors. The word "always" gives people the impression that their faults are worse than they are. "Usually" or "sometimes" are better words for describing people's behaviors and this shouldn't put them on the defensive. The word "never" is often used in place of "seldom." There is a big difference between "seldom" and "never," and people will often resent the word "never" when it is used to describe their behaviors. People will always react less defensively to the words "usually" and "seldom."

Criticize A Person At The Time Of The Act

The best time to criticize someone is right after the unfavorable act is committed. If you are unable to correct a person's actions as they do something wrong. You can also do so later when you're alone with that person and you can discuss the situation openly. An example is; "You fell on purpose." Or "You deliberately told him." Or "You took it when I told you not to."

Give A Person Expectations To Live Up To, Not A Reputation To Live a Down

Always give people positive expectations to live up to, not negative reputations to live down. This is an excellent way to motivate people to work for you. Give people standards to work up to. Establish high standards, and they will work up to them. Constructively tell people what you know they can achieve. Your confidence in them increases their confidence in themselves. The expectations you place on others will be realized by them. If you tell someone what you want them to do and then you say questionable remarks like, "I don't know if you can do it," "You probably won't do it" then they will not be motivated to do more. If you tell them, "I know you can do it," they will live up to your expectations. Here are some examples of phrases you can use: "I know I can count on you to do well because of your great job experience."; "I know you can do a great job because you are so good at …….." You could have gotten a college degree because you are so bright. You are such a good person; you could easily have been married to a pretty girl. With your type of job skills, you could have earned $62,000 a year. An expectation with praise works wonderfully.

Don't Get Angry

Other people may frustrate and anger you. Losing your temper with another person could hurt you and them. Anger and frustration will never solve your problems, reasoning and logic will. Don't let personal feelings and resentment get in your way. Be cheerful and smile and laugh to avoid anger and ugly tempers. Keep trying to do this so that you are calm and reasonable as you communicate.

If you feel the urge to be angry, it is better to wait before you let out your anger and embarrass yourself, or you could just walk away or do something else. If you can't avoid the angry confrontation then use the following technique. If you feel angry or frustrated, count from one to five and take slow breaths as you count to five. That is one, two, three, four and five. This should give you time to release your anger and become calm and collect.

Criticism With Comparison Can Create Resentment

Comparing one person to another unfavorably will cause that person to resent you. Try not to make any type of comparison that will put a person down. Critical comparisons that make a person look good have the opposite effect. "You are not as good as Sid", create bad feelings. Try saying "You are the best person here, but Sid is

better at accounting. An example of critical comparisons is, "Judy is better than you," may create bad feelings. Try saying "Judy is a better card player then you, but you are a fun person to be with."

Don't Criticize People In Front Of Others

Criticizing someone is pointing out their faults. Giving criticism helps another person. I know I like getting criticism for my work for it helps me to learn and do better. I use the criticism constructively to improve my work. However, public criticism will cause people to feel degraded and embarrassed, and they will resent you for doing that to them. If you criticize someone, criticize them privately and constructively, this way you don't make them look bad in front of others. It is better to criticize a person at the time of the act. Tell the person at the time of the act, that you want to talk to them. An example is: "Could you step outside so we can talk." Or "Can I have a word with you."

Say Something Good Then Criticize

Use the technique where you say something good about them, then you add the criticism. Do this and you will have more friends. Here are examples, "You are the best salesman at work, but you should stop selling those securities. "You are the best dancer here, but you are clumsy and you broke the glass vase as you danced." "You are the best looking person here, but you have to stop being so pushy." "You earn the highest commissions at work, but don't flash your money in the air." "You are a very good listener, but you yell too much."

HOW TO PUNISH & CRITICIZE

You must only punish people to a degree relative to the wrongdoing. If you go overboard, the people you punish will resent you. If you don't punish people for their "bad behavior", they will take advantage of you. The best way to punish someone is to have the other person set the punishment. Ask the other person what should be done to them because of what they have done. Some of the time, the person will give themselves a more severe punishment than you would give. In this case, lower the punishment. They will look upon you favorably for it. If a person names a punishment for themselves that is too weak to suit their wrongdoing, say, "I'm sorry, but that is not what I had in mind. I think that .this ...... is fair."

Improving Other People's Actions With Praise

People increase or decrease their actions depending upon how others react to them. Praise is a strong reward. The best way to get people to do what you want them to do, is to praise them for their progress. By rewarding them with praise for their improvements, you will get better results from them. Remember, that too much praise and reward tends to spoil a person, if they didn't earn it. Try to be as honest and sincere when praising.

Criticize Again, If Necessary

You may have to speak to a person more than once if there has been very little improvement in their behavior. If you speak to them a second time, you must be harder on them. If you have to speak to them more than two or three times, you must review your criticizing skills. You must be tougher. Again, be sure that you don't criticize a person for a behavior that they cannot change.

HOW TO DEAL WITH USELESS CRITICISM

Some criticism is in poor taste. We must often deal with unconstructive criticism, such as, "You look terrible today," or "You don't know anything, you idiot." Don't let this type of criticism bother you. When you find yourself faced with such useless criticism, follow these steps:

Agree With The Facts

Carefully evaluate the criticism the other person presents you with, and be sure to agree with them on the facts, if they are true. In the examples you could reply, "I haven't been feeling too well lately," and "No, I don't know much about this subject." When you respond to the other person, answer only respond to what they actually say, not what they imply.

Answer The Criticism

Stay calm and collected throughout the conversation. Don't lose your temper. The only way you will feel degraded is if you take criticism personally, and not constructively. Don't waste their time and your emotions by reading more into their criticism than is actually stated. By accepting criticism constructively, not personally, you won't need to defend your pride or attack the other person. An example is; A person tells you, "You are a fool to drop the plate." You would ignore "You are a fool" and you would say, "I walked by the table and the tablecloth must have slipped."

Accept Your Mistakes

If you make a mistake, accept it, but don't feel guilty. If you are in error, apologize sincerely and take any actions necessary to remedy the situation. If you do this, there is no reason for a teary, dramatic apology. Such scenes will only embarrass you more and make the other person feel uncomfortable as well.

HOW TO GAIN THE MOST FROM CRITICISM

When you get constructive criticism, try to gain the most from it. Constructive criticism is one of the best ways to mold yourself into a better person. The following steps will show you how to get the most from constructive criticism.

Ask For Feedback

Find out exactly what others object to about you. If someone tells you that they don't like your behavior, find out exactly what they don't like about your behavior. Be very persistent, and insist that the person be explicit (specific) in their criticism. Ask the other person what you can do to change the objectionable action in the future. Vague criticism is worthless to you.

Use Deduction To Find Your Faults

If a person criticizes you vaguely, but can't bring themselves to tell you clearly what that person disapproves of, then consider faults that others have criticized you for in the past. Often, the same faults will displease different people. This may be the only way to find out what displeases the other person.

Don't Be Defensive

If you act defensively, you will not be able to benefit from constructive criticism. Don't be sarcastic or hostile toward the other person. Remember that the other person is criticizing you. Try to better yourself and better your relationship with them. The purpose of relationships is that people get along with each other and can work together well.

DEALING WITH DIFFICULT RELATIONSHIPS WITH PEOPLE

When all else fails and a relationship starts to go bad and if you continue the relationship you may be hurt or even injured, then you must find alternatives to remedy the situation.

Contact Relatives And Friends

Contact relatives of either the people in your conflict or your own relatives and talk to them about the problems you are having in a relationship. Call up either your or their mother or father, brother, sister or even older children and explain the situation, believe me, they will look into the problem and resolve some of it. Don't forget to also contact either their or your good friends, or even distant relatives, they can easily help resolve the problem you are having and also get advice. I always use this method of communicating with others and it really works.

Regular Therapy Or Counseling

If you can't score with their relatives and friends, you must find another solution to resolve the problem that you have with other people. Therapy or counseling is a great solution. You can get counseling at your local church or synagogue. A priest, pastor or rabbi can help you and your family or friends with all situations. Regular counseling where one party is a moderator is good because it helps many people communicate and settle their differences. In private therapy which is expensive, a therapist could talk to one to two people and get out, deep reasons for difficulties. It really works. Get therapy or counseling, like marriage counseling, or family

SUMMARY

- People that criticize are always blaming others and are looking for faults in others.
- Criticism is helpful in solving problems.
- If you are expressive and honest, then go with your feelings and criticize objectionable behavior in others.
- Use praise with criticism to make criticism more positive.
- Add humor to your criticism and end criticism with praise.
- Try to be fair and unbiased and not angry when being critical of faults and mistakes.
- Punish people for their "wrong actions" or they will take advantage of you.
- When listening to useless criticism, reply to the criticism and not the attacks.
- To get the most out of criticism, don't be defensive and ask for feedback.
- When dealing with difficult situations, contact friends, relatives and associates for solutions to the problem.
- If the problem is severe, counseling or therapy can help the problem.
- Take the problem to superior court, small claims court or arbitration to remedy the wrong doings and to recover financial damages.

counseling with problem people in your life. Working with a licensed therapist, priest, pastor, rabbi or councilor could really help you.

Physical Violence

Yelling and hitting to resolve a dispute is unnecessary, but happens in many cases. Sometimes it can't be avoided because you are in the wrong situation or the wrong place. People can be hurt and property can be damaged, but some say it was worth the effort, because it did resolve some issues. While this is considered unacceptable behavior, this type of behavior does take place in many households. Some families may end up in jail or family court for this type of behavior. A lesser punishment is regular therapy sessions to resolve the differences.

Take the problem court And Sue

If all else fails, you can take them to court and sue them. You have a choice of superior court or small claims court. Small claims court is for claims under $10,000. While superior court is for judgments more than $10,000, but it is expensive, due to attorney fees and court costs. The other party could be liable for your court costs and attorney fees, so Superior Court could be free, if you can collect. Remember, even if you get a judgment for a large sum of money you still have to collect the money. Collecting the money may be difficult.

Many attorneys will take your case for free, if you are due money and the party you are suing has substantial money. Attorneys may gladly take the accident, divorce and even product liability cases. You can contact an attorney to determine if they will take your legal case. The Superior Court Judges preside over cases involving misdemeanors, contract disputes, liability, and other actions. The Superior Court also has jurisdiction over cases involving divorce, title to land, felonies involving jury trials, and even death penalty cases.

Small Claims Court

For small cases involving about $10,000 or less in damages, take your problems to small claims court. If you are on a budget you will find the costs being very low. You can defend yourself or sue a plaintiff. A small claims court is cheap, simple, and quick and the judgment you get is binding in all courts. You can attach wages and levy bank accounts with the small claims judgment. If it is a claim under $10,000, go to small claims court for a quick and binding money judgment.

Settle Your Differences With Arbitration

If you want to resolve a claim outside the court system, you can try arbitration. Arbitration is usually for commercial cases and it is sometimes a clause in contracts to save money in case of a disagreement. Arbitration is an informal hearing where arbitrators help disagreeing parties resolve a dispute. The awards won from arbitration are legally binding on both sides and the judgments are enforceable in the courts. It can cost you a moderate amount. You can contact the American Arbitrators Association at website https://www.adr.org/Arbitration, or call to file a new case at 800-778-7879 or General Inquiry 800-778-7879

Chapter Twenty Six

Wealth Secrets To Removing Debt

"Novanetics" can definitely help you to become more prosperous. If you are debt, you must devise some plan to get out of the red. You can declare bankruptcy, but that will tarnish your credit and financial records. An alternative is a "wage-earner" plan which allows you to meet your debts methodically without bankruptcy. Remember, creditors hate bankruptcy because they may be left with no payments, but if you can't get on the wage-earner plan, there is another solution. Sit down with your creditors and negotiate a payment plan, it could be to pay them 20 percent of what you owe them. To them, 20 percent of what you owe is better than nothing. Tell them how much you can pay. Believe me, they will settle for less than the actual amount owed.

A wage-earner plan (Chapter 13 bankruptcy) lets individuals restructure their debts in order to repay their debts over a period of time. For the wage earners plan, you still owe the debts, but you can restructure the amount you owe to a lesser amount, in a payment plan over a period of time. You can also keep some of your assets with a wage-earner plan.

Wipe Out Debts Without Bankruptcy

In 1938, federal law established the wage-earner plan (Chapter 13 bankruptcy), and is now administered by the same branch of our judicial system that handles bankruptcy. To take advantage of the plan, you must be a wage earner and most of your income must come from your wages, regardless of how much you make. You can discharge any amount of your debt under this law.

Here's how it works: Call the nearest U.S. District Court and find out the name of the trustee who administers the wage-earner plan (Chapter 13 bankruptcy); make an appointment to see him. Bring to your appointment all relevant financial records, such as payment books, contracts, etc. The trustee will examine your finances and set up a plan by which a portion of your debts is paid over a three-year period. Within 3 days you can get relief from your debtors. You then make monthly payments to the trustee who, in turn, pays each of your creditors. You can also contact an attorney that can help you administer the wage-earner plan.

The Outcome

A possible side effect of the wage-earner plan (Chapter 13 bankruptcy) is the reduction of much of your debt, because a provision of your filing requires your creditors to appear in court. Statistics show that 40 percent of creditors fail to appear in court -- in this case, you owe only 60 percent of your creditors their claims. In some cases, none of your creditors will appear. If this happens, all your debts are wiped out, without the pain of bankruptcy. If some of your creditors do appear in court, the court allows you to divide your payments into smaller amounts to be paid over a three-year period. Once you file, you will stop bill collectors, law suits, judgments, assignments, seized bank accounts, and other actions against you and you can even negotiate to keep some of your assets in the final agreement. Indeed, in many cases, your credit rating may improve because you have made an honest effort to work with the lending parties to pay off your debts.

Your debt may be wiped out entirely if a creditor used deceptive trade practices to induce your purchase, as defined by the Uniform Commercial Code. You should also be aware that, under the Homestead Act, your residence may be exempted from levy to the extent determined by local law. This means that a certain amount of your home equity is except from creditors that have gotten a court judgment against you. The equity exempt limit which is determined by your state could be $25,000 to $50,000. Check with a lawyer or your local courthouse for more details.

Establishing credit

When first establishing credit, there are several things you should do:

Open a checking account at a bank. A checking account verifies that you have some dealings in the financial world; mortgage banks will almost certainly check how you've maintained your account, and most importantly, your average bank account balance.

Open as many charge accounts as you can. If any company will make you a loan, it is a department store, by means of a charge card. They know how closely their business is tied to charging. Use the charge cards liberally; making sure you will be able to pay off the accounts exactly according to the terms. You could consider a debit card only to establish credit. A debit card is easy to get and this type of card could help you establish your credit. The next few sections will show you how to get large amounts of money from credit cards.

Use a cosigner. This frequently used method allows someone with no credit to get a loan by relying on the good credit rating of someone else, like a parent. Banks are willing to risk the loan because the cosigner is just as liable for paying back the money as the true borrower.

Use a private loan company. These companies, such as Marcus, Lendingtree and Credible, are more willing than banks to take a risk when lending money; for that risk, they charge higher interest rates. Borrow up to your limit; pay it back religiously. https://www.marcus.com, , https://www.lendingtree.com, https://www.credible.com, https://www.us.hsbc.com. (Which was Household Finance)

FREE CREDIT BUREAU REPORTS

Contact the following credit bureaus to get a free credit report. You might even offer a credit report from all three credit bureaus.

Equifax
P.O. Box 740241
Atlanta, GA 30374
Web Site: https://www.equifax.com
Toll Free: (800) 685-1111
Toll Free Voice: 1-866-640-2273

Experian
P.O. Box 2104
Allen, TX 75013-2104
Web Site: https://www.experian.com
Toll Free: 1-888-397-3742
Toll Free Voice: 1-800-493-1058

TransUnion
P.O. Box 1000
Chester, PA 19022
800-888-4213
Toll Free Voice:1-800 916-8800
Web Site: https://www.transunion.com

METHODS OF GETTING CREDIT

If you want to establish credit at a fast, but sure pace, follow these instructions. Open a savings account, and deposit money on a regular basis. Soon after, open a checking account. Have no overdrafts. Pay your rent and utility bills on time. To eliminate or reduce the large deposit usually required by utilities, have your employer verify that you have worked for him for more than 18 months. If you apply for credit and are turned down, find out why. By law, the party that turned you down for credit must tell you why. When you find out why you were refused, improve that aspect of your credit history.

Buy things on lay-away plans and pay them off in a week or two. After doing this a few times, apply for credit at the stores, and make sure the credit officers know about your layaways. Apply for credit from all the stores you know. If you do establish credit, make all payments early and don't miss a single one. Make sure you can pay back all the debts you incur.

Protecting Your Credit

It is your job to protect your credit. Here is a list of what you should do to protect it: If your loan application is rejected, ask if the reason is your credit report. If it is, get that credit report and correct any errors on it, no matter what time and effort are required. When the corrections are made, reapply for the loan. If disaster strikes -- and you become ill or lose your job -- and can't make payments, tell your banker. Don't lie and hide.

Know the laws that protect you:

1) Fair Debt Collection Practices Act, which prohibits creditors from using false or misleading threats or abuse and harassment.
2) Fair Credit Reporting Act, which allows you to get a copy of your credit report and correct errors.
3) Truth in Lending Act, which makes lenders detail exactly how much the loan is going to cost you.
4) Equal Credit Opportunity Act, which forbids lenders denying you credit because of your age, sex, race or marital status.

Get Credit Cards

If you establish credit using the above procedure, you should have no trouble getting any credit card you want, but there are still a few guidelines you should follow to ensure you have no difficulties:

1) Apply for pre-paid debit cards or debit cards. Some banks will issue you a debit card when you open an account with them. Debit cards are easy to get and they can establish your credit.
2) Apply for department store cards. Purchase something, and then pay the balance off when it comes due. The easiest department store cards to get are Macys and Victoria's Secret.
3) Apply for gasoline credit cards using your department store cards as references.
4) Apply for bank cards, such as MasterCard, Visa, Discover and American Express.

5) Apply for entertainment and travel cards and any other card you can get.

The Corporate Method Of Raising Money

You can get money you need by forming a corporation. Besides being easy to form, there are many advantages. For instance, you can raise money by selling corporate stock. You can be authorized to sell one million shares of stock at no par value when creating the charter for the corporation.

Let me show you an example of how your corporation will work. First, issue one million shares of stock once you are authorized to do so. Keep 300,000 shares for yourself and reserve another 300,000 for future sales to the public. The remaining 400,000 shares should be issued for public sale at about $1 per share. If you sell 100,000 shares, you will have raised $80,000 after deducting a 20 percent broker's fee. In time, your stock may go up to $5 per share. Your stock that was worth $300,000 will then be worth $1.5 million. You will have quadrupled the worth of your stock. And this doesn't include the stock that you reserved for future sale.

You may find this example hard to believe, but the truth is, people just like you make it work. If you have a worthwhile venture, this may be your best option. I must point out one drawback of this method. You must go through the Security And Exchange Commission in order to incorporate. For this, you will need legal counsel, which is expensive. However, many lawyers will accept shares of stock in your corporation as payment for their services.

You can contact LegalZoom for online legal agreements at https://www.legalzoom.com or LegalZoom at Toll Free (800) 773-0888. Or contact: LegalZoom at Website: https://www.legalzoom.com or LegalZoom at Toll Free (800) 773-0888, Or contact: LegalShield Get Access to Attorneys for only $24.95/Month. LegalShield One Pre-Paid Way Ada, OK 74820, Website: https://www.legalshield.com, Member Services Phone 844-428-3756 or email memberservices@legalshield.com.

Getting A Cosigner For A Business Loan

Getting a business loan is difficult. It is not only hard but it is time consuming to go through the effort of getting a business loan. Businesses do not have the same equity as real estate so it is difficult to get approval. The lengthy paperwork can leave any person in disarray. The Small Business Administration will guarantee your business loan with a local bank in your area. Small Business Administration can help prepare extensive paperwork needed by banks, especially in 2020. Contact the SBA to find out about their Business Financing Programs.

Small Business Administration
409 3rd Street, SW, Ste 7800
Washington, DC 20416
Web Site: www.sba.gov
Phone: (202) 205-6605 (Fed Relay Srvs
TDD): 1-800-877-8339
SBA Answer Desk: 1-800-U-ASK-SBA
(1-800-827-5722)
Emails: answerdesk@sba.gov
Answer Desk TTY: (704) 344-6640

OTHER SOURCES OF INCOME

Go To School And Earn A Degree Or Certificate

Go to school and increase your education. Get a college degree, or get a certificate in training from a vocational school. Vocational schools and junior colleges can provide training for hair stylists, electricians, construction work, truck drivers, medical assistants, lab technicians, emergency technicians and others. You can get financial assistance including grants and loans for attending almost any type of an educational program. Contact the career center of the school you would like to attend and they can personally give you details of education funding and financing. Consider going back to school and getting hired for a higher paying job.

Get Married.

Getting married to someone with a high paying job or a person with cash assets can help you get rich quickly. It is overlooked, but many people marry for money. Consider marrying a rich, highly educated and/or highly skilled person to improve your financial standing and get all of the ritzy things you want in your life.

If the person has rich parents but is not

SUMMARY

- To wipe out debts without bankruptcy, just use the wage earner plan to lower your debts and keep some of your assets.
- Fix your credit rating by obtaining free credit reports.
- Establish a better credit rating and you will be able to borrow more money.
- Obtain credit cards such as department store and debit cards to establish your credit.
- The corporate method of raising money involves selling shares in your company.
- The Small Business Administration can help you get a business loan.
- Go to school and get a college degree or retrain for a new job for more income.
- Get married to either a foreigner or domestic partner to increase your income.
- Get welfare, unemployment, and other government benefits.

necessarily very rich, calculate this formula to determine future wealth. Take their parents total worth and divide that amount by the number of children in the family. Let's say both parents are worth 5 million dollars and these parents have five children,(five million divided by 5 children) then each child could possibly inherit one million dollar each at a future date, which could be ten to fifty years from now, depending on the age of the parents of your intended spouse.

This simple ritual called marriage, could greatly improve anyone's financial balance sheet. Be careful and do your homework get a background check of finances and criminal activity done by your intended spouse. Get married to improve your finances.

Marry A Foreigner.

Would you marry a person from a foreign country to increase your wealth? Many people do this, but there are many rules that have to be followed when marrying a foreigner. Check with the customs and immigration for rules concerning getting a foreigner citizenship by marriage.

Looking for possible wives or husbands, look for these women or men on the internet. They did call them mail order brides or mail order grooms. Pick a doctor, nurse, engineer, corporate executive from a foreign country with a high paying job in their country. If they have a high paying job and money in the bank, you could be set for life with a foreigner who wants another citizenship and you in turn you want more money in your life. Many a person has been fooled by a foreigner who claimed to be rich or claimed to have earned a large salary. You could end up being married to an unskilled or poor foreigner, so hire an attorney to "certify legal documents", that the foreign person you marry is actually has a high paying job or money in the bank.

Three International Dating & Classified Websites.

- www.POF.com   (Plenty Of Fish)
- www.craigslist.com (Look in the CONNECTIONS section under activities or missed connections)
- www.match.com (Match.com)

Get Welfare, Unemployment Benefits And Other Government Benefits.

Government support for different people is called welfare. People of different income levels can get welfare, like social security, but welfare is intended to make sure different people can get basic human needs such as food and shelter. Welfare tries to make available financial aid or free or a subsidized amount of certain goods and social service, such as healthcare, education and job skill training. If you are poor and struggling, it is a very good way to support yourself and your family. Apply for government programs such as retirement benefits, military programs, affordable rental housing, food assistance and other benefits. Go to the website https://www.usa.gov/benefits. For unemployment benefits contact the Department Of Labor.

Chapter Twenty Seven

Your Ultimate Doctor

All through this book I have shown you how to be successful and prosperous, but a chapter is missing. What else should this book include? I will give you a hint. It is included in the oldest quote that every person understands. Well, let me tell you. Money will not bring you success, if you don't have your health. That's right you heard me. You must have good health. We don't live forever, we all die. It should be our goal to make the best of the time that we have and to extend our lives for as long as we can. If you are ill, all of the money in the world will not make you happy. I am sure that you will agree that your health is the most important thing in your life, more important even than money. No amount of money or power can make you well, if you are sick. I am going to show you how to use the powers of your mind to improve your health. I know what you are thinking. Does it really work? I want you to try these techniques and see for yourself.

If you are unhealthy you should seek the services of a doctor, in addition using your mind could help you to create a more virile and healthy body. Using your mind and modern medical treatment could improve your health, if you exercise on a regular basis and eat the proper foods.

Many people wait until they become ill before they start taking care of themselves. Don't fall into this trap. Take care of yourself now. I will show you how you can use your mind and faith to help you stay healthier and also overcome pain and disease. Have you seen other people do it? Have you ever wondered how you can use your subconscious mind to improve your health? You don't have to wonder anymore. In addition to seeing a medical professional, I am going to reveal to you how you can use your ultimate doctor, your mind to keep yourself healthier.

I want you to understand that a diet consisting of healthy food and a regulated exercise schedule are necessary for good health, but the use of your subconscious mind can help you, in addition to the directions from your doctor.

One Of The Greatest Healers Is Faith

Religious faith and modern medicine are the greatest healers of all. Religious faith helps communities by teaching morality, nurturing its culture, and making people compassionate but faith and a belief in god could also help your health. A wise man once told me, *"He who believes, has everything."* Where your health is concerned, this statement could be true.

Your health is dependent on your emotional well-being. That is why it is important to be in good spirits at all times. In this chapter I am going to describe miracles that others have witnessed with their own eyes. I am going to tell you how other people healed themselves and how you could possibly heal yourself. Your mind and your faith have created what you are. Can a belief in god heal you? Can your mind heal you? It's up to you. You decide.

You have heard of people miraculously recovering from a sickness. Is this true? Did they discover their hidden potential? Did they use their subconscious mind? As you read on, you be the judge. Can a licensed doctor's care work with these mind techniques? The answer is yes. Your mind can't replace a doctor's care, but it can help. What I am saying is that together they can create magic. Magic that is priceless; magic that creates miracles.

Forget Your Aches And Pains

What does complaining about your aches and pains do for you? Stress and negative feelings can make it worse. You see, your subconscious mind can help. If you were ill and you had stress and negative thoughts, then those messages go to your mind and your condition may get worse. It is like a self-fulfilling prophesy. Your subconscious mind just acts. It can't distinguish between a command that is positive for your well-being or one that is negative. It just listens and does what it is told. What if you told your mind to heal your body? Can you imagine being healthier? If that were true, then minor aches and pains would no longer bother you. If you can use the power of your mind to help yourself, then recovery from any type of illness is swifter. Can you imagine all those healthful benefits resulting simply by giving positive instructions to your mind? Well, let's try it out in this chapter. You have nothing to lose and you can be the judge. Can your mind use subliminal relaxing, positive and healing suggestions to help heal? Why not give it those instructions? In this life, your health is all you have, so let's try it in this chapter.

Can Your Sins Make You Sick?

Time and time again I hear this question. I personally believe that the result of certain sins can be illness. People that do the right things with the lives are healthier then people that do the wrong things. I have provided bible quotes, to give you an idea of the bible's interpretation of sickness and health. **Psalm**: Praise the LORD, my soul, and forget not all his benefits- who forgives all your sins and heals all your diseases. Here is another one. **James**: And the prayer of faith shall save the sick, and the Lord shall raise him up; and if he have committed sins, they shall be forgiven him. Here is another interpretation of the general meaning of the holy bible and illness. "The Bible explains the causes of physical illness. All physical illness is a result of the curse God placed upon the world when mankind fell into sin (**Isa**). In addition, physical illness is sometimes caused by

Satan and demons, as the four gospels show. Other times physical illness is a result of sin in one's life."

Bad Influences

You should remove bad influences from your life. You have heard the phrase that, some people make you sick. There is evidence to prove that this is true and many people swear by this. If you want to stay healthier stay away from negative and stressful people that you feel unhealthy with. Some people could be a bad influence to your good health. If that is the case, then you should distance yourself from these people. Another bad influence could be a location or an area that makes you feel sick. People complain that being in certain areas or locations make them feel worse. People complain of areas like garbage dumps. If that is the case with you, then you must avoid these locations in order to be healthier.

Heal Yourself

What is the secret of self-healing? Could it be belief in god and yourself and your doctor? Many say belief is the secret. Believe that you will get better. Believing that you will get worse isn't good. Try these healing instructions in addition to seeing a doctor. The results will show you how simple and amazing the art of healing is. I want you to believe, regardless of any conflicting evidence. I want you to believe that your mind can work wonders. But to work wonders, you must believe.

Imagine Yourself Well

The method of imagining will not substitute the services of a medical facility or a doctor. Get the best quality care from a licensed doctor. Get spiritual guidance from your church, synagogue, mosque or temple. In addition you can try the imagination techniques as outlined in this book.

I want you to imagine that you are feeling great. Imagine how well you feel, regardless of any medical evidence. Imagine and think about all of the fun activities that you can participate in because you feel so much better. Think how well and how refreshed you will feel when the pain leaves you. Imagine and adopt the frame of mind in which you are already healed and you are feeling better than you have ever felt in your life.

Imagine your mind as being in control of your whole body. Imagine your mind healing your body, after all, it was your mind that runs your body. Imagine all of the healing information is located in your mind. I also want you to imagine your body as being cleansed by your mind. Imagine bad cells are leaving; good cells are being produced and replacing the bad. Imagine damaged cells are being replaced. Imagine your white blood cells are fighting off all of the bad foreign substances in your body. I want you to visualize the fight taking place in your body. Imagine the forces of your mind overpowering any disease or ailment. Imagine your body winning the battle. Visualize the battle in your mind, because the battle is real. Imagine your mind fighting off disease, and healing ailments. Imagine it is healing and replacing every bone, tissue and substance in your body. Imagine your mind not letting you down, and making you healthier.

One Main Ingredient

It is very important that you don't moan and groan about your pain. Don't even think about it, if you can. Think about how good you feel; tell yourself over and over that you are well. If someone asks you how you are feeling, tell them that you feel fine. Keep telling yourself how good you feel. If you tell someone that you are feeling bad, you could actually start to make yourself feel worse.

Regardless of any evidence a doctor or medical professional may present, you should get emotional about feeling good. Have faith in yourself. Imagine yourself in a very pleasing situation. Let your mind wander into a setting that has you feeling very comfortable. Create in your mind the emotional sensation of feeling good.

I don't let thoughts of getting sick settle in my mind. I visit my doctor for checkups on a regular basis. I used to suffer from severe headaches, but no more. I now concentrate on feeling good. I used to try to figure out how bad my headaches could get; this made them get worse. Now, I just visit a doctor and take an aspirin and ignore the headaches by doing other activities and then telling myself that I feel good. In fact, I use the super-influencing technique to take care of my headaches. You could try this technique to remove your pain. It works for me.

Lucy's Mind Didn't Let Her Down

This reminds me of a courageous woman I heard of many years ago. Lucy was loved by all her friends and family. She was an inspiration to all who knew her. One day in early December, Lucy bent over to pick up a heavy bag of sugar. When the bag was already off the ground, Lucy realized that the bag was just too heavy. She lost control of the bag, and she wound up falling hard to the ground. The fall hurt her back badly.

The doctor told her it would take time for her to recover; he wasn't sure, in fact, that her back would recover fully. He advised her to get plenty of rest and relaxation and to hope for a miracle. Lucy couldn't go on her weekly outings to the park, and her back injury forced her to quit her part-time job as a bookkeeper. Lucy became depressed because she missed the enjoyment that physical activity had always brought her.

But Lucy was a fighter. She believed she could heal herself quickly. She gave others courage. She said in a weak voice, *"I am going to get well, I will fight off the pain. You'll see, in a matter of a month, I'll be as good as new."* This woman's courage moved others, and respected her strength.

One month later, Lucy was in great shape. She was looking really good; even her doctor was surprised. She was one of the lucky ones. What did she do to get well? 'The first thing she did was to start believing that she would get better. Regardless of what her doctor told her, she believed that with the right medical treatment, she would recover quickly. She had lots of confidence in herself.

'The second thing she did, was to remain positive. She didn't sit there and complain about her aches and pains. It hurt sometimes, but when she put the pain out of her mind. She felt a lot better. Besides, who wants to think about pain? She dreamt that the pain was leaving her body. She could see herself walking around and feeling better and better each day. She could feel the joy of feeling good.

STEPS TO LOSE WIEGHT

- **First**, You must set your goals to lose weight and diet.
- **Second,** Refer your diet and exercise plan to a medical professional.
- **Third,** Keep a diary or calendar and write down on a daily basis your weight and your exercise regiment.
- **Forth,** Use pictures and videos and imagine yourself as thin and energetic.
- **Fifth**, Create the emotional sensation of feeling joyful and good
- **Sixth**, Repeat your goals at least three times a day.

She laid back and dreamt that her body was revitalized; she could actually feel the healing take place. It still gives her a tingling feeling. As she continued to recover, she can see her mind healing her back. One of the things that I think helped her was a prayer that she repeated to herself four times each day, some days even more often. It may seem dumb, but I know it helped heal her.

Lucy's Prayer

This is my version of what she said to herself for ten minutes. *"I will use the immense power of my mind to heal my back. I have full confidence in the powers locked within me. I invest in full faith in myself to regain excellent health and inner peace."* Lucy helped make a miracle happen; a miracle that will bring joy to her heart for the rest of her life, a miracle that could not have happened without faith.

See Your New Thinner Body

I am going to show you the method that could make your figure more attractive in a matter of days. I will show you how to use the power of your mind to sculpt your body. You could succeed, and I can show you how. If you want to try to take pounds off using this technique follow the imagination techniques. It is also advisable that before any weight loss regiment, that you see a licensed physician.

This is the technique I want you to follow. I want you to visualize your body as thin and lean. Get some pictures taken when you were thin, or get some pictures of other people you want to look like. Look over these pictures and visualize the kind of body that you want. Imagine you are walking on the beach and stirring a lot of attention. Visualize how everyone around you feels about your new body. Notice small details like the looks on their faces and every little curve of your new body. Do this visualizing for about 25 minutes every day.

See Your New Activities

If you want to lose weight, you should take up two new activities. One is an exercise program and the other is a good food diet program. I want you to visualize what both these activities will be like. I want you to imagine that you are exercising or aerobicizing to dance music. Feel the sweat running down your body. Visualize who you are with. Every little detail should be noticeable to you.

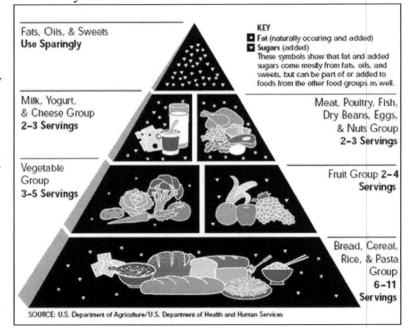

190

Imagine the type of food you will eat. Imagine also the type of food you will not eat. Imagine that you are sitting at a table and eating a wonderful green salad and high protein foods, like meats. Imagine that you will lose pounds with this food diet that you can certify with medical professionals. While you diet drink plenty of glasses of water each day. Visualize that you have no desire for sweets. You dislike sweets, for the harm they will do to your body. You know how unattractive and unhealthy, these things can make you. Your mind will accept what you want it to accept. Tell subconscious mind to visualize and to accept these new habits for you. You will also start to enjoy these new exercise activities. The new activities that will help you lose weight. The subconscious mind could help weight loss.

Repeat Your Desires To Yourself

Also, I want you to repeat your dieting goals to yourself three times every day. The best time to repeat these goals to yourself is just before you go to sleep, when you are sleepy. Another good time is when you just wake up. At these times, your subconscious mind is very easily influenced by suggestions.

A Woman Who Lost 47 Pounds

Janice was thin when she was young, but is heavy now. She had a desire to be thin again, which, for her - meant losing 50 or 60 pounds. She decided to shed that excess fat. Janice wanted to use the powers of her subconscious mind to lose weight. Janice was going to try to use her mind to sculpt her body to a thinner shape. Janice had old pictures of herself that she was going to use. She was going to feel and visualize herself, when she was 120 pounds, 15 years ago and this included visualizing even the small details of being thinner. . Janice thought it was a challenge, but she could use this visualizing technique. She said she was going to go on a low-calorie, grapefruit diet and she was also going to ride a stationary bike for 30 minutes or more each day, Janice said she would visualize what her new diet activities and while she peddled her exercise bike in her home, she imagined pounds melting off as she was riding. Janice imagined herself becoming thinner and thinner. She was also told to visualize the type of diet food she would eat and

SUMMARY

- One of the greatest healers is faith.
- The result of certain sins can be illness.
- There are six steps that can help the dieting, exercising and the healing process.
- **First**, You must set your dieting and exercising goals. **Second,** Refer your diet and exercise plan to a medical professional. **Third**, Write your progress in a diary or a calendar. **Forth**, Visualize and imagine yourself as being thinner. **Fifth**, Enjoy yourself and create the emotional sensation of feeling good. **Sixth**, Repeat your goals to yourself three times a day.
- You could use the same six steps when trying to heal yourself.
- To lose weight and to be healthy stay on a proper diet, and follow the food pyramid guidelines, exercise on regular basis and drink three to six glasses of water a day.
- Participate and look forward to new activities.
- When dieting, think of the rewards of being thin and visualize your new body.
- Repeat your weight-loss goals and desires to yourself three times a day.

she imagined that pounds were burned off because the food that she ate helped her lose weight. She drank plenty of water. Janice said she could easily do all of those things and hoped that she could lose weight. She was told, "You can do it."

Janice set her goals. She set her goal at four pounds a week. She put a small chart on the wall to mark her progress, and underneath it she pinned her old picture. There was one more thing that Janice had to do for her successful weight loss. Janice was going to repeat her weight-loss instruction to herself three times a day. Once before she went to sleep, once in the morning and once in the afternoon.

Here is my version of what you should repeat to yourself; adapt it as you see fit. *'The power of my mind will create a slender, attractive body for me. I enjoy eating the delicious foods I prepare for myself that will help me lose weight. I also look forward to the physical enjoyment that I get from riding my bike. I can see myself losing four pounds a week until I am a vibrant 120 pounds.'*

THE GRAPEFRUIT DIET: Popular since the 30's, it was thought that grapefruit juice tainted food so effortless weight loss was possible. The grapefruit diet generally, is a diet where, a person eats one grapefruit to 1/2 grapefruit at each meal, along with meat, eggs, other foods that are rich in fat and protein, and certain vegetables. Sugar, fruits, sweet vegetables, grains, starchy vegetables and high calorie foods are avoided. Three to six glasses of water are consumed every day.

Well, losing 47 pounds in 13 weeks, is a great goal. Janice was determined to lose weight and following a diet, an exercise program and the use of the powers of the subconscious mind. What about your weight loss program? Do you want to lose weight? Try this method of losing weight and see how much weight you lose. When dieting or trying to stay healthy stick with the Department Of Agriculture food pyramid and remember to drink three to six glasses of water a day.

Chapter Twenty Eight

Novanetics: The Power Of The Mind, Directs You

"Novanetics" can show you the way to success. With *"Novanetics"* and the power of your subconscious mind many things that you want could be yours. This book gave you specialized information and told you what other people have done. You saw how they found success. Now it is time for you to find and enjoy your own success.

The secret way success is to use the magical powers of *"Novanetics"* to find love, health, beauty prosperity and harmony within yourself and with others. This book will assist you in getting anything or being anything that you desire. That is the purpose of this book. If you want to live out your dreams use the powers of *"Novanetics"*.. Use it and be successful and prosperous.

A Man Who Wished For A Promotion

Carl was a quiet man. He worked for the same company for seven and a half years, but he was there only for the paycheck. He didn't enjoy what he did because he didn't have the position that he wanted. He was filled with resentment. He didn't have many friends at work, and he wasn't well liked. There was no way he was going to get a promotion in his present state.

I met Carl about three years ago, and he was just as I described him. I asked Carl if he desired a promotion. He told me in a harsh voice, "I think that I am capable of any upper-level management position. It's just too much of a responsibility to take on."

Carl limited his thoughts. He considered a promotion to be too much responsibility. With this type of negative thinking, he was able to talk himself out of any kind of promotion. His problem was his attitude. I sat down with Carl and talked over his situation. I explained to him that he had the ability to be promoted and could put it to use. I gave Carl some suggestions and asked him to come back in a few months. When he did, he described how he had visualized himself as the marketing director of his company.

"Every day I went to work, I modeled myself after the present marketing director. When I had free moments, I would go to him and show him my new ideas. It was stressful at times. I began to appreciate his ability to work with people and to get various jobs done properly. I became very enthusiastic about everything that I did at work. The guys at work began to treat me nicer and I now enjoy my day at work much more." Just hearing this made me happy. I just had to ask Carl what he did to make all of this happen.

"It all started when I began using my imagination," he said. "I would sit at home and visualize that I was the marketing director. I sat there and imagined I did all the work he does. I visualized sitting in his office and delegating duties to the whole marketing department. I even imagined working over some new plans with the president and vice president." I just had to compliment him. 'That's great," I told Carl.

"Well, you haven't heard it all," he said. "Every night now, before I go to sleep, I repeat this prayer to myself: *I love all people. I use my full effort to do my best at work. I'm a very capable, hard worker. My dedication will earn me a promotion."*

I was really impressed by the improvement in Carl's attitude. He had done so much for himself. A few years later, I heard from him again. At 2 p.m. I got a phone call from Carl. "Dave," he told me excitedly. "I got it, I got it." "What did you get?" I asked. "I'm the new marketing manager. The old marketing manager retired and they gave the position to me. What do you think, Dave?" "Very good, very good," I told him. As I left the office that warm, sunny day, I couldn't help thinking how believing in himself had made this man's dream come true.

Getting The Man Of Her Dreams

A lot of people tell me that the thing that would make them most happy is having someone to share their lives with. It is very difficult, living a lonely life. I know many people who go through life lonely. It does not have to be that way!

I want to share a story with you. It is the story of a woman who wanted someone to care for and someone who would care for her; a woman who wanted to share her life with someone else. Gloria was an attractive woman in her early 30s. She had a steady secretarial job and a beautiful ten-year-old girl. She confided in me one day. She told me that she was tired of being lonely. "My marriage just didn't work out. I want to experience a relationship with a man with whom I can love and grow." I asked her if she knew exactly what she wanted in a man. She told me that she didn't. I told her the following.

"Gloria, when you go home tonight, I want you to visualize the man of your dreams. I want you to think about him and what he is like. Pretend both of you are going out and are having fun together. Look at this man and notice every single detail about him. Write down these details. In this way you will know exactly which qualities you desire."

"I also want you to ask your mind to find this man for you. Your mind knows exactly which man will make you happy. Instruct your mind to select him for you. Do this and you could have the man that you want." After writing down what I told her, she asked me, "How will I know this man when I meet him?"

"Gloria, you will know this man because of a feeling that will fill your body," I said. "Some call it chemistry, but whatever it is, you will feel it. It is like a strong hunch. Believe me, you will find him. There is one more thing I must tell you. When you know exactly which qualities you want in a man, make sure that you have the same qualities in yourself. No one will give you honesty or sincerity if you can't give the same. You must be willing to give as much as you receive. 'Thanks so much," she said as she left.

A few days before Thanksgiving, I got a call from Gloria. She told me an enchanting story. In her small voice, she said: "I went to a party on a Friday night many months ago. There was this tall, dark gentleman there, his name was Phil. He slowly walked over to me and introduced himself. He was so charming. As he talked to me I was feeling something special. I knew at that moment that chemistry was taking place. After a few hours of getting to know Phil, I let my feelings take over and told Phil that I was attracted to him. He was so flattered that he asked me out for Saturday night. I could have used the old *I'm busy* line because he gave me such short notice. But I wanted to be honest, so I said, *Sure.*

"He took me to a nice restaurant. He told me that I was very honest and sincere and that I didn't play games. He admired these qualities in me. He also told me that he admired my confidence. He said that he appreciated a woman who knows what she wants and goes after it. We've been seeing each other for months now, it's been wonderful."

The Road Is Yours

"Novanetics" should not be a mystery to you any longer. You should understand its principals. They are yours for the rest of your life. Yours to use and to achieve success with. I have shown you throughout this book how many people just like you have used these techniques and realized their dreams. Let me ask you one question. Do you want to succeed? I have shown you what you have to do to succeed. I have shown you what behavior ensures failure; you see, success is a matter of choice. I have left the decision in your hands. I earnestly hope you have chosen the road to success. It is a road that can be traveled more easily with a wagon, and I have given you the wagon. The road is already marked for you. All you have to do is to pull your wagon up the road. Pull the wagon all the way to the city of success.

Let's Review Novanetics

"Novanetics" is a method of tapping into your subconscious mind to unleash your total potential. The effects of using *"Novanetics"* may give you extreme success, unlimited prosperity and overwhelming happiness. It is a compilation of the greatest success secrets ever assembled in one book. It contains knowledge from the greatest minds on earth and also knowledge from the mystical philosophy of the Far East and the wisdom of Christianity. *"Novanetics"* will give you the answers to becoming very successful. Much of *"Novanetics"* is being used by the Japanese in their quest to become the, most successful nation on this earth; and we know how well it has worked for them. They have the highest income group in the U.S., and they have the lowest crime rate as well as living longer than any other people on earth. They understand methods in *"Novanetics"* and use them. *It is time that the rest of the world used the advanced knowledge of "Novanetics" to better themselves.*

Let's Try The Quiz Again

I know you have learned a lot by reading this book. I want to make sure that you got the most out of it. I urge you to read this book as many times as you can. Reading this book twice a year will allow you to get the most out of it. I hope that you learn its secrets. I know that if you do, they will help you to become more successful and get what you want. Now it is time to try the quiz again.

When answering this quiz, follow the same rules as before. Trust the first answer that comes to your mind, it is usually the best. Answer A if you agree with the statement and D if you disagree with the statement.

The Quiz

1)   The power of your mind can give you many things that you want.

2)   Luck has a lot to do with getting rich.

3)   Some people are poor by their own choice.

4)   Recognizing and admitting to your weaknesses is wise?

5)   It is not necessary to write down a goal to finish it effectively.

6)   Specific goals are unnecessary.

7)   Planning ahead takes the fun out of activities.

8)   Visualizing or dreaming of your desires is natural?

9)   Commonly made decisions should be solved at your first compulsion.

10)   Hunches are valid only some of the time.

11)   No specific time limit should be placed on goals.

12)   Perusing a goal will make you happy?

13)   For the most part, you should fully expose your feelings to supportive people.

14)   You should give to others because they expect you to.

15)   Speaking about anything on your mind is healthy.

16) High expectations are not good because they lead to disappointments.

17) Creating a funny and cheerful personality will make you less likable with friends, because this is not a serious personality.

18) It is better do a funny "ballet" dance when doing something peculiar in front of people like sneaking away?

19) A person begin to be funnier within one hour with the comedy techniques in "Novanetics".

20) It is to your advantage to concentrate on more than one thing at a time.

21) Strong persistence will not help you get what you want because it irritates people.

22) You learn more when you feel that you know nothing or don't have a set opinion.

23) It is better to know something about everything then to specialize in one area.

24) Scientific studies show that the power of the mind may improve body healing by 30%.

25) You can drastically reduce your debt to creditors and still keep some of assets without declaring bankruptcy with a wage earners plan.

26) Can a person earn a rental income of $9,600 a year with a $975 investment that includes locks on two doors and installing one exterior door?

27) Of the five ways to earn money from income property which are cash flow, equity, depreciation, appreciation and interest payments, can depreciation and interest payments be deducted on your tax return.

28) Refinancing your mortgage at a higher interest rate is a great way to lower your monthly mortgage payments.

29) Will building a rental apartment on your property guarantee that the market price of your home will go up?

30) You can bring your mortgage payment down to zero, and earn a rental income, even after the cost of the construction, by building accessory apartments.

31) The government doesn't offer special home financing programs that can reduce the mortgage payment for home owners.

32) Some people just lock the doors in a section of their home that has a separate entry way, then rent out that part of the house to save 60% on their mortgage payments.

33) Can anyone with little money and the right instructions become a millionaire from real estate?

About the Answers

How did you enjoy taking this quiz for the second time? Fun, wasn't it. I am sure you finished the quiz quickly. I have gone through the answers to these questions all through the book. Now you can grade yourself.

Here are the answers: 1-A, 2-D, 3-A, 4-A, 5-D, 6-D, 7-D, 8-A, 9-A, 10-D, 11-D, 12-A, 13-A, 14-D, 15-A, 16-D, 17-D, 18-A, 19-A, 20.-D, 21-D, 22-A, 23-D, 24-A, 25-A, 26-A, 27-A, 28-D, 29-A, 30-A, 31-D, 32-A, 33-A.

Here is a refresher as to what these scores mean? Multiply your score by three to see your score as a percentage of 100. So if you got 30, that would be 90% and if you got 25, that would be 75%. A score of over 90% is an A+. A score of 80% to 89% is an A. A score of over 70% to 79% is a B. A score of 60% to 69% is a C.

If you scored less than 33, you need *"Novanetics"*. A score of less than 33 means you don't know something that you should know. All of the answers to these questions can be found in this course. As you read, you will see topics that correspond to each question. This test was given to you to see how well you understood the principals of success.

After you have finished this educational course you may want a *"NOVANETICS"* certificate to hang on your wall in the same decorative frame you would use for a college degree. With this certificate you can show others you have completed the *"NOVANETICS"* course. A *"NOVANETICS"* certificate is impressive with family and friends. This certificate may also get you jobs and business opportunities with people that will see the certificate. Some of the information covered in this course is included in the curriculum for a real estate license and a psychology degree.

Only after you have read and studied this course and have taken the 200 question final examination can you earn the certificate. Send a total of $9 for the grading and the *"NOVANETICS"* personalized educational certificate which includes shipping & handling. Write David Bendah, PO Box 152808, Dept. DD2, San Diego, CA 92195 and send $9 with your name and address in capital letters.

SUMMARY

- *Novanetics* is a method of tapping into your subconscious mind to unleash your total potential.
- *Novanetics* is not reserved for the talented few. It is for everyone who wants success and prosperity.
- There is one simple three step formula to begin the success process. Create a desire for what you want. Believe that it will be yours. .Know exactly what you want.
- Your subconscious mind can help you to excel in your job or in your personal life. This book has given you a wagon to pull to the city of success.
- Anyone can be successful. Use my techniques and you will prosper.
- I would be happy if you write me, with any success stories you would like to share.
- Write David Bendah if you would like a "Novanetics" course certificate that you can handsomely present on your wall. Also write David Bendah if you would like to be on his mailing list for the latest wealth opportunities or write him if you would like to be a registered student of "Novanetics" either buy the book or send a copy of your sales receipt for the book or any proof of purchase.

Who Can Be Successful?

Is *"Novanetics"* only reserved for the talented few? Not at all. It can be used by anyone in any situation. I'm just a regular guy who uses *"Novanetics"* and it has created miracles for me. All you need to start with, is faith and the ability to believe. To become successful you must follow three principals. You must create a burning desire for what you want. You must believe that it will be yours. You must know exactly what you want. If you can follow these three principals, you can start the success process, but above all you must believe in yourself.

I have shown you what you must do to succeed. Follow my simple steps and wealth and health success can be yours. You have the tools to succeed. Now that you have them, use them. Use them correctly and a new world will be yours. If you have read this book, I know you have chosen to succeed. I hope this book has helped you; I hope that you will see the same amazing results that many others have. If there is anything I can do to further assist your quest for success, please don't hesitate to let me know. I want to help you. I really want to hear from you. I want to know what you are doing. I really want to know how the book has helped you. Please let me know by writing me your story. Your feedback and stories means a lot to me. Write David Bendah, PO Box 152808, Dept. DD2, San Diego, CA 92195.

A PERSONAL NOTE FROM THE WRITER

I am constantly aware of outstanding moneymaking and personal-growth opportunities. I would be very happy to share any of the information I have with you. If you would like to be kept up-to-date with the latest wealth opportunities, please send your name and address to me. I will put it on my personal mailing list. If For more information or sales please write, David Bendah, PO Box 152808, Dept. DD2, San Diego, CA 92195

BECOMING A REGISTERED STUDENT:

"NOVANETICS" is an educational school course, whose purpose is to increase your income. In order to take the final examination and earn the *"NOVANETICS"* certificate you must be a registered student. Buying this book makes you a registered student.. To become a registered student and buy the book *"NOVANETICS"* send **$34.95** USD plus $3.95 USD for shipping for any quantity of books. For international registered students send **$34.95** USD + $15 USD for shipping. If you have bought the book through a book store or other retail outlet send a copy of your sales receipt or proof of purchase. Write, David Bendah, PO Box 152808, Dept. DD2, San Diego, CA 92195

Novanetics Part One Examination
Real Estate & Business Certificate

You will be given 80 real estate multiple choice questions and 120 business and psychology multiple choice questions and in which you must get a score of at least 65%. Number the two scantron test sheets from part one to part two. Take the examination by using a pencil and then blacken out the right answer for each question on the scantron test sheets. Do not blacken out more than one choice per question. The answer is either (a) or (b) or (c) or (d). The scantron test sheets are included with this book or purchase scantron test sheets at any office supply store. When you have completed the test Write David Bendah, PO Box 152808, Dept. DD2, San Diego, CA 92195 and send the completed scantron tests and $9 with your name and address in capital letters.

Becoming A Registered Student:

"NOVANETICS" is an educational school course, whose purpose is to increase your income. In order to take the final examination and earn the *"NOVANETICS"* certificate you must be a registered student. Buying this book makes you a registered student. To become a registered student and buy the book *"NOVANETICS"* send **$34.95** USD plus $3.95 USD for shipping for any quantity of books. For international registered students send **$34.95** USD + $15 USD for shipping. If you have bought the book through a book store or other retail outlet send a copy of your sales receipt or proof of purchase. Write, David Bendah, PO Box 152808, Dept. DD2, San Diego, CA 92195. **TEST AA11**

CHAPTER 8 Wealth Apartment Additions To Pay Your Mortgage Payments (Part One)

(01) What four chapter business start up plan is included in *Novanetics*?
a) none (b) real estate (c) mail order (d) internet sales

(02) How many walls to a home can you add when getting a building permit?
a) none (b) as many as the permit allows (c) one (d) two

(03) If your mortgage payment is $2,000 a month, then how much money can you earn in rents to pay your mortgage payment?
a) Any amount (b) $2,000 (c) $1,000 (d) $2,500

(04) How many walls can you add to your home?
a) one (b) two (c) any amount in the plans (d) only interior walls

(05) When closing off a door in your home for an apartment, you should?

a) paint the door (b) lock and nail the door (c) replace the door (d) install a glass door

(06) How much of a positive cash flow can you earn when creating apartments?
a) half the mortgage payment (b) the full mortgage payment (c) none (d) a & b

(07) What type of door is the best door to install for an exterior or interior door?
a) glass door (b) wooden door (c) pre-hung door (d) any door

(08) What doors can be locked when building apartments?
a) any door (b) 36 inch doors (c) exterior doors (d) 30 inch door

(09) How many bids do you need when hiring a contractor?
a) Ten (b) three (c) one (d) none

(10) How much money can a contractor overcharge you by?

a) any amount (b) 50% (c) it never happens (d) 100%

(11) How much money will your home go up in value when building apartments?
   a) significant amount (b) very little (c) none (d) a & b & c

(12) To save money when installing more electrical wiring and more water plumbing for apartments you should?
   a) use a gas generator (b) install meters (c) install separate systems (d) Use one system and share

(13) When building a new home, what should you add to get more rental income?
   a) outside stairways (b) exterior doors (c) bathrooms (d) a & b & c

(14) Where should you install outside stairways for separate apartment entrances.
   a) only to the second floor (b) only to the third floor (c) to all floors (d) none are needed

(15) When building a new home or remodeling where should you add electrical, plumbing and sewer hookups.
   a) add none (b) only kitchen and bathroom (c) everywhere you can build additions (d) a & b

(16) What do separate apartments need?
   a) Separate entrance (b) bathroom (c) wine cellar (d) a & b

(17) Where can you not build an apartment?
   a) back yard (b) basement (c) neighbors lot (d) garage

(18) Range hood fans above the stove could be.
   a) vent less (b) vented to the outside (c) vented to the floor (d) a & b

(19) What is your standard bathtub length size?
   a) 5 feet (b) 4 feet (c) 7 feet (d) 6 feet

(20) What is your standard shower stall size?

a) 6 feet by 3 feet (b) 32" x 32" (c) 48" x 48" (d) 24" x 24"

(21) When building an apartments in your basement, you should add.
   a) Tiled floors (b) a bathroom (c) a drop ceiling (d) textured walls

CHAPTER 9   Wealth Apartment Additions To Pay Your Mortgage Payments (Part Two)

(22) What part of a church can be easily converted into apartments?
   a) class rooms (b) parking lot (c) sanctuary (d) steeple

(23) Church rental income property can.
   a) increase church income (b) decrease church income (c) is not needed (d) be too expensive

(24) Churches can earn rental income.
   a) during church holidays (b) with certain religions (c) in certain parts of the country (d) at any time

(25) Most barn or garage kits that can be purchased will cost:
   a) $1,000 (b) $3,000 to $20,000 (c) over $20,000 (d) over $50,000

(26) A type of home where people share bathrooms, kitchens and living rooms is called a.
   a) rooming house (b) tiny home (c) duplex (d) fourplex

(27) When planning construction in your home who should you contact for a building permit?
   a) Federal government (b) city or county building dept. (c) Fire dept. (d) Police dept.

(28) What building permit is needed for minor repairs or painting.
   a) none (b) regular permit (c) police permit (d) building permit

(29) What permit do you need when adding a manufactured home to your property?

a) no permit   (b) the manufacturer's permit
    (c) city or county building permit   (d) a
    sales receipt for the home

(30) For what type of construction do you contact
the city or county for a building permit?
  a) commercial   (b) residential   (c) rural
      (d) any construction

(31) To save on real estate taxes you can deduct:
  a) property improvements   (b) title costs
      (c) depreciation   (d) a & b & c

(32) An installment sale to save on taxes is paid
over:
  a) the same year   (b) many years   (c) the
      year after the sale   (d) no years

(33) To qualify for a "long term" sale for capital
gain tax benefits you must hold on to your
property at least:
  a) thirty years   (b) twenty years   (c) one
      year   (d) ten years

(34) Capital gain taxes do not apply to:
  a) building   (b) shares of stock   (c) payroll
      income   (d) land

CHAPTER 10   Making A Fortune With Real Estate

(35) How often can you invest in real estate with
other people's money?
  a) about ten percent   (b) with commercial
      frequently   (c) not at all   (d) frequently

(36) What type of a tax write-off does real estate
provide?
  a) lucrative   (b) none   (c) small   (d)
      measly

(37) When buying real estate the location of the
property should be?
  a) good location   (b) average location   (c)
      doesn't matter   (d) any location

(38) When buying real estate the condition of the
property should be?
  a) doesn't matter   (b) bad   (c) relatively
      good   (d) run down

(39) When buying real estate the price of the
property should be?
  a) doesn't matter   (b) below market value
      (c) market value   (d) above market value

(40) What conditions are important when buying
real estate?
  a) owner anxious to sell   (b) good finance
      terms   (c) above market prices   (d) a &
      b

(41) What are the most important factors when
buying a real estate?
  a) expensive appearance   (b) can be resold,
      rented or improved easily   (c) large
      property   (d) close to main streets

(42) Owners become anxious to sell when?
  a) tenants refuse to pay or pay late   (b) high
      vacancy rate   (c) condition of the
      building is bad   (d) a & b & c

(43) Owners will give you a bargain in real estate
if?
  a) owner retires or is in poor health   (b)
      property is left to heirs that want to sell
      (c) partners break up partnership   (d) a &
      b & c

(44) To get a very low price on a real estate
building the property must be:
  a) in a flood zone   (b) in bad condition, like
      with old plumbing and termites   (c)
      located in the city   (d) located in the
      suburbs

(45) Who can you hire to help you find a
property?
  a) lawyer   (b) accountant   (c) real estate
      agent   (d) finance officer

(46) Cash flow in finance is the:
  a) tax debt   (b) profit after expenses   (c)
      cash movement   (d) investment money

(47) When looking for real estate should you:
  a) place classifieds   (b) put up signs   (c)
      consult attorneys   (d) a & b

(48) Depreciation in real estate is:
   a) building value   (b) land value   (c) tax
      (d) deducted over a period of 27.5 years

(49) Appreciation in real estate is:
   a) an increase in value   (b) taxes   (c) debt
      (d) a building code

(50) Mortgage interest payments are a:
   a) legitimate expense   (b) building code
      (c) loan income   (d) profits

(51) Equity in real estate is:
   a) expenses   (b) taxes   (c) profits you can
      borrow against   (d) tax debt

(52) When refinancing a property how much
cash can you get?
   a) not much   (b) the market value   (c) loan
      amount   (d) approximate equity

(53) When you refinance your property for a
lower interest rate you can get:
   a) better interest rate   (b) lower mortgage
      payment   (c) no benefits   (d) a & b

(54) If your monthly mortgage payments are
$1,135 at 5.5%   for 30 years and you refinance
to 3.5%, your mortgage payments would:
   a) be less by $10   (b) be less by about $250
      (c) be higher by $250   (d) not change

(55) A second mortgage on a property is:
   a) for car financing   (b) usually at a higher
      interest rate   (c) property insurance   (d)
      fire insurance

(56) A reverse mortgage is a:
   a) home equity converted to mortgage
      payments   (b) a loan with no interest
      payments   (c) car loan (d) credit card
      loan

(57) With a depreciation expense you can deduct.
   a) land value   (b) building value   (c)
      mortgage amount   (d) interest payments

(58) Over many years appreciation values in real
estate

   a) keep pace with inflation   (b) change only
      in the summer   (c) fall slightly   (d)
      don't change

(59) Return on investment is:
   a) insurance rate   (b) tax debt   (c) profit
      divided by investment   (d) down
      payment

CHAPTER 11   Income Property Wealth

(60) If a six unit apartment building earned $600
a unit how much would it earn in a month?
   a) $3,600   (b) $1,200   (c) $3,000 (d)
      $4,200

(61) What is the vacancy rate?
   a) Insurance rate   (b) rate the rentals are
      empty   (c) fire insurance rate   (d)
      mortgage rate

(62) Operating expenses are?
   a) insurance expense   (b) property taxes
      (c) all expenses except for mortgage
      expense   (d) all expenses

(63) The Cap Rate is?
   a) Net income divided by asking price   (b)
      highest rate   (c) mortgage rate   (d) fire
      code

(64) How many ways does "Novanetics" show
you how to reduce mortgage payments up to
%100?
   a) four   (b) one   (c) two   (d) ten

(65) When negotiating real estate you should?
   a) act eager and enthusiastic   (b) act
      uninterested   (c) get angry   (d) do not
      say one word

(66) When negotiating real estate what should
you ask about property offers?
   a) how long has the property been listed
      (b) how many offers have you had   (c)
      did you turn down offers   (d) a & b & c

(67) When negotiating real estate what should
you ask about the property.

a) what capital improvements were made (b) how much was paid for the property and when was it paid (c) who owned the property over 20 years ago (d) a & b

(68) When buying a property you should.
a) ask all of the questions you can (b) don't ask questions (c) ask five questions (d) ask few questions

(69) When buying real estate with no money down expect to.
a) pay a 15% down payment (b) purchase the property with no money (c) pay a large down payment (d) pay a 10% down payment

(70) Can a buyer refinance a property and use the equity money to buy the property with no money down?
a) seldom (b) yes (c) only one time (d) only in Canada

(71) How many ways does "*Novanetics*" show you how to buy property with no money down?
a) none (b) one (c) eight (d) two

CHAPTER 26 Wealth Secrets To Removing Debt

(72) What is a good method of removing all of your debts?
a) bankruptcy (b) wage earners plan (c) no method (d) a & b

(73) What is the first thing you should do to establish credit?
a) invest in gold and silver (b) invest in antiques (c) open a checking account (d) do nothing

(74) If you are attempting on fixing your credit rating you should?
a) ask the state tax department (b) do nothing (c) ask the IRS for help (d) Get free credit reports

(75) When you establish a good credit rating you can?
a) borrow more money (b) have better financial references (c) get a lower tax rate (d) a & b

(76) The easiest credit cards to get are?
a) American express (b) debit cards (c) MasterCard & Visa (d) a & b

(77) What does the corporate method of raising money use to raise money?
a) future commodities (b) real estate (c) stock (d) taxes

(78) What will help advance your job opportunities?
a) Marriage (b) having children (c) more education (d) nothing

(79) What type of funding can you get when attending school for a degree, diploma or a certificate?
a) no funding (b) government grants and loans (c) trading stamps (d) postage stamps

(80) How does a person meet a marriage partner to improve their finances?
a) by Internet (b) by mail (c) by phone or introduction (d) a & b & c

Novanetics Part Two Examination
Real Estate & Business Certificate

You will be given 80 real estate multiple choice questions and 120 business and psychology multiple choice questions and in which you must get a score of at least 65%. Number the two scantron test sheets from part one to part two. Take the examination by using a pencil and then blacken out the right answer for each question on the scantron test sheets. Do not blacken out more than one choice per question. The answer is either (a) or (b) or (c) or (d). The scantron test sheets are included with this book or purchase scantron test sheets at any office supply store. When you have completed the test Write David Bendah, PO Box 152808, Dept. DD2, San Diego, CA 92195 and send the completed scantron test sheets and $9 with your name and address in capital letters. **TEST AA11**

CHAPTER 1 Tapping Into The Power Of *Novanetics*

(81) What type of a desire do you need to obtain wealth?
  a) realistic (b) creative (c) burning (d) no nonsense

(82) What type of thoughts limit wealth creating powers of the mind?
  a) positive (b) happy (c) funny (d) negative

CHAPTER 2 Wealth Is Your Choice

(83) What atmosphere is the best for you to succeed?
  a) negative (b) chilling (c) positive (d) suspicious

(84) A successful person learns from their mistakes by?
  a) ignoring them (b) correcting them (c) denying them (d) rejecting them

(85) The lessons of failure?
  a) are funny (b) bore you (c) should be ignored (d) teach you to succeed

(86) To be successful what is a good choice?
  a) being poor (b) being wealthy (c) being fearful (d) distrustful

CHAPTER 3 The Power Of *Novanetics* Is Within You

(87) What type of suggestions will your mind obey?
  a) negative (b) exciting (c) positive (d) a & b & c

(88) What can you do to help your mind to perform different routine tasks?
  a) program it (b) listen to the nature (c) do nothing (d) attach electrodes

(89) What type of a thinker is a creative thinker?
  a) open to ideas (b) curious (c) have ideas (d) a & b & c

(90) How much of the mind did the unconscious take up in Sigmund Freud's iceberg model?
  a) 1/7 (b) 6/7 (c) 4/7 (d) 7/7

CHAPTER 4 How To Get The Wealth You Want

(91) What must you do to get what you want?
  a) Work faithfully for what you want (b) know exactly what you want (c) undergo hypnosis (d) both a & b

(92) What can you use to program your mind?
  a) fresh air b) warm air c) goals d) sleep

(93) Your goals should be?
  a) specific (b) written down (c) within a time frame (d) a & b & c

(94) What should you do three times a day with

your goals?

a) repeat them   (b) visualize them   (c) become enthusiastic   (d) a & b & c

(95) When should you repeat your goals about ten times?

a) Only in the evening   (b) only in the morning   (c) once a day   (d) at least three times a day.

(96) Before you go to sleep and wake up your goals should be?

a) visualized   (b) repeated and visualized   (c) tucked away   (d) swayed

(97) How much of a money limit should you put on your written goals?

a) an average limit   (b) spending limit   (c) opinion of others limit   (d) no limit

(98) When one of your goals is to own a Mercedes Benz car, you should.

a) buy a toy Mercedes car   (b) put up a Mercedes car poster   (c) get Mercedes car pictures   (d)   a & b & c

CHAPTER 5   Making Your Wealth Dreams Come To Life

(99) Visualizing your goals is:

a) necessary   (b) not necessary   (c) an option   (d) a choice

(100) What should you do when wanting to be successful?

a) create sensations and feeling of already being successful   (b) positive enthusiasm   (c) dream and visualize   (d) a & b & c

(101) What feeling should you have with your goals?

a) critical   (b) chilling   (c) enthusiastic   (d) objective

CHAPTER 6   Securing Your Wealth Goals

(102) To complete your goals you should.

a) make your goals realistic   (b) use a worksheet with a time frame   (c) ignore them   (d) start new goals

(103) Money, time and education are important for?

a) workshops   (b) goal requirements   (c) taxes   (d) real estate

(104) Obstacles, solutions, rewards and due dates are part of?

a) goal chart   (b) profit and loss statement   (c) income statement   (d) cash flow statement

(105) How much of a time limit should you set for goals?

a) five year to one week   (b) no time limit   (c) only one week   (d) yearly limits

(106) When should you reward the completion of your goals?

a) before you start them   (b) during the day   (c) when you have completed them   (d) a & b & c

(107) What time of the year should you repeat, visualize and become enthusiastic about your goals.

a) in the summer   (b) in the winter   (c) in the fall   (d) any time of the year

CHAPTER 7   Laugh Your Way To Wealth

(108) Having a funny cheerful personality will make you?

a) more likable   (b) hated   (c) not liked   (d) boring

(109) People with a sense of humor have?

a) less friends   (b) low paying jobs   (c) better jobs and marriages   (d) shorter marriages

(110) Smiling more often will make you.

a) more likable   (b) happier   (c) disliked   (d) a & b

(111) Laughing is good for?

a) being likable (b) being funny (c) skin complexion (d) a & b

(112) What happens when you talk in a whimsical tone on the phone?
   a) people hang up (b) you sound interesting and funny (c) you are put on hold (d) people turn down the volume

(113) When should you practice loud laughter?
   a) morning (b) evening (c) late at night (d) any time

(114) Comically singing criticism should be done?
   a) never (b) so people understand (c) only late at night (d) only early in the morning

(115) People think that when you use more face, hand and body gestures you are?
   a) dumb (b) funny (c) dangerous (d) boring

(116) When should you do a funny dance like funny ballet dancing?
   a) when you leave and take things (b) never (c) only at twilight (d) early morning

(117) When you use funny props like glasses, hats and clothes people think you are?
   a) dangerous (b) boring (c) funny (d) dumb

CHAPTER 12   The Super Influencing Wealth Technique

(118) When can the super influencing technique be used to alter your personality?
   a) when under water (b) after an argument (c) when asleep (d) any time of day

(119) What is the super influencing technique supposed to do?
   a) help with sports (b) imprint suggestions (c) grow muscle (d) make a person funny

(120) When you reach deep relaxation your suggestions will be.
   a) ready for another day (b) imprinted (c) ignored (d) suppressed

(121) What should you do when angry?
   a) use shocking device (b) get angrier (c) count from one to five before losing your cool (d) nothing

(122) What is the best way to repeat suggestions?
   a) in a calm repetitive manner (b) not at all (c) on the phone (d) while driving

CHAPTER 13   Using Your Hidden Computer To Solve Complicated Problems

(123) Routine decisions are.
   a) made quickly (b) made slowly (c) suppressed (d) ignored

(124) Firm decisions are changed.
   a) Angrily (b) quickly (c) slowly (d) suppressed

(125) When should you identify reasons, study the reasons and know your resources.
   a) on tax returns (b) income statements (c) profit and loss statements (d) when problem solving

(126) According to the decision making model, when should you 1) choose the best decision. 2) carry out the best decision   and 3) evaluate the final decision .
   a) in the beginning of the model (b) at the end of the model (c) not at all (d) seldom

CHAPTER 14   How To Achieve Happiness With Success

(127) What will make you happier?
   a) serious attitude (b) cheerfulness and smiling (c) frowning (d) anger

(128) Why should you do fun things and have pleasant thoughts?
   a) to be angrier (b) to be critical (c) to be happier (d) to be angrier

(129) What will reading a business book, watching a business movie or going to a library do?
   a) make a person dull   (b) create confusion   (c) waste time   (d) lessen boredom

(130) What exercises will make you happier?
   a) Jogging   (b) laughing and smiling exercises   (c) weight lifting   (d) gymnastics

(131) People are happy when they are.
   a) perusing goals   (b) miserable   (c) angry   (d) sad

CHAPTER 15   The Wealth And Love Relationships

(132) Do attached people have a tendency to get bored and detached people have a tendency to get lonely?
   a) never   (b) Only in the summer   (c) yes   (d) only winter

(133) A non attached attitude can make you?
   a) good looking (b) richer   (c) unhappy   (d) a & b

(134) Going from detached to non attached means contemplating.
   a) staying with the relationship (b) leaving the relationship   (c) exercising   (d) anger feelings

(135) Going from attached to non attached means contemplating.
   a) exercising   (b) leaving the relationship   (c) getting married   (d) having children

CHAPTER 16   Creating The Wealth Attitude

(136) Expressing your feelings to supportive people is good for.
   a) a weak ego   (b) understanding others   (c) anger tantrums   (d) a & b

(137) What does being close minded do to your mind?
   a) limits your mind   (b) encourages growth   (c) creates happiness   (d) creates joy

(138) When should you have high expectations but prepare for the worst?
   a) never   (b) all of the time   (c) only when angry   (d) during the day

(139) What time of the day will people live up to your high expectations?
   a) Morning   (b) evening   (c) after lunch   (d) anytime

CHAPTER 17   The Treasure Chest Of Feelings

(140) By expressing your feelings honestly to supportive people you will get.
   a) better at sleeping   (b) more understanding   (c) nothing   (d) more wasted time

(141) By having a deep sense of honesty in sales you will get.
   a) respect and admiration   (b) no sales   (c) more wasted time   (d) less sales

(142) Expressing the honest details of your product and service will get you.
   a) no sales   (b) bored on the job   (c) more sales   (d) less sales

(143) You should do what you feel, but after you act you should.
   a) ignore feedback   (b) do nothing   (c) ignore comments   (d) pay attention to feedback

CHAPTER 18   The Secret Of Making You Rich With "Novanetics"

(144) By paying attention to details you will be able to.
   a) enjoy the world   (b) be better with people   (c) hate everything   (d) a & b

(145) People will pay attention to the activities or things that they.
   a) don't care about   (b) dislike   (c) hate   (d) like or love

(146) What will telephone conversations, conversations, games, and school help you do?
  a) nothing   (b) pay attention to details   (c) waste time   (d) a & b & c

(147) What is a good idea when wanting to pay attention to activities?
  a) look the other way   (b) get angry   (c) watch and empty your mind of all pre-conceived thoughts   (d) do another activity

(148) What are good activities to practice?
  a) school lessons   (b) sports activities   (c) chapters in this book   (d) a & b & c

(149) What should you do when wanting to do an activity well?
  a) practice and study it for weeks and days   (b) don't do it often   (c) do it first thing in the morning everyday   (d) do another activity

CHAPTER 19   Using Persistence To Gain Success

(150) What is the best way to create persistence?
  a) constant exercise   (b) create a burning desire to achieve a goal   (c) a lot of practice   (d) expressing your feelings

(151) If you want something what should you do?
  a) keep asking for it   (b) ignore it   (c) deny it   (d) look at it

(152) When should you agree to an agreement? When you have?
  a) half of the facts   (b) don't know the details   (c) when you are sure of the facts   (d) a & b & c

(153) When negotiating?
  a) talk a lot   (b) give out your complete position   (c) type out all facts and pass them out   (d) the first person that speaks loses.

(154) What technique uses the concept, "let the other person talk while you take the benefits"?
  a) acting   (b) time management   (c) negotiating   (d) improve comedy.

CHAPTER 20   Others Will Make You Wealthy

(155) By writing down qualities you admire in others, you will know.
  a) what qualities you want from others   (b) time management   (c) real estate   (d) develop comedy.

(156) Can the people you know (1) help you succeed or (2) help you fail?
  a) neither   (b) just succeed   (c) just fail   (d) both

(157) Knowing successful people will either (1) earn you money or (2) save you time?
  a) both   (b) just save time   (c) just earn money   (d) neither

(158) When joining a support group should you (1) associate with people better than you or (2) show appreciation of others?
  a) just associate with people better than you   (b) just show appreciation   (c) neither   (d) both

(159) When should you reward others for helping you?
  a) anytime they help you   (b) never   (c) half the time   (d) just once

(160) What do studies show indoor plants do?
  a) are too messy   (b) make people feel better   (c) take up too much water   (d) do nothing

CHAPTER 21   Listening To Riches

(161) When is a benefit oriented message good?
  a) all the time   (b) never   (c) half the time   (d) some of the time

(162) To draw on a point and avoid arguments you should start your discussions with?
  a) denial   (b) agreements   (c) plain talk   (d) silence

(163) What technique does not give you a chance to say no?
a) silence (b) denial (c) an argument (d) a choice in your favor

(164) When handling adversity should you (1) prepare for adversity or (2) focus on your goal?
a) just prepare for adversity (b) neither (c) both (d) just focus on your goal

(165) How often do you have to pay a price for success?
a) always (b) never (c) just a few times (d) just once

CHAPTER 22 Knowledge: The Key To Riches

(166) If you don't know all of the information you need what should you do?
a) Pick a different project (b) know where to find the information you need (c) limit your project (d) a & c

(167) What are sources of information?
a) people (b) books (c) videos (d) a & b & c

(168) In order to succeed you must?
a) study old material (b) specialize in certain information (c) study anything (d) do nothing

(169) When you are not close-minded how often are you open to new ideas?
a) always (b) just once (c) just four times (d) never

(170) To get through difficult situations you must?
a) be silent (b) do nothing (c) practice the situation before it happens (d) be calm and don't worry

(171) Study at home correspondence courses are good for.
a) earning a certificate (b) not good (c) earning a degree (d) a & c

CHAPTER 23 Managing Your Time For Wealth

(172) Evaluate your time schedule so you?
a) use up more time (b) are more productive with time (c) waste time (d) a & c

(173) Evaluate your activities so you are?
a) more productive (b) less productive (c) ready to move locations (d) b & c

(174) In order to make un-enjoyable activities productive you must?
a) make people like them (b) you can't (c) offer more rewards (d) a & c

(175) Time wasters are?
a) being a perfectionist (b) timing your activities (c) doing work you don't know (d) a & c

(177) What things must you do to become more productive?
a) take breaks often (b) don't procrastinate (c) plan your whole day (d) b & c

(178) What things must you do to become more productive?
a) take breaks often (b) don't procrastinate (c) plan your whole day (d) b & c

(179) If you create deadlines and you combine activities you will?
a) confuse people (b) be more productive (c) be disorganized (d) a & c

CHAPTER 24 How To Win People Over

(180) You should give people praise and appreciation when.
a) they deserve a reward (b) not at all (c) all the time (d) once a day

(181) When mistakes are admitted by others.
a) say nothing (b) tell them what they must hear to improve (c) get angry (d) leave

(182) Being arrogant and only concerned with yourself.

a) makes good conversation   (b) creates laughter   (c) makes others dislike you   (d) creates love

(183) Wave, shake hands, say hello and talk to everyone you meet.
   a) is too forward   (b) c & d   (c) will earn you friends   (d) makes you likable

(184) When making the final close you should.
   a) explain your needs and ask for action   (b) walk away   (c) become shy   (d) demand attention

(185) To convince others to do what you want you should.
   a) visualize in words the future results   (b) say nothing   (c) say little   (d) b & c

(186) If you are well groomed and your appearance and dress are good, people will think.
   a) You are good   (b) they can trust you   (c) you may be bad   (d) a & b

CHAPTER 25   Persuade People To Your Point Of View

(187) When using constructive criticism, tell them.
   a) what the problem is   (b) what to do to solve the problem   (c) as little as possible (d) a & b

(188) When criticizing another person.
   a) don't degrade them   (b) try to add humor   (c) be silent   (d) a & b

(189) When is the best time to criticize a person.
   b) anytime   (b) never   (c) at the time of the act   (d) when you are angry

(190) Criticizing people in front of others will cause them to.
   a) be embarrassed and degraded   (b) be happy   (c) become angry   (d) a & c

(191) What is better when criticizing a person.
   a) just criticism   (b) just praise   (c) just praise and criticism   (d) just silence

(192) When dealing with bad relationships should you (1) contact relatives and friends or (2) attend regular therapy and counseling.
   a) just the first option   (b) just the second option   (c) none of the options   (d) both options

(193) If you have lost minimal money due to another person's fault . What should you do?
   a) send nasty notes   (b) call their friends and relatives   (c) sue them in small claims court   (d) forget your loses

CHAPTER 27   Your Ultimate Doctor

(194) Religious faith is?
   a) improves communities   (b) one of the greatest healers   (c) no available to some people   (d) a & b

(195) When losing weight should you (1) visualize and imagine yourself thinner or (2) repeat your dieting goals to yourself three times a day?
   a) just the second option   (b) none (c) just the first option (d) both options

(196) Will imagining yourself well and feeling better help you heal?
   a) studies suggest they help   (b) seldom   (c) only in church (d) only at work

(197) What should you remove from your life to improve your health?
   a) parties (b) water sports (c) warm weather (d) bad influences

(198) To stay healthy should you (1) follow the food pyramid diet guidelines or (2) exercise daily?
   a) both options one and two (b) just option one (c) just option two (d) none of the options

CHAPTER 28   *Novanetics*: The Power Of The Mind, Directs You

(199) Do the steps to succeeding include, (1) creating a desire for what you want or (2) believe that it will be yours or (3) know exactly what you

want.

a) number one two and three   (b) just number one and two   (c) just number one   (d) just number three

(200) Is "*Novanetics*" reserved for the talented few?

a) just the talented few   (b) it can be used by anyone in any situation   (c) only the rich   (d) Only for foreigners

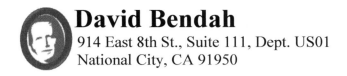

David Bendah

914 East 8th St., Suite 111, Dept. US01
National City, CA 91950

9/21/2020

Department Of Veteran Affairs
810 Vermont Ave NW
Washington, DC   20420

Dear Department Of Veteran Affairs:

I have just published a book that I know is the best American book ever published since 1776.   It is an American book, published in the United States and it is the best book in the world.   Like the liberating of Europe in 1945 and the moon landing in 1969, Americans could be celebrating again in 2020 for another first in the world.   The best book in the whole world has been printed in the United States and Americans could be joyful in showing the whole world another first.   While there isn't a ticker tape parade planned, the plans for a celebration are not known at this time.   This book could make about 5,000 Americans famous worldwide (from the recognition of the best book in the world published in the United States), that does not include the increase of millions of new jobs for Americans from American companies some of which are sponsors in this book.

While top American books have been published during the great depression and other times in American history that aided in economic and recession recovery.   There is some controversy on the impact of "*NOVANETICS*" the best book in the world, on economic periods like the American Civil War, World War I and World War II.   Who knows, if this book was published before the American civil war (1859), they may have decided not to have an American civil war.   Who knows about World War I?   Do the studies and see for yourself.

Since the book is so good, the American *"NOVANETICS"* could be translated into 200 languages.   A special large library building could be allocated in Washington D.C. with translations of "*NOVANETICS*"? Having the best book in the world translated in different languages will keep all world languages alive.   Even rare American Indian and European languages could be kept alive, with the best book in the world.

Some countries would like to publish this book and add mini-biographies with their native industrialists, so as to add a national identity to their foreign version of the American book.   Like the space program the book is under heavy investigation due to it's American origin and "best in the world" title.   There may be prejudice on who can own the book, since the book will make determinations on who is rich and who is poor. I would appreciate any help you could give me in marketing the book that earns the title "The United States First."

The manual *"NOVANETICS"* was written to boost the American economy and to help people that have been hurt by the pandemic.   During the COVID-19 pandemic, in the end of March, 2020 I started to re-write the book *"NOVANETICS"*.I combined sections of other books I wrote with the 50,000 word 1985 version, which had a different title.   I did a lot of my own personal research into fields that have not been published before.   So much of the information in the book is original work and has never been published before.   I don't know how many Swedish Nobel prizes the book could earn for original research, new developments and original work, but I think the number is considerable.   The book, *NOVANETICS* is so good, it could start a school, so I have decided to issue certificates of completion for those reading, studying and taking the final 200 question final exam.

Though only preferred individuals will own this book, I know it will help people get financial assistance they need to keep their homes and assistance to keep their credit clean.   It is absolutely essential to own during the pandemic.   You will find that the book *"NOVANETICS"* is the best book ever written and that is in the whole world.   This is the truth.   If you can get a copy consider yourself lucky.   I am willing to put my money where my mouth is.   To help the United States, I am offering a reward.   I am willing to give out a **$3,000 reward** if you can find better books that can help the whole economy during the pandemic.   I have sent copies to the United States Department Of Commerce, the Small Business Administration, Walt Disney Co, Chrysler Motors, Ford Motors, Mercedes Benz, Walmart and AT&T. No book has beaten me yet. Send my book to a local university or college to do the study.

The conditions for the reward are:
- To compare books against each other, you must show financial net worth per reader, before and after the use of the book. The book that shows the highest increase in financial wealth per reader is the winner.
- I will give out the reward once for each title and I will give out a total of $3,000, for 1st, 2nd and 3rd rewards. I will not give out the award multiple times per title.
- It cannot be a book that plagiarized "*NOVANETICS*" or it cannot be another book written by David Bendah. It can't be a book that is re-written or the same topic matter as "*NOVANETICS*". It can't be a book that works in conjunction with the same material in my book.
- The increase in financial wealth per reader must be based on the readers earning money with their own skills and work efforts, by using the techniques and methods in the book.
- You must do this study so that you will know that "*NOVANETICS*" by David Bendah is the best book ever written.

Since it is the best book ever published in the whole world, I have decided to create an educational course with the book. "*NOVANETICS*" is like a correspondence course and as soon as you finish this excellent educational course I will ask you for $7 to grade your final examination and for a prestigious "*NOVANETICS*" Business and Real Estate certificate you can proudly hang on your wall in the same decorative frame you would use for a college degree. Like other educational programs, even if you pay the $7, I am not giving you the "*NOVANETICS*" certificate. You can only earn the prestigious certificate after you have read and studied the program material in the book and you have taken the final 200 question examination. With this certificate you can show others you have completed the "*NOVANETICS*" course. A "*NOVANETICS*" certificate is impressive with family and friends and could get you jobs and business opportunities with people that will see the certificate. Some of the information covered in this course is included in the curriculum for a real estate license, business administration degree and a psychology degree.

It is another first for the United States. I am planning a second printing with a two column format, a 200 question exam in the back of the book, and the chapters are in a different order. The four real estate chapters which are located in chapters 24, 25, 26 & 27, will move to chapters 6, 7, 8 & 9. I have included one to two copies of my book with this letter. If you would like more copies of the book, please let me know and I will send you copies of the best book in the whole world.

Could you send me any grants and/or prizes that I have earned and that I can use to help me sell and promote my original United States book. I deserve the grants and prizes, since my book is an excellent investment for the United States. Every one dollar I get could earn the entire United States government tens of thousands of dollars. "*NOVANETICS*" is an excellent investment for the United States since it could make about 5,000 Americans famous worldwide (from the recognition of the best book in the world published in the United States), that does not include the increase of millions of new jobs for Americans from American companies some of which are sponsors of this book. Please send me any grants and/or prizes that I have earned for my contributions to the United States.

36

Sincerely yours

David Bendah

WHAT NOVANETICS CAN DO FOR YOU

Success need not elude you. It is not hard to attain. Thousands of people just like you have become successful. What do they have that you don't? They have the key to wealth. The key that unlocks its mysterious doors to prosperity. You are holding that key now, the same key that has made fortunes and helped build empires for people all over the world. Use this key wisely and you will prosper.

You may have asked yourself why *you* needed to read this book called, *"Novanetics"*. Let me ask you one question. Why shouldn't you have to read it? I am giving you the chance of a lifetime; a chance to become everything that you have ever wanted to be. I can tell you that there are thousands upon thousands of people who have studied the concepts in this book and who are successful today because they did. Don't you think that you are worth it? Don't you think it's worth taking the chance? Make the decision today that will make you rich.

What secrets does *"Novanetics"* hold? There's no mystery. It shows you how you can use the magical powers of your subconscious mind to get what you want. You see, most people have the potential to be successful. They just don't believe in themselves or have the confidence. The reason that they are not successful is because their hidden powers are asleep. Take the first step is to wake up those hidden powers, by reading this book. Take the second step and use the powers of *"Novanetics"* *"THE BEST BOOK IN THE WHOLE WORLD"* to succeed and to prosper.

NOVANETICS: *HOW TO USE ADVANCED WEALTH TECHNIQUES & YOUR SUBCONSCIOUS MIND TO GET RICH.*

> **THE BEST BOOK IN THE WHOLE WORLD.**

> *To practice the success concepts, this book includes a free special "start-up" business plan on ten mortgage assistance plans to pay your mortgage payments and a second free special "start-up" business plan on high profit rental real estate and "no money down" offers.*

ABOUT THE AUTHOR

David Bendah has written numerous books including books on using the subconscious mind's power to help achieve success. Thousands of people have attended his business activities. His latest American book "*NOVANETICS*" which is possibly the best book in the world (based on a contest with a "$3,000 reward" on books that increase income). His books and seminars have given birth to a new breed of successful people all over this nation. He is one of the foremost authorities on advanced wealth techniques, real estate mortgage reduction programs and using the mind to its full potential. If you would like to attend one of his activities, please contact him at David Bendah, PO Box 152808, Dept. DD2, San Diego, CA 92195.

After being more than $12,000 in debt, David Bendah was able to turn his life around. In a short period of time, by using advanced wealth techniques, he was able to climb out from under his debts and buy the luxury home of his choice and a new Mercedes Benz sports car that he had always dreamed of owning. He started a large San Diego, publishing company that had over a hundred employees and sold about eighty different books and published one monthly national magazine and one bi-monthly national magazine and he also started a seminar education school.